DATE DUE

THE
WINTER
OF OUR
DISCONTENT

THE
WINTER
OF OUR
DISCONTENT

The Viking Press · New York

JOHN
STEINBECK

To Beth, my sister,
whose light burns clear

A serial version of this novel appeared in *McCall's*

Readers seeking to identify the fictional people and places here described would do better to inspect their own communities and search their own hearts, for this book is about a large part of America today.

PART ONE

CHAPTER I

W̲ʜᴇɴ the fair gold morning of April stirred Mary Hawley awake, she turned over to her husband and saw him, little fingers pulling a frog mouth at her.

"You're silly," she said. "Ethan, you've got your comical genius."

"Oh say, Miss Mousie, will you marry me?"

"Did you wake up silly?"

"The year's at the day. The day's at the morn."

"I guess you did. Do you remember it's Good Friday?"

He said hollowly, "The dirty Romans are forming up for Calvary."

"Don't be sacrilegious. Will Marullo let you close the store at eleven?"

"Darling chicken-flower—Marullo is a Catholic and a wop. He probably won't show up at all. I'll close at noon till the execution's over."

"That's Pilgrim talk. It's not nice."

"Nonsense, ladybug. That's from my mother's side. That's pirate talk. It *was* an execution, you know."

"They were not pirates. You said yourself, whalers, and you said they had letters of what-you-call-it from the Continental Congress."

"The ships they fired on thought they were pirates. And those Roman G.I.'s thought it was an execution."

"I've made you mad. I like you better silly."

"I am silly. Everybody knows that."

"You always mix me up. You've got every right to be proud—Pilgrim Fathers and whaling captains right in one family."

"Have they?"

"What do you mean?"

"Would my great ancestors be proud to know they produced a goddam grocery clerk in a goddam wop store in a town they used to own?"

"You are not. You're more like the manager, keep the books and bank the money and order the goods."

"Sure. And I sweep out and carry garbage and kowtow to Marullo, and if I was a goddam cat, I'd be catching Marullo's mice."

She put her arms around him. "Let's be silly," she said. "Please don't say swear words on Good Friday. I do love you."

"Okay," he said after a moment. "That's what they all say. Don't think that lets you lie jaybird naked with a married man."

"I was going to tell you about the children."

"They in jail?"

"Now you're silly again. Maybe it's better if they tell you."

"Now why don't you—"

"Margie Young-Hunt's going to read me again today."

"Like a book? Who's Margie Young-Hunt, what is she, that all our swains—"

"You know if I was jealous—I mean they say when a man pretends he don't notice a pretty girl—"

"Oh, that one. Girl? She's had two husbands."

"The second one died."

"I want my breakfast. Do you believe that stuff?"

"Well Margie saw about Brother in the cards. Someone near and dear, she said."

"Someone near and dear to me is going to get a kick in the pants if she doesn't haul freight—"

"I'm going—eggs?"

"I guess so. Why do they call it Good Friday? What's good about it?"

"Oh! You!" she said. "You always make jokes."

The coffee was made and the eggs in a bowl with toast

beside them when Ethan Allen Hawley slid into the dinette near the window.

"I feel good," he said. "Why do they call it Good Friday?"

"Spring," she said from the stove.

"Spring Friday?"

"Spring fever. Is that the children up?"

"Fat chance. Lazy little bastards. Let's get 'em up and whip 'em."

"You talk terrible when you're silly. Will you come home twelve to three?"

"Nope."

"Why not?"

"Women. Sneak 'em in. Maybe that Margie."

"Now Ethan, don't you talk like that. Margie's a good friend. She'd give you the shirt off her back."

"Yah? Where'd she get the shirt?"

"That's Pilgrim talk again."

"I bet you anything we're related. She's got pirate blood."

"Oh! You're just silly again. Here's your list." She tucked it in his breast pocket. "Seems like a lot. But it's Easter weekend, don't forget—and two dozen eggs, don't forget. You're going to be late."

"I know. Might miss a two-bit sale for Marullo. Why two dozen?"

"For dyeing. Allen and Mary Ellen asked specially. You better go."

"Okay, bugflower—but can't I just go up and beat the hell out of Allen and Mary Ellen?"

"You spoil them rotten, Eth. You know you do."

"Farewell, oh ship of state," he said, and slammed the screen door after him and went out into the green-gold morning.

He looked back at the fine old house, his father's house and his great-grandfather's, white-painted shiplap with a fanlight over the front door, and Adam decorations and a widow's walk on the roof. It was deep-set in the greening garden among lilacs a hundred years old, thick as your waist, and swelling with buds. The elms of Elm Street joined their tops and yellowed out in new-coming leaf. The sun had just cleared the bank building and flashed on the silvery gas tower, starting the kelp and salt smell from the old harbor.

Only one person in early Elm Street, Mr. Baker's red setter, the banker's dog, Red Baker, who moved with slow dignity, pausing occasionally to sniff the passenger list on the elm trunks.

"Good morning, sir. My name is Ethan Allen Hawley. I've met you in pissing."

Red Baker stopped and acknowledged the greeting, with a slow sway of his plumed tail.

Ethan said, "I was just looking at my house. They knew how to build in those days."

Red cocked his head and reached with a hind foot to kick casually at his ribs.

"And why not? They had the money. Whale oil from the seven seas, and spermaceti. Do you know what spermaceti is?"

Red gave a whining sigh.

"I see you don't. A light, lovely rose-smelling oil from the head cavity of the sperm whale. Read *Moby Dick*, dog. That's my advice to you."

The setter lifted his leg on the cast-iron hitching post at the gutter.

Turning to walk away, Ethan said over his shoulder, "And make a book report. You might teach my son. He can't even spell spermaceti, or—or anything."

Elm Street runs at an angle into High Street two blocks from the old Ethan Allen Hawley house. Halfway down the first block a delinquent gang of English sparrows were fighting on the new-coming lawn of the Elgar house, not playing but rolling and picking and eye-gouging with such ferocity and so noisily that they didn't see Ethan approach. He stopped to watch the battle.

"Birds in their little nests agree," he said. "So why can't we? Now there's a bunch of horse crap for you. You kids can't get along even on a pretty morning. And you're the bastards Saint Francis was nice to. Screw!" He ran at them, kicking, and the sparrows rose with a whispered roar of wings, complaining bitterly in door-squeak voices. "Let me tell you this," Ethan said after them. "At noon the sun will darken and a blackness will fall on the earth and you will be afraid." He came back to the sidewalk and proceeded on his way.

The old Phillips house in the second block is a boarding house now. Joey Morphy, teller at the First National, came out of the front door. He picked his teeth and straightened his Tattersall waistcoat and said, "Hi," to Ethan. "I was just going to call on you, Mr. Hawley," he said.

"Why do they call it Good Friday?"

"It's from the Latin," said Joey. "Goodus, goodilius, goodum, meaning lousy."

Joey looked like a horse and he smiled like a horse, raising a long upper lip to show big square teeth. Joseph Patrick Morphy, Joey Morphy, Joey-boy—"the Morph"— a real popular guy for one only a few years at New Baytown. A joker who got off his gags veily-eyed like a poker player, but he whinnied at other people's jokes, whether or not he had heard them. A wise guy, the Morph, had the inside dope on everything—and everybody from Mafia to Mountbatten—but he gave it out with a rising inflection, almost like a question. That took the smart-aleck tone out of it, made his listener a party to it so that he could repeat it as his own. Joey was a fascinating monkey— a gambler but no one ever saw him lay down a bet, a good bookkeeper and a wonderful bank teller. Mr. Baker, First National president, trusted Joey so completely that he let the teller do most of the work. The Morph knew everyone intimately and never used a first name. Ethan was Mr. Hawley. Margie Young-Hunt was Mrs. Young-Hunt to Joey, even though it was whispered that he was laying her. He had no family, no connections, lived alone in two rooms and private bath in the old Phillips house, ate most of his meals at the Foremaster Grill and Bar. His banking past was known to Mr. Baker and the bonding company and it was immaculate, but Joey-boy had a way of telling things that had happened to someone else in a way that made you suspect they had happened to Joey, and if that was so, he had really been around. Not taking credit made people like him even more. He kept his fingernails very clean, dressed well and sharply, and always had a clean shirt and a shoeshine.

The two men strolled together down Elm Street toward High.

"I've been meaning to ask you. You related to Admiral Hawley?"

"Don't you mean Admiral Halsey?" Ethan asked. "We've had lots of captains but I never heard of an admiral in the family."

"I heard your granddad was a whaling captain. Kind of connected up in my mind with the admiral, I guess."

"Town like this has got myths," said Ethan. "Like they say people on my dad's side did some pirating way back and my mother's family came over in the *Mayflower*."

"Ethan Allen," Joey said. "My God—you related to him too?"

"Might be. Must be," said Ethan. "What a day—ever see a prettier? What was it you wanted to see me about?"

"Oh, yes. I guess you're closing the store twelve to three. Would you make me a couple of sandwiches about half past eleven? I'll run in and get them. And a bottle of milk."

"Bank's not closing?"

"Bank is. I'm not. Little Joey'll be right in there, chained to the books. Big weekend like this—everybody and his dog cashing checks."

"I never thought of that," said Ethan.

"Oh, sure. Easter, Memorial Day, Fourth of July, Labor Day—any long weekend. If I wanted to stick up a bank, I'd do it just before a long weekend. The stuff's right there all laid out, waiting."

"You ever get stuck up, Joey?"

"No. But I had a friend that did twice."

"What did he say about it?"

"Said he was scared. Just took orders. Laid down on the floor and let 'em have it. Said the money was better insured than he was."

"I'll bring you the sandwiches when I close up. I'll knock on the back door. What kind you want?"

"Don't bother, Mr. Hawley. I'll slip across the alley—one ham and one cheese on rye, lettuce and mayonnaise, and maybe one bottle of milk and a Coke for later."

"Got some nice salami—that's Marullo."

"No, thanks. How's the one-man Mafia holding up?"

"All right, I guess."

"Well, even if you don't like guineas, you got to admire a guy can build a pushcart into all the property he owns. He's pretty cute. People don't know how much he's got salted away. Maybe I shouldn't say that. Banker's not supposed to tell."

"You didn't tell."

They had come to the corner where Elm angles into High Street. Automatically they stopped and turned to look at the pink brick and plaster mess that was the old Bay Hotel, now being wrecked to make room for the new Woolworth's. The yellow-painted bulldozer and the big crane that swung the wrecking ball were silent like waiting predators in the early morning.

"I always wanted to do that," Joey said. "Must be a kick to swing that steel ball and see a wall go down."

"I saw enough go down in France," Ethan said.

"Yeah! Your name's on the monument down by the waterfront."

"Did they ever catch the robbers that stuck up your friend?" Ethan was sure the friend was Joey himself. Anyone would have been.

"Oh, sure. Caught 'em like mice. It's lucky robbers aren't smart. If Joey-boy wrote a book how to rob a bank, the cops would never catch anybody."

Ethan laughed. "How'd you go about it?"

"I got a pipeline, Mr. Hawley. I just read the papers. And I used to know a guy pretty well was a cop. You want the two-dollar lecture?"

" 'Bout six bits' worth. I've got to open the store."

"Ladies and gentlemen," said Joey, "I am here this morning— No, look! How do they catch bank robbers? Number one—record, got caught before. Number two—get fighting over the profits and someone blows it. Number three—dames. Can't let dames alone, and that ties into number four—they got to spend that money. Watch new spenders and you got them."

"So what's your method, professor, sir?"

"Simple as socks. Everything opposite. Never rob a bank if you ever got caught or booked for anything. No confederates—do it alone and don't tell a soul, nobody. Forget dames. And don't spend it. Put it away, maybe for years. Then when you've got some excuse for having some money, bring it out a little at a time and invest. Don't spend."

"How about if the robber got recognized?"

"If he covers his face and don't talk, who's going to recognize him? You ever read descriptions by eyewitnesses? They're nuts. My cop friend says sometimes when they'd plant him in the line-up, he got picked out over and over again. People swore their eyes out he did whatever it was. That'll be six bits, please."

Ethan put his hand in his pocket. "I'll have to owe you."

"I'll take it out in sandwiches," said Joey.

The two crossed High Street and entered the alley that right-angled from the other side. Joey went in the back door of the First National Bank on his side of the alley, and Ethan unlocked the alley door of Marullo's Fruit and Fancy Groceries on his side. "Ham and cheese?" he called.

"On rye—lettuce and mayonnaise."

A little light, grayed by the dusty iron-barred window, came into the storeroom from the narrow alley. Ethan paused in the twilight place shelved to the ceiling and stacked with the cartons and wooden cases of canned fruits, vegetables, fish, processed meats, and cheese. He sniffed for mice among the seminal smells of flour and dried beans and peas, the paper-and-ink odor of boxed cereals, thick rich sourness of cheeses, and sausage, reek of hams and bacon, ferment of cabbage trimmings, lettuce, and beet tops from the silvery garbage cans beside the back door. Perceiving no rusty must of mouse, he opened the

alley door again and rolled the covered garbage cans into the
alley. A gray cat darted to get in, but he drove it away.

"No, you don't," he remarked to the cat. "Mice and rats
are fee for cats, but you're a sausage nibbler. Aroint! You
hear me—aroint!" The seated cat was licking a curled pink
paw but at the second "aroint" he hightailed away and
scrambled over the board fence behind the bank. "That
must be a magic word," Ethan said aloud. He returned to
the storeroom and closed the door after him.

Now through the dusty room to the swinging door of the
grocery—but at the cubicle of the toilet he heard the whispering of seeping water. He opened the plywood door,
switched on the light, and flushed the toilet. Then he
pushed open the wide door with wire-netted glass peek-
hole and wedged it open, kicking the wood block firmly in
with his toe.

The store was greeny from the drawn shades over the big
front windows. Again shelves to the ceiling, filled neatly
with gleaming canned and glassed foods, a library for the
stomach. On one side—counter, cash register, bags, string,
and that glory in stainless steel and white enamel, the cold
cabinet, in which the compressor whispered to itself. Ethan
flipped a switch and flooded the cold cuts, cheeses, sausage,
chops, steaks, and fish with a cold bluish neon glare. A re-
flected cathedral light filled the store, a diffused cathedral
light like that of Chartres. Ethan paused to admire it, the
organ pipes of canned tomatoes, the chapels of mustard
and olives, the hundred oval tombs of sardines.

"Unimum et unimorum," he intoned in a nasal litanic
tone. "Uni unimouse quod unibug in omnem unim, do-
mine—ahhhhhmen," he sang. And he could hear his wife
commenting, "That's silly and besides it might hurt somebody's feelings. You can't go around hurting feelings."

A clerk in a grocery store—Marullo's grocery store—a man
with a wife and two darling children. When is he alone,
when can he be alone? Customers in the daytime, wife and
kiddies in the evening; wife at night, customers in the daytime, wife and kiddies in the evening. "Bathroom—that's
when," Ethan said loudly, and right now, before I open

the sluice. Oh! the dusky, musky, smelly-welly, silly-billy time—the slovenly-lovely time. "Now whose feelings can I hurt, sugarfoot?" he said to his wife. "There ain't nobody nor nobody's feelings here. Just me and my unimum unimorum until—until I open that goddam front door."

From a drawer behind the counter by the cash register he took a clean apron and unfolded it and straightened the tapes, put it around his thin middle, brought the tapes around and back again. He reached behind his back with both hands and fumbled a bowknot.

The apron was long, halfway down his shins. He raised his right hand, cupped loosely, palm upward, and he declaimed, "Hear me oh ye canned pears, ye pickles and ye piccalilli—'As soon as it was day, the elders of the people and the chief priests and the scribes came together and led Him into their council—' *as soon as it was day.* The buggers went to work early, didn't they? They didn't waste no time nohow. Let's see now. 'And it was about the sixth hour'—that's maybe twelve o'clock— 'and there was a darkness over all the earth until the ninth hour. And the sun was darkened.' Now how do I remember that? Good God, it took Him a long time to die—a dreadful long time." He dropped his hand and looked wondering at the crowded shelves as though they might answer him. "You don't speak to me now, Mary, my dumpling. Are you one of the Daughters of Jerusalem? 'Weep not for me,' He said. 'Weep for yourselves and for your children. . . . For if they do these things in a green tree, what shall be done in the dry?' Still breaks me up. Aunt Deborah wrought better than she knew. It's not the sixth hour yet—not yet."

He raised the green shades on the big windows, saying, "Come in, day!" And then he unlocked the front doors. "Enter, world." He swung the iron-barred doors open and latched them open. And the morning sun lay softly on the pavement as it should, for in April the sun arose right where the High Street ran into the bay. Ethan went back to the toilet for a broom to sweep the sidewalk.

A day, a livelong day, is not one thing but many. It changes not only in growing light toward zenith and decline again, but in texture and mood, in tone and meaning, warped by a thousand factors of season, of heat or cold, of still or multi winds, torqued by odors, tastes, and the fabrics of ice or grass, of bud or leaf or black-drawn naked limbs. And as a day changes so do its subjects, bugs and birds, cats, dogs, butterflies and people.

Ethan Allen Hawley's quiet, dim, and inward day was done. The man who swept the morning pavement with metronomic strokes was not the man who could sermonize to canned goods, not a unimum unimorum man, not even a silly-billy man. He gathered cigarette ends and gum wrappers, bud cases from the pollenizing trees, and simple plain dust in the sweep of his broom and moved the windrow of derelict toward the gutter, to await the town men with their silver truck.

Mr. Baker took his measured decent way from his house on Maple Street toward the red brick basilica of a First National Bank. And if his steps were not of equal length, who was to know that out of ancient habit he avoided breaking his mother's back?

"Good morning, Mr. Baker," Ethan said and held his stroke to save the banker's neat serge pants from dust.

"Morning, Ethan. Fine morning."

"Fine," said Ethan. "Spring's in, Mr. Baker. Groundhog was right again."

"He was, he was." Mr. Baker paused. "I've been wanting to talk to you, Ethan. That money your wife got by her brother's will—over five thousand, isn't it?"

"Sixty-five hundred after taxes," Ethan said.

"Well, it's just lying in the bank. Ought to be invested. Like to talk to you about that. Your money should be working."

"Sixty-five hundred dollars can't do much work, sir. It can only stand by for emergencies."

"I'm not a believer in idle money, Ethan."

"Well, this also serves—just standing and waiting."

The banker's voice became frosty. "I don't understand." His inflection said he did understand and found it stupid, and his tone twisted a bitterness in Ethan, and the bitterness spawned a lie.

The broom traced a delicate curve against the pavement. "It's this way, sir. That money is Mary's temporary security if anything should happen to me."

"Then you should use part of it to insure your life."

"But it's only temporary, sir. That money was Mary's brother's estate. Her mother is still living. She may live many years."

"I understand. Old people can be a burden."

"They can also sit on their money." Ethan glanced at Mr. Baker's face as he said his lie, and he saw a trace of color rise out of the banker's collar. "You see, sir, if I invested Mary's money I might lose it, the way I lost my own, the way my father lost the pot."

"Water under the bridge, Ethan—water under the bridge. I know you got burned. But times are changing, new opportunities opening up."

"I had my opportunity, Mr. Baker, more opportunity than good sense. Don't forget I owned this store right after the war. Had to sell half a block of real estate to stock it—the last of our business property."

"I know, Ethan. I'm your banker. Know your business the way your doctor knows your pulse."

"Sure you know. Took me less than two years to damn near go bankrupt. Had to sell everything but my house to pay my debts."

"You can't take all the blame for that. Fresh out of the Army—no business experience. And don't forget you ran smack into a depression, only we called it recession. Some pretty seasoned businessmen went under."

"I went under all right. It's the first time in history a Hawley was ever a clerk in a guinea grocery."

"Now that's what I don't understand, Ethan. Anybody can go broke. What I don't see is why you stay broke, a man of your family and background and education. It doesn't have to be permanent unless your blood has lost its guts. What knocked you out, Ethan? What kept you knocked out?"

Ethan started an angry retort— Course you don't understand; you've never had it—and then he swept a small circle of gum wrappers and cigarette butts into a pyramid and moved the pyramid toward the gutter. "Men don't get knocked out, or I mean they can fight back against big things. What kills them is erosion; they get nudged into failure. They get slowly scared. I'm scared. Long Island Lighting Company might turn off the lights. My wife needs clothes. My children—shoes and fun. And suppose they can't get an education? And the monthly bills and the doctor and teeth and a tonsillectomy, and beyond that suppose I get sick and can't sweep this goddam sidewalk? Course you don't understand. It's slow. It rots out your guts. I can't think beyond next month's payment on the refrigerator. I hate my job and I'm scared I'll lose it. How could you understand that?"

"How about Mary's mother?"

"I told you. She sits on it. She'll die sitting on it."

"I didn't know. I thought Mary came from a poor family. But I know when you're sick you need medicine or maybe an operation or maybe a shock. Our people were daring men. You know it. They didn't let themselves get nibbled to death. And now times are changing. There are opportunities our ancestors never dreamed of. And they're being picked up by foreigners. Foreigners are taking us over. Wake up, Ethan."

"And how about the refrigerator?"

"Let it go if you have to."

"And how about Mary and the children?"

"Forget them for a while. They'll like you better if you climb out of the hole. You're not helping them by worrying about them."

"And Mary's money?"

"Lose it if you have to but risk it. With care and good advice you don't have to lose it. Risk isn't loss. Our people have always been calculated-risk people and they didn't lose. I'm going to shock you, Ethan. You're letting down the memory of old Cap'n Hawley. You owe his memory something. Why, he and my daddy owned the *Belle-Adair* together, one of the last built and finest of all whaling bottoms. Get off your ass, Ethan. You owe the *Belle-Adair* something you haven't paid in guts. The hell with the finance company."

Ethan coaxed a reluctant piece of cellophane over the gutter's edge with his broom tip. He said softly, "The *Belle-Adair* burned to the waterline, sir."

"I know she did, but did that stop us? It did not."

"She was insured."

"Of course she was."

"Well, I wasn't. I saved my house and nothing else."

"You'll have to forget that. You're brooding on something past. You've got to scrape up some courage, some daring. That's why I said you should invest Mary's money. I'm trying to help you, Ethan."

"Thank you, sir."

"We'll get that apron off you. You owe that to old Cap'n Hawley. He wouldn't believe it."

"I guess he wouldn't"

"That's the way to talk. We'll get that apron off."

"If it wasn't for Mary and the children—"

"Forget them, I tell you—for their own good. There's some interesting things going to happen here in New Baytown. You can be part of it."

"Thank you, sir."

"Just let me think about it."

"Mr. Morphy says he's going to work when you close at noon. I'm making him some sandwiches. Want me to make you some?"

"No thanks. I'm letting Joey do the work. He's a good man. There's some property I want to look up. In the County Clerk's office, that is. Nice and private there from twelve till three. Might be something in that for you. We'll talk soon. So long." He took a long first step to miss a crack and crossed the alley entrance to the front door of the First National Bank, and Ethan smiled at his retreating back.

He finished his sweeping quickly, for people were trickling and fresheting to work now. He set the stands of fresh fruit at the entrance of the store. Then, making sure no one was passing, he removed three stacked cans of dog food and, reaching behind, brought out the grim little bag of currency, replaced the dog food, and, ringing "no sale" on the cash register, distributed the twenties, tens, fives, and one-dollar bills in their places under the small retaining wheels. And in the oaken cups at the front of the cash drawer he segregated the halves, quarters, dimes, nickels, and pennies, and slammed the drawer shut. Only a few customers showed up, children sent for a loaf of bread or a carton of milk or a pound of forgotten coffee, little girls with sleep-messy hair.

Margie Young-Hunt came in, pert-breasted in a salmon sweater. Her tweed skirt clung lovingly in against her thighs and tucked up under her proud fanny, but it was in her eyes, her brown myopic eyes, that Ethan saw what his wife could never see because it wasn't there when wives were about. This was a predator, a huntress, Artemis for pants. Old Cap'n Hawley called it a "roving eye." It was in her voice too, a velvet growl that changed to a thin, mellow confidence for wives.

"Morning, Eth," Margie said. "What a day for a picnic!"

"Morning. Want to take a bet you ran out of coffee?"

"If you guess I ran out of Alka-Seltzer, I'm going to avoid you."

"Big night?"

"In a small way. Traveling-salesman story. A divorced woman's safe. Brief case of free samples. Guess you'd call him a drummer. Maybe you know him. Name of Bigger or Bogger, travels for B. B. D. and D. Reason I mention it is he said he was coming in to see you."

"We buy from Waylands mostly."

"Well, maybe Mr. Bugger's just drumming up business, if he feels better than I do this morning. Say, could you give me a glass of water? I'll take a couple of fizzers now."

Ethan went to the storeroom and brought back a Dixie cup of water from the tap. She dropped three of the flat tablets in and let them fizz. Then, "Mud in your eye," she said and tossed it back. "Get to work, you devils," she said.

"I hear you're going to read Mary's fortune today."

"Oh, Lord! I nearly forgot. I should go in the business. I could made my own fortune."

"Mary loves it. Are you good at it?"

"Nothing to be good at. You let people—women, that is —talk about themselves and then tell it back to them and they think you've got second sight."

"And tall dark strangers?"

"There's that, sure. If I could read men, I wouldn't have pulled the bellywhoppers I have. Brother! did I misread a couple of characters."

"Didn't your first husband die?"

"No, my second, peace be to his ashes, the son of a— No, let it ride. Peace be to his ashes."

Ethan greeted the entering elderly Mrs. Ezyzinski solicitously and lingered over the transference of a quarter of a pound of butter, even passed a complimentary word or two about the weather, but Margie Young-Hunt, relaxed and smiling, inspected the gold-sealed cans of *pâté de foie gras* and the minuscule jewel-cases of caviar in back of the counter by the cash register.

"Now," said Margie when the old lady tottered out, muttering to herself in Polish.

"Now—what?"

"I was just thinking—if I knew as much about men as I do about women, I'd put out my shingle. Why don't you teach me about men, Ethan?"

"You know enough. Maybe too much."

"Oh, come on! Don't you have a silly bone in your body?"

"Want to start now?"

"Maybe some evening."

"Good," he said. "A group. Mary and you and the two kids. Subject: men—their weakness and stupidity and how to use them."

Margie ignored his tone. "Don't you ever work late— accounts first of the month, that stuff?"

"Sure. I take the work home."

She raised her arms over her head and her fingers moused in her hair.

"Why?" she asked.

"Cat's why to make kittens' britches."

"See what you could teach me if you would?"

Ethan said, " 'And after that they had mocked Him, they took the robe off from Him and put His own raiment on Him and led Him away to crucify Him. And as they came out they found a man of Cyrene, Simon by name. Him they compelled to bear His cross. And when they were come unto a place called Golgotha—that is to say, a place of a skull—' "

"Oh, for God's sake!"

"Yes—yes—that is correct. . . ."

"Do you know what a son of a bitch you are?"

"Yes, O Daughter of Jerusalem."

Suddenly she smiled. "Know what I'm going to do? I'm going to read one hell of a fortune this morning. You're going to be a big shot, did you know? Everything you touch will turn to gold—a leader of men." She walked quickly to the door and then turned back, grinning. "I dare you to live up to it and I dare you not to. So long, Savior!" How strange the sound of heeltaps on pavement, striking in anger.

At ten o'clock everything changed. The big glass doors of the bank folded open and a river of people dipped in for money and brought the money to Marullo's and took away the fancy foods Easter calls for. Ethan was busy as a water skater until the sixth hour struck.

The angry firebell from its cupola on the town hall clanged the sixth hour. The customers drifted away with their bags of baked meats. Ethan brought in the fruit stands and closed the front doors, and then for no reason except that a darkness fell on the world and on him, he pulled down the thick green shades and the darkness fell on the store. Only the neon in the cold counter glared a ghostly blue.

Behind the counter he cut four fat slices of rye bread and buttered them liberally. He slid open the cold doors and picked out two slices of processed Swiss cheese and three slices of ham. "Lettuce and cheese," he said, "lettuce and cheese. When a man marries he lives in the trees." He mortared the top slices of bread with mayonnaise from a jar, pressed the lids down on the sandwiches, and trimmed the bits of lettuce and ham fat from the edges. Now a carton of milk and a square of waxed paper for wrapping. He was folding the ends of the paper neatly when a key rattled in the front door and Marullo came in, wide as a bear and sack-chested so that his arms seemed short and stood out from his body. His hat was on the back of his head so that his stiff iron-gray bangs showed like a cap. Marullo's eyes were wet and sly and sleepy, but the gold caps on his front teeth shone in the light from the cold counter. Two top buttons of his pants were open, showing his heavy gray underwear. He hooked little fat thumbs in the roll of his pants under his stomach and blinked in the half-darkness.

"Morning, Mr. Marullo. I guess it's afternoon."

"Hi, kid. You shut up good and quick."

"Whole town's shut. I thought you'd be at mass."

"No mass today. Only day in the year with no mass."

"That so? I didn't know that. Anything I can do for you?"

The short fat arms stretched and rocked back and forth on the elbows. "My arms hurt, kid. Arthritis. . . . Gets worse."

"Nothing you can do?"

"I do everything—hot pads, shark oil, pills—still hurts. All nice and shut up. Maybe we can have a talk, eh, kid?" His teeth flashed.

"Anything wrong?"

"Wrong? What's wrong?"

"Well, if you'll wait a minute, I'll just take these sandwiches to the bank. Mr. Morphy asked for them."

"You're a smart kid. You give service. That's good."

Ethan went through the storeroom, crossed the alley, and knocked on the back door of the bank. He passed the milk and sandwiches in to Joey.

"Thanks. You didn't need to."

"It's service. Marullo told me."

"Keep a couple of Cokes cold, will you? I got dry zeros in my mouth."

When Ethan returned, he found Marullo peering into a garbage can.

"Where do you want to talk, Mr. Marullo?"

"Start here, kid." He picked cauliflower leaves from the can. "You cutting off too much."

"Just to make them neat."

"Cauliflower is by weight. You throwing money in the garbage. I know a smart Greek fella owns maybe twenty restaurants. He says the big secret is watch the garbage cans. What you throw out, you don't sell. He's a smart fella."

"Yes, Mr. Marullo." Ethan moved restlessly toward the front of the store with Marullo behind him bending his elbows back and forth.

"You sprinkling good the vegetables like I said?"

"Sure."

The boss lifted a head of lettuce. "Feels dry."

"Well, hell, Marullo, I don't want to waterlog them—they're one-third water now."

"Makes them look crisp, nice and fresh. You think I don't know? I start with one pushcart—just one. I know. You got to learn the tricks, kid, or you go broke. Meat, now—you paying too much."

"Well, we advertise Grade A beef."

"A, B, C—who knows? It's on the card, ain't it? Now, we going to have a nice talk. We got dead wood on our bills. Anybody don't pay by the fifteenth—off the books."

"We can't do that. Some of these people have been trading here for twenty years."

"Listen, kid. Chain stores won't let John D. Rockefeller charge a nickel."

"Yes, but these people are good for it, most of them."

"What's 'good for it'? It ties up money. Chain stores buy carloads. We can't do that. You got to learn, kid. Sure—nice people! Money is nice too. You got too much meat scraps in the box."

"That was fat and crust."

"Okay if you weigh before you trim. You got to look after number one. You don't look after number one, whose'll do it? You got to learn, kid." The gold teeth did not glitter now, for the lips were tight little traps.

Anger splashed up in Ethan before he knew it and he was surprised. "I'm not a chiseler, Marullo."

"Who's a chiseler? That's good business, and good business is the only kind of business that stays in business. You think Mr. Baker is giving away free samples, kid?"

Ethan's top blew off with a bang. "You listen to me," he shouted. "Hawleys have been living here since the middle seventeen hundreds. You're a foreigner. You wouldn't know about that. We've been getting along with our neighbors and being decent all that time. If you think you can barge in from Sicily and change that, you're wrong. If you want my job, you can have it—right here, right now. And don't call me kid or I'll punch you in the nose—"

All Marullo's teeth gleamed now. "Okay, okay. Don't get mad. I just try to do you a good turn."

"Don't call me kid. My family's been here two hundred years." In his own ears it sounded childish, and his rage petered out.

"I don't talk very good English. You think Marullo is guinea name, wop name, dago name. My *genitori*, my name, is maybe two, three thousand years old. Marullus is from Rome, Valerius Maximus tells about it. What's two hundred years?"

"You don't come from here."

"Two hundred years ago you don't neither."

Now Ethan, his rage all leaked away, saw something that makes a man doubtful of the constancy of the realities outside himself. He saw the immigrant, guinea, fruit-peddler change under his eyes, saw the dome of forehead, the strong beak nose, deep-set fierce and fearless eyes, saw the head supported on pillared muscles, saw pride so deep and sure that it could play at humility. It was the shocking discovery that makes a man wonder: If I've missed this, what else have I failed to see?

"You don't have to talk dago talk," he said softly.

"Good business. I teach you business. Sixty-eight years I got. Wife she's died. Arthritis I hurt. I try to show you business. Maybe you don't learn. Most people they don't learn. Go broke."

"You don't have to rub it in because I went broke."

"No. You got wrong. I'm try to learn you good business so you don't go broke no more."

"Fat chance. I haven't got a business."

"You're still a kid."

Ethan said, "You look here, Marullo. I practically run this store for you. I keep the books, bank the money, order the supplies. Keep customers. They come back. Isn't that good business?"

"Sure—you learned something. You're not no kid no more. You get mad when I call you kid. What I'm going to call you? I call everybody kid."

"Try using my name."

"Don't sound friendly. Kid is friendly."

"It's not dignified."

"Dignified is not friendly."

Ethan laughed. "If you're a clerk in a guinea store, you've got to have dignity—for your wife, for your kids. You understand?"

"Is a fake."

"Course it is. If I had any real dignity, I wouldn't think about it. I nearly forgot something my old father told me not long before he died. He said the threshold of insult is in direct relation to intelligence and security. He said the words 'son of a bitch' are only an insult to a man who isn't quite sure of his mother, but how would you go about insulting Albert Einstein? He was alive then. So you go right on calling me kid if you want to."

"You see, kid? More friendly."

"All right then. What were you going to tell me about business that I'm not doing?"

"Business is money. Money is not friendly. Kid, maybe you too friendly—too nice. Money is not nice. Money got no friends but more money."

"That's nonsense, Marullo. I know plenty of nice, friendly, honorable businessmen."

"When not doing business, kid, yes. You going to find

out. When you find out is too late. You keep store nice, kid, but if it's your store you maybe go friendly broke. I'm teaching true lesson like school. Goo-by, kid." Marullo flexed his arms and went quickly out the front door and snapped it after him, and Ethan felt darkness on the world.

A sharp metallic rapping came on the front door. Ethan pushed aside the curtain and called, "We're closed till three."

"Let me in. I want to talk to you."

The stranger came in—a spare man, a perpetually young man who had never been young, a smart dresser, hair gleaming thinly against his scalp, eyes merry and restless.

"Sorry to bother you. Got to blow town. Wanted to see you alone. Thought the old man'd never go."

"Marullo?"

"Yeah. I was across the street."

Ethan glanced at the immaculate hands. On the third finger of the left hand he saw a big cat's eye set in a gold ring.

The stranger saw the glance. "Not a stick-up," he said. "I met a friend of yours last night."

"Yes?"

"Mrs. Young-Hunt. Margie Young-Hunt."

"Oh?"

Ethan could feel the restless sniffing of the stranger's mind, searching for an opening, for a bond on which to build an association.

"Nice kid. She gave you a big build-up. That's why I thought— My name's Biggers. I cover this territory for B. B. D. and D."

"We buy from Waylands."

"I know you do. That's why I'm here. Thought you might like to spread it out a little. We're new in this district. Building up fast. Have to make some concessions to get a foot in the door. It would pay you to take advantage of that."

"You'd have to see Mr. Marullo about that. He's always had a deal with Waylands."

The voice didn't lower but its tone became confidential. "You do the ordering?"

"Well, yes. You see Marullo has arthritis, and besides he has other interests."

"We could shave prices a little."

"I guess Marullo's got them shaved as close as they'll shave. You'd better see him."

"That's what I didn't want to do. I want the man that does the ordering, and that's you."

"I'm just a clerk."

"You do the ordering, Mr. Hawley. I can cut you in for five per cent."

"Marullo might go for a discount like that if the quality was the same."

"You don't get it. I don't want Marullo. This five per cent would be in cash—no checks, no records, no trouble with the tax boys, just nice clean green cabbage from my hand to your hand and from your hand to your pocket."

"Why can't Marullo get the discount?"

"Price agreements."

"All right. Suppose I took the five per cent and turned it over to Marullo?"

"I guess you don't know them like I do. You turn it over to him, he'll wonder how much more you aren't turning over. That's perfectly natural."

Ethan lowered his voice. "You want me to double-cross the man I work for?"

"Who's double-crossed? He don't lose anything and you make a buck. Everybody's got a right to make a buck. Margie said you were a smart cooky."

"It's a dark day," Ethan said.

"No, it's not. You got the shades pulled down." The sniffing mind smelled danger—a mouse confused between the odor of trap wire and the aroma of cheese. "Tell you what," Biggers said, "you think about it. See if you can throw some business our way. I'll drop in to see you when I'm in the district. I make it every two weeks. Here's my card."

Ethan's hand remained at his side. Biggers laid the card

on top of the cold counter. "And here's a little memento we got out for new friends." From his side pocket he brought a billfold, a rich and beautiful affair of pin seal. He placed it beside the card on the white porcelain. "Nice little item. Place for your driver's license, lodge cards."

Ethan did not reply.

"I'll drop by in a couple of weeks," Biggers said. "You think about it. I'll sure be here. Got a date with Margie. There's quite a kid." With no reply, he said, "I'll let myself out. See you soon." Then suddenly he came close to Ethan. "Don't be a fool. Everybody does it," he said. "Everybody!" And he went rapidly out the door and closed it quietly after him.

In the darkened silence Ethan could hear the low hum of the transformer for the neon light in the cold counter. He turned slowly to the piled and tiered audience on the shelves.

"I thought you were my friends! You didn't raise a hand for me. Fair-weather oysters, fair-weather pickles, fair-weather cake-mix. No more unimus for you. Wonder what Saint Francis would say if a dog bit him, or a bird crapped on him. Would he say, 'Thank you, Mr. Dog, *grazie tanto*, Signora Bird'?" He turned his head toward a rattling and a knocking and a pounding on the alley door, went quickly through the storeroom, muttering, "More customers than if we were open."

Joey Morphy staggered in, clutching his throat. "For God's sake," he groaned. "Succor—or at least Pepsi-Cola, for I dieth of dryth. Why is it so dark in here? Are mine eyes failething too?"

"Shades pulled down. Trying to discourage thirsty bankers."

He led the way to the cold counter and dug out a frosted bottle, uncapped it, and reached for another. "Guess I'll have one too."

Joey-boy leaned against the lighted glass and poured down half the bottle before he lowered it. "Hey!" he said. "Somebody's lost Fort Knox." He picked up the billfold.

"That's a little gift from the B. B. D. and D. drummer. He's trying to hustle some of our business."

"Well, he ain't hustling peanuts. This here's quality, son. Got your initials on it, too, in gold."

"It has?"

"You mean you don't know?"

"He just left a minute ago."

Joey flipped open the folded leather and rustled the clear plastic identification envelopes. "You better start joining something," he said. He opened the back. "Now here's what I call real thoughtful." Between first and second fingers he extracted a new twenty-dollar bill. "I knew they were moving in but didn't know with tanks. That's a remembrance worth remembering."

"Was that in there?"

"You think I planted it?"

"Joey, I want to talk to you. The guy offered me five per cent of any business I threw their way."

"Well, bully-bully! Prosperity at last. And it wasn't no idle promise. You should set up the Cokes. This is your day."

"You don't mean I should take it—"

"Why not, if they don't add it on the cost? Who loses?"

"He said I shouldn't tell Marullo or he'd think I was getting more."

"He would. What's the matter with you, Hawley? You nuts? I guess it's that light. You look green. Do I look green? You weren't thinking of turning it down?"

"I had trouble enough not kicking him in the ass."

"Oh! It's like that—you and the dinosaurs."

"He said everybody does it."

"Not everybody can get it. You're just one of the lucky ones."

"It's not honest."

"How not? Who gets hurt? Is it against the law?"

"You mean you'd take it?"

"Take it—I'd sit up and beg for it. In my business they got all the loopholes closed. Practically everything you can do in a bank is against the law—unless you're president. I don't get you. What are you hoggle-boggling about? If you were taking it away from Alfio lad, I'd say it wasn't quite straight—but you're not. You do them a favor, they do you a favor—a nice crisp green favor. Don't be crazy. You've got a wife and kids to think of. Raising kids ain't going to get any cheaper."

"I wish you'd go away now."

Joey Morphy put his unemptied bottle down hard on the counter. "Mr. Hawley—no, Mr. Ethan Allen Hawley," he said coldly, "if you think I would do anything dishonest or suggest that you do—why you can go and screw yourself."

Joey stalked toward the storeroom.

"I didn't mean that. I didn't mean it. Honest to God I didn't, Joey. I just had a couple of shocks today and besides —this is a dreadful holiday—dreadful."

Morphy paused. "How do you mean? Oh! yes, I know. Yes, I do know. You believe I know?"

"And every year, ever since I was a kid, only it gets worse because—maybe because I know more what it means, I hear those lonely 'lama sabach thani' words."

"I do know, Ethan, I do. It's nearly over—nearly over now, Ethan. Just forget I stomped out, will you?"

And the iron firebell clanged—one single stroke.

"It's over now," said Joey-boy. "It's all over—for a year." He drifted quietly out through the storeroom and eased the alley door shut.

Ethan raised the shades and opened the store again, but there wasn't much trade—a few bottle-of-milk and loaf-of-bread kids, a small lamb chop and can of peas for Miss Borcher for her hot-plate supper. People were just not moving about in the street. During the half-hour before six o'clock, while Ethan was getting things ready to close up, not a soul came in. And he locked up and started away before he remembered the groceries for home—had to go back and assemble them in two big bags and lock up over again. He had wanted to walk down to the bayside and watch the gray waves among the pilings of the dock and smell the sea water and speak to a seagull standing beak into the wind on a mooring float. He remembered a lady-poem written long ago by someone whipped to frenzy by the gliding spiral of a gull's flight. The poem began: "Oh! happy fowl—what thrills thee so?" And the lady poet had never found out, probably didn't want to know.

The heavy bags of groceries for the holidays discouraged the walk. Ethan moved wearily across the High Street and took his way slowly along Elm toward the old Hawley house.

CHAPTER II

MARY came from the stove and took one of the big grocery bags from him.

"I've got so much to tell you. Can't wait."

He kissed her and she felt the texture of his lips. "What's the matter?" she asked.

"Little tired."

"But you were closed three hours."

"Plenty to do."

"I hope you aren't gloomy."

"It's a gloomy day."

"It's been a wonderful day. Wait till you hear."

"Where are the kids?"

"Upstairs with the radio. They've got something to tell you too."

"Trouble?"

"Now why do you say that?"

"I don't know."

"You don't feel well."

"Damn it, I do too."

"With all the lovely things—I'll wait till after dinner for our part. Are you going to be surprised."

Allen and Mary Ellen boiled down the stairs and into the kitchen. "He's home," they said.

"Pop, you got Peeks in the store?"

"You mean that cereal, sure, Allen."

"I wish you'd bring some. It's the one with a mouse mask on the box that you cut out."

"Aren't you a little old for a mouse mask?"

Ellen said, "You send the box top and ten cents and you

get a ventriloquism thing and instructions. We just heard it on the radio."

Mary said, "Tell your father what you want to do."

"Well, we're going to enter the National I Love America Contest. First prize is go to Washington, meet the President—*with* parents—lots of other prizes."

"Fine," said Ethan. "What is it? What do you have to do?"

"Hearst papers," Ellen cried. "All over the country. You just write an essay why you love America. All the winners get to go on television."

"It's the grapes," said Allen. "How about going to Washington, hotel, shows, meet the President, the works. How's that for the grapes?"

"How about your schoolwork?"

"It's this summer. They announce the winners Fourth of July."

"Well, that might be all right. Do you really love America or do you love prizes?"

"Now, Father," said Mary, "don't go spoiling it for them."

"I just wanted to separate the cereal from the mouse mask. They get all mixed up."

"Pop, where would you say we could look it up?"

"Look it up?"

"Sure, like what some other guys said—"

"Your great-grandfather had some pretty fine books. They're in the attic."

"Like what?"

"Oh, like Lincoln's speeches and Daniel Webster and Henry Clay. You might take a look at Thoreau or Walt Whitman or Emerson—Mark Twain too. They're all up there in the attic."

"Did you read them, Pop?"

"He was my grandfather. He used to read them to me sometimes."

"Maybe you could help us with the essays."

"Then they wouldn't be yours."

"Okay," said Allen. "Will you remember to bring home some Peeks? They're full of iron and stuff."

"I'll try."

"Can we go to the movies?"

Mary said, "I thought you were going to dye the Easter eggs. I'm boiling them now. You can take them out on the sun porch after dinner."

"Can we go up in the attic and look at the books?"

"If you turn out the light after. Once it burned for a week. You left it on, Ethan."

When the children had gone, Mary said, "Aren't you glad they're in the contest?"

"Sure, if they do it right."

"I can't wait to tell you—Margie read me in cards today, three times, because she said she never saw anything like it. Three times! I saw the cards come up myself."

"Oh! Lord!"

"You won't be so suspicious when you hear. You always poke fun about tall dark strangers. You can't guess what it was about. Well—you want to guess?"

He said, "Mary, I want to warn you."

"Warn me? Why, you don't even know. My fortune is *you.*"

He spoke a harsh, bitter word under his breath.

"What did you say?"

"I said, 'Slim pickings.' "

"That's what you think, but that's not what the cards think. Three times, she threw them."

"Cards think?"

"They know," said Mary. "Here she read my cards and it was all about you. You're going to be one of the most important men in this town—that's what I said, *most* important. And it's not going to be long either. It's very soon. Every card she turned showed money and more money. You're going to be a rich man."

"Darling," he said, "please let me warn you, please!"

"You're going to make an investment."

"With what?"

"Well, I was thinking about Brother's money."

"No," he cried. "I wouldn't touch it. That's yours. And it's going to stay yours. Did you think that up or did—"

"She never mentioned it. And the cards didn't. You are going to invest in July and from then on, it's one thing after another—one right after another. But don't it sound nice? That's the way she said it— 'Your fortune is Ethan. He is going to be a very rich man, maybe the biggest man in this town.' "

"God damn her! She's got no right."

"Ethan!"

"Do you know what she's doing? Do you know what you're doing?"

"I know I'm a good wife and she's a good friend. And I don't want to quarrel with the children hearing. Margie Young is the best friend I've got. I know you don't like her. What I think is you're jealous of my friends—that's what I think. I had a happy afternoon and you want to spoil it. That's not nice." Mary's face was mottled with angry disappointment, and vengeful toward this obstacle to her daydreaming.

"You just sit there, Mr. Smart, and tear people down. You think Margie made it all up. She didn't, because I cut the cards three times—but even supposing she did, why would she do it except to be kind and friendly and offer a little help. You tell me that, Mr. Smart! You find some nasty reason."

"I wish I knew," he said. "It might be pure mischief. She hasn't a man or a job. It might be mischief."

Mary lowered her voice and spoke with scorn. "You talk about mischief—you wouldn't know mischief if it slapped you in the face. You don't know what Margie goes through. Why, there are men in this town after her all the time. Big men, married men, whispering and urging—nasty. Sometimes she don't know where to turn. That's why she needs me, a woman friend. Oh, she told me things—men you just wouldn't believe. Why some of them even pretend they don't like her in public, and then they sneak to her house or call her up and try to get her to meet them—sanctimonious men, always preaching morals and then doing like that. You talk about mischief."

"Did she say who they were?"

"No, she didn't and that's another proof. Margie don't want to hurt anybody even if they hurt her. But she said there was one I just wouldn't believe. She said it would turn my hair gray if I knew."

Ethan took a deep breath and held it and let it out as a huge sigh.

"Wonder who it could be," Mary said. "The way she said it was like it was somebody we know well and just couldn't believe."

"But she would tell under certain circumstances," Ethan said softly.

"Only if she was forced. She said that herself. Only if she had to if like her—honor, or her good name, you know . . . Who do you s'pose it could be?"

"I think I know."

"You know? Who?"

"Me."

Her mouth fell open. "Oh! You fool," she said. "If I don't watch you, you trap me every time. Well it's better than gloomy."

"A pretty kettle. Man confesses to sins of the flesh with wife's best friend. Is laughed to scorn."

"That's not nice talk."

"Perhaps man should have denied it. Then at least his wife would have honored him with suspicion. My darling, I swear to you by all that's holy, that never by word or deed have I ever made a pass at Margie Young-Hunt. Now will you believe I'm guilty?"

"You!"

"You don't think I'm good enough, desirable enough, in other words you don't think I could make the grade?"

"I like jokes. You know it—but that's not something to joke about. I hope the children haven't got into the trunks up there. They never put anything back."

"I'll try once more, fair wife. A certain woman, initials M. Y.-H., has surrounded me with traps, for reasons known only to herself. I am in grave danger of falling into one or more of them."

"Why don't you think of your fortune? The cards said

July and they said it three times—I saw it. You are going to get money and lots of money. Think about that."

"Do you love money so much, cottontail?"

"Love money? What do you mean?"

"Do you want money enough so that even necromancy, thaumaturgy, juju, or any other dark practices are justified?"

"You said it! You started it. I'm not going to let you hide in your words. Do I love money? No, I don't love money. But I don't love worry either. I'd like to be able to hold up my head in this town. I don't like the children to be hangdog because they can't dress as good—as well—as some others. I'd love to hold up my head."

"And money would prop up your head?"

"It would wipe the sneers off the faces of your holy la-de-das."

"No one sneers at Hawley."

"That's what you think! You just don't see it."

"Maybe because I don't look for it."

"Are you throwing your holy Hawleys up at me?"

"No, my darling. It's not much of a weapon any more."

"Well, I'm glad you found it out. In this town or any other town a Hawley grocery clerk is still a grocery clerk."

"Do you blame me for my failure?"

"No. Of course I don't. But I do blame you for sitting wallowing in it. You could climb out of it if you didn't have your old-fashioned fancy-pants ideas. Everybody's laughing at you. A grand gentleman without money is a bum." The word exploded in her head, and she was silent and ashamed.

"I'm sorry," Ethan said. "You have taught me something —maybe three things, rabbit footling mine. Three things will never be believed—the true, the probable, and the logical. I know now where to get the money to start my fortune."

"Where?"

"I'll rob a bank."

The little bell of the timer on the stove took up a slow-spaced pinging.

Mary said, "Go call the children. The casserole's ready. Tell them to turn out the light." She listened to his tread.

CHAPTER III

My wife, my Mary, goes to her sleep the way you would close the door of a closet. So many times I have watched her with envy. Her lovely body squirms a moment as though she fitted herself into a cocoon. She sighs once and at the end of it her eyes close and her lips, untroubled, fall into that wise and remote smile of the ancient Greek gods. She smiles all night in her sleep, her breath purrs in her throat, not a snore, a kitten's purr. For a moment her temperature leaps up so that I can feel the glow of it beside me in the bed, then drops and she has gone away. I don't know where. She says she does not dream. She must, of course. That simply means her dreams do not trouble her, or trouble her so much that she forgets them before awakening. She loves to sleep and sleep welcomes her. I wish it were so with me. I fight off sleep, at the same time craving it.

I have thought the difference might be that my Mary knows she will live forever, that she will step from the living into another life as easily as she slips from sleep to wakefulness. She knows this with her whole body, so completely that she does not think of it any more than she thinks to breathe. Thus she has time to sleep, time to rest, time to cease to exist for a little.

On the other hand, I know in my bones and my tissue that I will one day, soon or late, stop living and so I fight against sleep, and beseech it, even try to trick it into coming. My moment of sleep is a great wrench, an agony. I know this because I have awakened at this second still feeling the crushing blow. And once in sleep, I have a very busy time. My dreams are the problems of the day stepped up to absurdity, a little like men dancing, wearing the horns and masks of animals.

I sleep much less in time than Mary does. She says she needs a great deal of sleep and I agree that I need less but I am far from believing that. There is only so much energy stored in a body, augmented, of course, by foods. One can use it up quickly, the way some children gobble candy, or unwrap it slowly. There's always a little girl who saves part of her candy and so has it when the gobblers have long since finished. I think my Mary will live much longer than I. She will have saved some of her life for later. Come to think of it, most women live longer than men.

Good Friday has always troubled me. Even as a child I was deep taken with sorrow, not at the agony of the crucifixion, but feeling the blighting loneliness of the Crucified. And I have never lost the sorrow, planted by Matthew, and read to me in the clipped, tight speech of my New England Great-Aunt Deborah.

Perhaps it was worse this year. We do take the story to ourselves and identify with it. Today Marullo instructed me, so that for the first time I understood it, in the nature of business. Right afterward I was offered my first bribe. That's an odd thing to say at my age, but I don't remember any other. I must think about Margie Young-Hunt. Is she an evil thing? What is her purpose? I know she has promised me something and threatened me if I don't accept it. Can a man think out his life, or must he just tag along?

So many nights I have lain awake, hearing my Mary's little purring beside me. If you stare into darkness, red spots start swimming on your eyes, and the time is long. Mary so loves her sleep that I have tried to protect her in it, even when the electric itch burned on my skin. She wakens if I leave the bed. It worries her. Because her only experience with sleeplessness has been in illness, she thinks I am not well.

This night I had to get up and out. Her breath purred gently and I could see the archaic smile on her mouth. Maybe she dreamed of good fortune, of the money I was about to make. Mary wants to be proud.

It is odd how a man believes he can think better in a special place. I have such a place, have always had it, but I know it isn't thinking I do there, but feeling and experiencing and remembering. It's a safety place—everyone must have one, although I never heard a man tell of it. Secret, quiet movement often awakens a sleeper when a deliberate normal action does not. Also I am convinced that sleeping minds wander into the thoughts of other people. I caused myself to need the bathroom, and when it was so, got up and went. And afterward I went quietly downstairs, carrying my clothes, and dressed in the kitchen.

Mary says I share other people's troubles that don't exist. Maybe that is so, but I did see a little possible scene play out in the dim-lighted kitchen—Mary awakening and searching the house for me, and her face troubled. I wrote a note on the grocery pad, saying, "Darling—I'm restless. Have gone for a walk. Be back soon." I think I left it squarely in the center of the kitchen table so that if the light was turned on at the wall switch it would be the first thing seen.

Then I eased the back door open and tasted the air. It was chilly, smelled of a crusting of white frost. I muffled up in a heavy coat and pulled a knitted sailor's cap down over my ears. The electric kitchen clock growled. It said quarter of three. I had been lying watching the red spots in the dark since eleven.

Our town of New Baytown is a handsome town, an old town, one of the first clear and defined whole towns in America. Its first settlers and my ancestors, I believe, were sons of those restless, treacherous, quarrelsome, avaricious seafaring men who were a headache to Europe under Elizabeth, took the West Indies for their own under Cromwell, and came finally to roost on the northern coast, holding charters from the returned Charles Stuart. They successfully combined piracy and puritanism, which aren't so unalike when you come right down to it. Both had a strong dislike for opposition and both had a roving eye for other people's property. Where they merged, they produced a hard-bitten, surviving bunch of monkeys. I know about them because my father made me know. He was a kind of high amateur ancestor man and I've always noticed that ancestor people usually lack the qualities of the ones they celebrate. My father was a gentle, well-informed, ill-advised, sometimes brilliant fool. Singlehanded he lost the land, money, prestige, and future; in fact he lost nearly everything Allens and Hawleys had accumulated over several hundred years, lost everything but the names—which was all my father was interested in anyway. Father used to give me what he called "heritage lessons." That's why I know so much about the old boys. Maybe that's also why I'm a clerk in a Sicilian grocery on a block Hawleys used to own. I wish I didn't resent it so much. It wasn't depression or hard times that wiped us out.

All that came from starting to say New Baytown is a pretty town. I turned right on Elm Street instead of left and walked fast up to Porlock, which is a cockeyed parallel with High. Wee Willie, our fat constable, would be dozing in his police car on the High, and I didn't want to pass the time of night with him. "What you doing up so late, Eth? Got yourself a little piece of something?" Wee Willie gets lonesome and loves to talk, and then later he talks about what he talked about. Quite a few small but nasty scandals have grown out of Willie's loneliness. The day constable is Stonewall Jackson Smith. That's not a nickname. He was christened Stonewall Jackson, and it does set him apart from all the other Smiths. I don't know why town cops have to be opposites but they usually are. Stoney Smith is a man who wouldn't give away what day it is unless he were on the stand under oath. Chief Smith runs the police work of the town and he's dedicated, studies the latest methods, and has taken the F.B.I. training in Washington. I guess he's as good a policeman as you are likely to find, tall and quiet and with eyes like little gleams of metal. If you were going in for crime, the chief would be a man to avoid.

All this came from my going over to Porlock Street to avoid talking to Wee Willie. It's on Porlock that the beautiful houses of New Baytown are. You see in the early eighteen hundreds we had over a hundred whaling bottoms. When the ships came back from a year or two out as far as the Antarctic or the China Sea, they would be loaded with oil and very rich. But they would have touched at foreign ports and picked up things as well as ideas. That's why you see so many Chinese things in the houses on Porlock Street. Some of those old captain-owners had good taste too. With all their money, they brought in English architects to build their houses. That's why you see so much Adam influence and Greek revival architecture on Porlock Street. It was that period in England. But with all the fanlights and fluted columns and Greek keys, they never neglected to put a widow's walk on the roof. The idea was that the faithful home-bound wives could go up there to watch for returning ships, and maybe some of them did. My family, the Haw-leys, and the Phillipses and the Elgars and the Bakers were older. They stayed put on Elm Street and their houses were what is called Early American, peak roofs and shiplap siding. That's the way my house, the old Hawley house, is. And the giant elms are as old as the houses.

Porlock Street has kept its gas street lamps, only there are electric globes in them now. In the summer tourists come to see the architecture and what they call "the old-world charm" of our town. Why does charm have to be old-world?

I forget how the Vermont Allens got mixed up with the Hawleys. It happened pretty soon after the Revolution. I could find out, of course. Up in the attic somewhere there will be a record. By the time father died, my Mary was pretty tired of Hawley family history, so when she suggested that we store all the things in the attic, I understood how she felt. You can get pretty tired of other people's family history. Mary isn't even New Baytown born. She came from a family of Irish extraction but not Catholic. She always makes a point of that. Ulster family, she calls them. She came from Boston.

No she didn't, either. I got her in Boston. I can see both of us, maybe more clearly now than then, a nervous, fright-ened Second Lieutenant Hawley with a weekend pass, and the soft, petal-cheeked, sweet-smelling darling of a girl, and triply all of those because of war and textbooks. How serious we were, how deadly serious. I was going to be killed and she was prepared to devote her life to my heroic memory. It was one of a million identical dreams of a million olive uniforms and cotton prints. And it might well have ended with the traditional Dear John letter except that she devoted her life to her warrior. Her letters, sweet with steadfastness, followed me everywhere, round, clear handwriting in dark blue ink on light blue paper, so that my whole company recognized her letters and every man was curiously glad for me. Even if I hadn't wanted to marry Mary, her constancy would have forced me to for the perpetuation of the world dream of fair and faithful women.

She has not wavered, not in the transplanting from Boston Irish tenancy to the old Hawley house on Elm Street. And she never wavered in the slow despondency of my failing business, in the birth of our children, or in the paralysis of my long clerkship. She is a waiter—I can see that now. And I guess she had at lengthy last grown weary of waiting. Never before had the iron of her wishes showed through, for my Mary is no mocker and contempt is not her tool. She has been too busy making the best of too many situations. It only seemed remarkable that the poison came to a head because it had not before. How quickly the pictures formed against the sound of frost-crunching footsteps on the night street.

There's no reason to feel furtive walking in the early morning in New Baytown. Wee Willie makes little jokes about it but most people seeing me walking toward the bay at three in the morning would suppose I was going fishing and not give it another thought. Our people have all sorts of fishing theories, some of them secret like family recipes, and such things are respected and respectable.

The street lights made the hard white frost on the lawns and sidewalks glint like millions of tiny diamonds. Such a frost takes a footprint and there were none ahead. I have always from the time I was a child felt a curious excitement walking in new unmarked snow or frost. It is like being first in a new world, a deep, satisfying sense of discovery of something clean and new, unused, undirtied. The usual night-folk, the cats, don't like to walk on frost. I remember once, on a dare, I stepped out barefoot on a frosty path and it felt like a burn to my feet. But now in galoshes and thick socks I put the first scars on the glittering newness.

Where Porlock crosses Torquay, that's where the bicycle factory is, just off Hicks Street, the clean frost was scarred with long foot-dragged tracks. Danny Taylor, a restless, unsteady ghost, wanting to be somewhere else and dragging there and wanting to be somewhere else. Danny, the town drunk. Every town has one, I guess. Danny Taylor—so many town heads shook slowly from side to side—good family, old family, last of the line, good education. Didn't he have some trouble at the Academy? Why doesn't he straighten up? He's killing himself with booze and that's wrong because Danny's a gentleman. It's a shame, begging money for booze. It's a comfort that his parents aren't alive to see it. It would kill them—but they're dead already. But that's New Baytown talking.

In me Danny is a raw sorrow and out of that a guilt. I should be able to help him. I've tried, but he won't let me. Danny is as near to a brother as I ever had, same age and growing up, same weight and strength. Maybe my guilt comes because I am my brother's keeper and I have not saved him. With a feeling that deep down, excuses—even valid ones—give no relief. Taylors—as old a family as Hawleys or Bakers or any of the others. In childhood I can remember no picnic, no circus, no competition, no Christmas without Danny beside me as close as my own right arm. Maybe if we had gone to college together this wouldn't have happened. I went to Harvard—luxuriated in languages, bathed in the humanities, lodged in the old, the beautiful, the obscure, indulged myself with knowledge utterly useless in running a grocery store, as it developed. And always I wished Danny could be with me on that bright and excited pilgrimage. But Danny was bred for the sea. His appointment to the Naval Academy was planned and verified and certain even when we were kids. His father sewed up the appointment every time we got a new Congressman.

Three years with honors and then expelled. It killed his

parents, they say, and it killed most of Danny. All that remained was this shuffling sorrow—this wandering night sorrow cadging dimes for a pint of skull-buster. I think the English would say, "He's let the side down," and that always wounds the let-downer more than the side. Danny's a night wanderer now, an early-morning man, a lonely, dragging thing. When he asks for a quarter for skull-buster his eyes beg you to forgive him because he can't forgive himself. He sleeps in a shack in back of the boat works where Wilburs used to be shipbuilders. I stooped over his track to see whether he was headed home or away. By the scuff of the frost he was going out and I might meet him any place. Wee Willie wouldn't lock him up. What would be the good?

There was no question where I was going. I had seen and felt and smelled it before I got out of bed. The Old Harbor is pretty far gone now. After the new breakwater went in and the municipal pier, sand and silt crept in and shallowed that once great anchorage sheltered by the jagged teeth of Whitsun Reef. And where once were shipways and rope-walks and warehouses and whole families of coopers to make the whale-oil casks, and docks too over which the bowsprits of whalers could project to their chain stays and figure- or fiddleheads. Three-masters they were usually, square-rigged; the after mast carried square sails as well as boom-and-gaff spanker—deep-hulled ships built to suffer the years at sea in any weather. The flying jib boom was a separate spar and the double dolphin-striker served as spritsail gaffs as well.

I have a steel engraving of the Old Harbor chockablock with ships, and some faded photographs on tin, but I don't really need them. I know the harbor and I know the ships. Grandfather rebuilt it for me with his stick made from a narwhal's horn and he drilled me in the nomenclature, rapping out the terms with his stick against a tide-bared stump of a pile of what was once the Hawley dock, a fierce old man with a white whisker fringe. I loved him so much I ached from it.

"All right," he'd say, in a voice that needed no megaphone from the bridge, "sing out the full rig, and sing it loud. I hate whispering."

And I would sing out, and he'd whack the pile with his narwhal stick at every beat. "Flying jib," I'd sing (whack), "outer jib" (whack), "inner jib, jib" (whack! whack!).

"Sing out! You're whispering."

"Fore skys'l, fore royal, fore topgal'n't s'l, fore upper tops'l, fore lower tops'l, fores'l"—and every one a whack.

"Main! Sing out."

"Main skys'l"—whack.

But sometimes, as he got older, he would tire. "Belay the main," he would shout. "Get to the mizzen. Sing out now."

"Aye, sir. Mizzen skys'l, mizzen royal, mizzen t'gal'n't, mizzen upper tops'l, mizzen lower tops'l, crossjack—"

"And?"

"Spanker."

"How rigged?"

"Boom and gaff, sir."

Whack—whack—whack—narwhal stick against the water-logged pile.

As his hearing got fuzzier, he accused more and more people of whispering. "If a thing's true, or even if it ain't true and you mean it, sing out," he would cry.

Old Cap'n's ears may have gone wonky toward the end of his life, but not his memory. He could recite you the tonnage and career of every ship, it seemed like, that ever sailed out of the Bay, and what she brought back and how it was divided, and the odd thing was that the great whaling days were nearly over before he was master. Kerosene he called "skunk oil," and kerosene lamps were "stinkpots." By the time electric lights came, he didn't care much or maybe was content just to remember. His death didn't shock me. The old man had drilled me in his death as he had in ships. I knew what to do, inside myself and out.

On the edge of the silted and sanded up Old Harbor, right where the Hawley dock had been, the stone foundation is still there. It comes right down to the low-tide level, and high water laps against its square masonry. Ten feet from the end there is a little passage about four feet wide and four feet high and five feet deep. Its top is vaulted. Maybe it was a drain one time, but the landward entrance is cemented in with sand and broken rock. That is my Place, the place everybody needs. Inside it you are out of sight except from seaward. There's nothing at Old Harbor now but a few clammers' shacks, rattlety things, mostly deserted in the winter, but clammers are a quiet lot anyway. They hardly speak from day's end to end and they walk with their heads down and their shoulders bowed.

That was the place I was headed for. I spent nighttide there before I went in the service, and the nighttide before I married my Mary, and part of the night Ellen was born that hurt her so bad. I was compelled to go and sit inside there and hear the little waves slap the stone and look out at the sawtooth Whitsun rocks. I saw it, lying in bed, watching the dance of the red spots, and I knew I had to sit there. It's big changes take me there—big changes.

South Devon runs along the shore, and there are lights aimed at the beach put there by good people to keep lovers from getting in trouble. They have to go somewhere else. A town ordinance says that Wee Willie has to patrol once an hour. There wasn't a soul on the beach—not a soul, and that was odd because someone is going fishing, or fishing, or coming in nearly all the time. I lowered myself over the edge and found the outcrop stone and doubled into the little cave. And I had hardly settled myself before I heard Wee Willie's car go by. That's twice I had avoided passing the time of night with him.

It sounds uncomfortable and silly, sitting cross-legged in a niche like a blinking Buddha, but some way the stone fits me, or I fit. Maybe I've been going there so long that my behind has conformed to the stones. As for its being silly, I don't mind that. Sometimes it's great fun to be silly, like children playing statues and dying of laughter. And sometimes being silly breaks the even pace and lets you get a new start. When I am troubled, I play a game of silly so that my dear will not catch trouble from me. She hasn't found me out yet, or if she has, I'll never know it. So many things I don't know about my Mary, and among them, how much

she knows about me. I don't think she knows about the
Place. How would she? I've never told anyone. It has no
name in my mind except the Place—no ritual or formula or
anything. It's a spot in which to wonder about things. No
man really knows about other human beings. The best he
can do is to suppose that they are like himself. Now, sitting
in the Place, out of the wind, seeing under the guardian
lights the tide creep in, black from the dark sky, I wondered
whether all men have a Place, or need a Place, or want one
and have none. Sometimes I've seen a look in eyes, a fren-
zied animal look as of need for a quiet, secret place where
soul-shivers can abate, where a man is one and can take
stock of it. Of course I know of the theories of back to the
womb and the death-wish, and these may be true of some
men, but I don't think they are true of me, except as easy
ways of saying something that isn't easy. I call whatever
happens in the Place "taking stock." Some others might call
it prayer, and maybe it would be the same thing. I don't believe it's thought. If I wanted to make a picture of it for myself, it would be a wet sheet turning and flapping in a lovely
wind and drying and sweetening the white. What happens
is right for me, whether or not it is good.

There were plenty of matters to consider and they were
jumping and waving their hands for attention like kids in
school. Then I heard the slow puttering of a boat engine,
a one-lunger, a fishing craft. Her masthead light moved
south beyond the Whitsun rocks. I had to put everything
aside until she turned her red and green lights safe in the
channel, a local boat to have found the entrance so easily.
She dropped anchor in the shallows and two men came
ashore in her skiff. Little wavelets brushed the beach and
the disturbed gulls took time to settle back on the mooring
floats.

Item: There was Mary, my dear, to think of, asleep with
the smile of mystery on her lips. I hoped she wouldn't
awaken and look for me. But if she did, would she ever tell
me? I doubt it. I think that Mary, for all that she seems to
tell everything, tells very little. There was the fortune to
consider. Did Mary want a fortune or did she want it for

me? The fact that it was a fake fortune, rigged by Margie Young-Hunt for reasons I didn't know, made no difference at all. A fake fortune was just as good as any and it is possible that all fortunes are a little fake. Any man of reasonable intelligence can make money if that's what he wants. Mostly it's women or clothes or admiration he really wants and they deflect him. The great artists of finance like Morgan and Rockefeller weren't deflected. They wanted and got money, just simple money. What they did with it afterward is another matter. I've always felt they got scared of the ghost they raised and tried to buy it off.

Item: By money, Mary meant new curtains and sure education for the kids and holding her head a little higher and, face it, being proud rather than a little ashamed of me. She had said it in anger and it was true.

Item: Did I want money? Well, no. Something in me hated being a grocery clerk. In the Army I made captain, but I know what got me into O. T. C. It was family and connections. I wasn't picked for my pretty eyes, but I did make a good officer, a good officer. But if I had really liked command, imposing my will on others and seeing them jump, I might have stayed in the Army and I'd have been a colonel by now. But I didn't. I wanted to get it over. They say a good soldier fights a battle, never a war. That's for civilians.

Item: Marullo was telling me the truth about business, business being the process of getting money. And Joey Morphy was telling it straight, and Mr. Baker and the drummer. They all told it straight. Why did it revolt me and leave a taste like a spoiled egg? Am I so good, or so kind, or so just? I don't think so. Am I so proud? Well, there's some of that. Am I lazy, too lazy to be involved? There's an awful lot of inactive kindness which is nothing but laziness, not wanting any trouble, confusion, or effort.

There is a smell and a feel of dawn long before the light. It was in the air now, a tempering of the wind; a new star or a planet cleared the horizon to eastward. I should know what star or planet but I don't. The wind freshens or steadies in the false dawn. It really does. And I would have to be going back soon. This rising star was too late to have much of a go before daylight. What is the saying— "The stars incline, they do not command"? Well, I've heard that a good many serious financiers go to astrologers for instruction in stock purchase. Do the stars incline toward a bull market? Is A. T. and T. influenced by the stars? Nothing as sweet and remote in my fortune as a star. A beat-up tarot deck of fortune-telling cards in the hands of an idle, mischievous woman, and she had rigged the cards. Do the cards incline but not command? Well, the cards inclined me out to the Place in the middle of the night, and they inclined me to give more thought than I wanted to, to a subject I detested. That's quite a bit of inclining right there. Could they incline me to a business cleverness I never had, to acquisitiveness foreign to me? Could I incline to want what I didn't want? There are the eaters and the eaten. That's a good rule to start with. Are the eaters more immoral than the eaten? In the end all are eaten—all—gobbled up by the earth, even the fiercest and the most crafty.

The roosters up on Clam Hill had been crowing for a long time and I had heard and not heard. I wished I could stay to see the sun rise straight out from the Place.

I said there was no ritual involved with the Place but that is not entirely true. Sometime on each visit I reconstruct Old Harbor for my mind's pleasure—the docks, the warehouses, the forests of masts and underbrush of rigging and canvas. And my ancestors, my blood—the young ones on the deck, the fully grown aloft, the mature on the bridge. No nonsense of Madison Avenue then or trimming too many leaves from cauliflowers. Some dignity was then for a man, some stature. A man could breathe.

That was my father talking, the fool. Old Cap'n remembered the fights over shares, the quibbling with stores, suspicion of every plank and keelson, the lawsuits, yes, and the killings—over women, glory, adventure? Not at all. Over money. It was a rare partnership, he said, that lasted more than one voyage, and blistering feuds ever afterward, continuing after the cause was forgotten.

There was one bitterness old Cap'n Hawley did not forget, a crime he could not forgive. He must have told me about it many times, standing or sitting on the rim of Old Harbor. We spent a goodly time there, he and I. I remember him pointing with his narwhal stick.

"Take that third rock on Whitsun Reef," he said. "Got her? Now, line her up with the tip of Porty Point at high water. See it there? Now—half a cable-length out on that line is where she lies, at least her keel."

"The *Belle-Adair*?"

"The *Belle-Adair*."

"Our ship."

"Half ours, a partnership. She burned at anchor—burned to the waterline. I never believed it was an accident."

"You think she was fired, sir?"

"I do."

"But—but you can't do that."

"I couldn't."

"Who did?"

"I don't know."

"Why?"

"Insurance."

"Then it's no different now."

"No different."

"There must be some difference."

"Only in a single man alone—only in one man alone. There's the only power—one man alone. Can't depend on anything else."

He never spoke to Cap'n Baker again, my father told me, but he didn't carry it to his son, Mr. Banker Baker. He wouldn't do that any more than he would burn a ship.

Good God, I've got to get home. And I got. I almost ran and I went up the High Street without thinking. It was still dark enough but a rim of lightness lay on the edge of the sea and made the waves gray iron. I rounded the war memorial and passed the post office. In a doorway Danny Taylor stood as I knew he must, hands in pockets, collar of his ragged coat turned up, and his old peaked shooter's cap with the earflaps turned down. His face was blue-gray with cold and sickness.

"Eth," he said, "I'm sorry to bother you. Sorry. I've got to have some skull-buster. You know I wouldn't ask if I didn't have to."

"I know. I mean I don't know, but I believe you." I gave him a dollar bill. "Will that do it?"

His lips were trembling the way a child's lips do when it's about to cry. "Thank you, Eth," he said. "Yes—that will put me away all day and maybe all night." He began to look better just thinking of it.

"Danny—you've got to stop this. Think I've forgotten? You were my brother, Danny. You still are. I'll do anything in the world to help you."

A little color came into his thin cheeks. He looked at the money in his hand and it was as though he had taken his first gulp of skull-buster. Then he looked at me with hard cold eyes.

"In the first place it's nobody's goddam business. And in the second place you haven't got a bean, Eth. You're as blind as I am, only it's a different kind of blindness."

"Listen to me, Danny."

"What for? Why, I'm better off than you are. I've got my ace in the hole. Remember our country place?"

"Where the house burned down? Where we used to play in the cellar hole?"

"You remember it all right. It's mine."

"Danny, you could sell it and get a new start."

"I won't sell it. The county takes a little bit of it for taxes every year. The big meadow is still mine."

"Why won't you sell it?"

"Because it's me. It's Daniel Taylor. Long as I have it no Christy sons of bitches can tell me what to do and no bastards can lock me up for my own good. Do you get it?"

"Listen, Danny—"

"I won't listen. If you think this dollar gives you the right to preach to me—here! Take it back."

"Keep it."

"I will. You don't know what you're talking about. You've never been a—drunk. I don't tell you how to wrap bacon do I? Now if you'll go your own way, I'll knock on a window and get some skull-buster. And don't forget—I'm better off than you are. I'm not a clerk." He turned around and put his head in the corner of the closed doorway like a child who abolishes the world by looking away from it. And he stayed there until I gave up and walked on.

Wee Willie, parked in front of the hotel, stirred out of his nap and rolled down the window of his Chevrolet. "Morning, Ethan," he said. "You up early or out late?"

"Both."

"Must have found yourself a fancy piece."

"Sure did, Willie, an houri."

"Now, Eth, don't tell me you'd take up with no street-walker."

"I swear it."

"Can't believe nothing no more. I bet you was fishing. How's Missus?"

"Asleep."

"That's where I'll be, come shift."

I went on without reminding him that's where he'd been.

I walked quietly up my back steps and switched on the kitchen light. My note was on the table a little left of center. I'd swear I left it right in the middle.

I put the coffee on and sat waiting for it to perk, and it had just begun to bounce when Mary came down. My darling looks like a little girl when she awakens. You couldn't think she is the mother of two big brats. And her skin has a lovely smell, like new-cut grass, the most cozy and comforting odor I know.

"What are you doing up so early?"

"Well may you ask. Please to know I have been up most of the night. Regard my galoshes there by the door. Feel them for wetness."

"Where did you go?"

"Down by the sea there is a little cave, my rumpled duck. I crawled inside and I studied the night."

"Now wait."

"And I saw a star come out of the sea, and since it had no owner I took it for our star. I tamed it and turned it back to fatten."

"You're being silly. I think you just got up and that woke me."

"If you don't believe me, ask Wee Willie. I spoke to him. Ask Danny Taylor. I gave him a dollar."

"You shouldn't. He'll just get drunk."

"I know. That was his wish. Where can our star sleep, sweet fern?"

"Doesn't coffee smell good? I'm glad you're silly again. It's awful when you're gloomy. I'm sorry about that fortune thing. I don't want you to think I'm not happy."

"Don't give it a worry, it's in the cards."

"What?"

"No joke. I'm going to make our fortune."

"I never know what you're thinking."

"That's the greatest difficulty with telling the truth. Can I beat the children a little to celebrate the day before Resurrection? I promise to break no bones."

"I haven't washed my face," she said. "I couldn't imagine who was rattling around in the kitchen."

When she had gone up to the bathroom, I put my note to her in my pocket. And I still didn't know. Does anyone ever know even the outer fringe of another? What are you like in there? Mary—do you hear? Who are you in there?

CHAPTER IV

THAT Saturday morning seemed to have a pattern. I wonder whether all days have. It was a withdrawn day. The little gray whisper of my Aunt Deborah came to me, "Of course, Jesus is dead. This is the only day in the world's days when He is dead. And all men and women are dead too. Jesus is in Hell. But tomorrow. Just wait until tomorrow. Then you'll see something."

I don't remember her very clearly, the way you don't remember someone too close to look at. But she read the Scripture to me like a daily newspaper and I suppose that's the way she thought of it, as something going on happening eternally but always exciting and new. Every Easter, Jesus really rose from the dead, an explosion, expected but nonetheless new. It wasn't two thousand years ago to her; it was now. And she planted something of that in me.

I can't remember wanting to open the store before. I think I hated every sluggish sloven of a morning. But this day I wanted to go. I love my Mary with all my heart, in some ways much better than myself, but it is also true that I do not always listen to her with complete attention. When she tells the chronicle of clothes and health and conversations which please and enlighten her, I do not listen at all, so that sometimes she exclaims, "But you should have known. I told you. I remember very clearly telling you on Thursday morning." And there's no doubt at all about that. She did tell me. She tells me everything in certain areas.

This morning I not only didn't listen, I wanted to get away from it. Maybe I wanted to talk myself and I didn't have anything to say—because, to give her fair due, she doesn't listen to me either, and a good thing sometimes. She listens to tones and intonations and from them gathers her facts about health and how my mood is and am I tired or gay. And that's as good a way as any. Now that I think of it, she doesn't listen to me because I am not talking to her, but to some dark listener within myself. And she doesn't really talk to me either. Of course when the children or some other hell-raising crises are concerned, all that changes.

I've thought so often how telling changes with the nature of the listener. Much of my talk is addressed to people who are dead, like my little Plymouth Rock Aunt Deborah or old Cap'n. I find myself arguing with them. I remember once in weary, dusty combat I called out to old Cap'n, "Do I have to?" And he replied very clearly, "Course you do. And don't whisper." He didn't argue—never did. Just said I must, and so I did. Nothing mysterious or mystic about that. It's asking for advice or an excuse from the inner part of you that is formed and certain.

For pure telling, which is another way of saying asking, my mute and articulate canned and bottled goods in the grocery serve very well. So does any passing animal or bird. They don't argue and they don't repeat.

Mary said, "You're not going already? Why you have half an hour. That's what comes of getting up so early."

"Whole flock of crates to open," I said. "Things to put on the shelves before I open. Great decisions. Should pickles and tomatoes go on the same shelf? Do canned apricots quarrel with peaches? You know how important color relations are on a dress."

"You'd make a joke about anything," Mary said. "But I'm glad. It's better than grumping. So many men grump."

And I was early. Red Baker wasn't out yet. You can set your watch by that dog, or any dog. He'd start his stately tour in exactly half an hour. And Joey Morphy wouldn't, didn't show. The bank wouldn't be open for business but that didn't mean Joey wouldn't be there working on the books. The town was very quiet but of course a lot of people had gone away for the Easter weekend. That and the Fourth of July and Labor Day are the biggest holidays. People go away even when they don't want to. I believe even the sparrows on Elm Street were away.

I did see Stonewall Jackson Smith on duty. He was just coming from a cup of coffee in the Foremaster Coffee Shop. He was so lean and brittle that his pistols and handcuffs seemed outsize. He wears his officer's cap at an angle, jaunty, and picks his teeth with a sharpened goose quill.

"Big business, Stoney. Long hard day making money."

"Huh?" he said. "Nobody's in town." What he meant was that he wished he weren't.

"Any murders, Stoney, or other grisly delights?"

"It's pretty quiet," he said. "Some kids wrecked a car at the bridge. But, hell, it was their own car. Judge'll make 'em pay for repairing the bridge. You heard about the bank job at Floodhampton?"

"No."

"Not even on television?"

"We don't have one, yet. Did they get much?"

"Thirteen thousand, they say. Yesterday just before closing. Three fellas. Four-state alarm. Willie's out on the highway now, bitching his head off."

"He gets plenty of sleep."

"I know, but I don't. I was out all night."

"Think they'll catch them?"

"Oh! I guess so. If it's money they usually do. Insurance companies keep nagging. Never let up."

"It would be nice work if they didn't catch you."

"Sure would," he said.

"Stoney, I wish you'd look in on Danny Taylor. He looks awful sick."

"Just a question of time," Stoney said. "But I'll go by. It's a shame. Nice fella. Nice family."

"It kills me. I like him."

"Well you can't do nothing with him. It's going to rain, Eth. Willie hates to get wet."

For the first time in my memory, I went into the alley with pleasure and opened the back door with excitement. The cat was by the door, waiting. I can't remember a morning when that lean and efficient cat hasn't been waiting **to** try to get in the back door and I have never failed to throw a stick at him or run him off. To the best of my knowledge, he has never got in. I call the cat "he" because his ears are torn up from fighting. Are cats strange animals or do they so resemble us that we find them curious as we do monkeys? Perhaps six or eight hundred times that cat has tried to get in and he has never made it.

"You're due for a cruel surprise," I told the cat. He was sitting in a circle of his tail, and the tip flicked up between his front feet. I went into the dark store, took a can of milk from the shelf, punched it open, and squirted it into a cup. Then I carried the cup to the storeroom and set it just inside and left the door open. He watched me gravely, looked at the milk, and then walked away and slid over the fence in back of the bank.

I was watching him go when Joey Morphy came into the alley with the key to the bank's back door ready in his hand. He looked seedy—grainy—as though he hadn't been to bed.

"Hi, Mr. Hawley."

"I thought you were closed today."

"Looks like I never close. Thirty-six-dollar mistake in the books. I worked till midnight last night."

"Short?"

"No—over."

"That should be good."

"Well, it ain't. I got to find it."

"Are banks that honest?"

"Banks are. It's only some men that aren't. If I'm going to get any holiday, I've got to find it."

"Wish I knew something about business."

"I can tell you all I know in one sentence. Money gets money."

"That doesn't do me much good."

"Me either. But I can sure give advice."

"Like what?"

"Like never take the first offer, and like, if somebody wants to sell, he's got a reason, and like, a thing is only as valuable as who wants it."

"That the quick course?"

"That's it, but it don't mean nothing without the first."

"Money gets money?"

"That cuts a lot of us out."

"Don't some people borrow?"

"Yeah, but you have to have credit and that's a kind of money."

"Guess I better stick to groceries."

"Looks like. Hear about the Floodhampton bank?"

"Stoney told me. Funny, we were just talking about it yesterday, remember?"

"I've got a friend there. Three guys—one talked with an accent, one with a limp. Three guys. Sure they'll get them. Maybe a week. Maybe two."

"Tough!"

"Oh, I don't know. They aren't smart. There's a law against not being smart."

"I'm sorry about yesterday."

"Forget it. I talk too much. That's another rule—don't talk. I'll never learn that. Say, you look good."

"I shouldn't. Didn't get much sleep."

"Somebody sick?"

"No. Just one of those nights."

"Don't I know. . . ."

I swept out the store and raised the shades and didn't know I was doing it or hating it. Joey's rules popped around and around in my head. And I discussed matters with my friends on the shelves, perhaps aloud, perhaps not. I don't know.

"Dear associates," I said, "if it's that simple, why don't more people do it? Why does nearly everyone make the same mistakes and over and over? Is there always something forgotten? Maybe the real basic weakness might be some form of kindness. Marullo said money has no heart. Wouldn't it be true then that any kindness in a money man would be a weakness? How do you get nice ordinary Joes to slaughter people in a war? Well, it helps if the enemy looks different or talks different. But then how about civil war? Well the Yankees ate babies and the Rebs starved prisoners. That helps. I'll get around to you, sliced beets and tinned button mushrooms, in a moment. I know you want me to talk about you. Everyone does. But I'm on the verge of it— point of reference, that's it. If the laws of thinking are the laws of things, then morals are relative too, and manner and sin—that's relative too in a relative universe. Has to be. No getting away from it. Point of reference.

"You dry cereal with the Mickey Mouse mask on the box and a ventriloquism gadget for the label and ten cents. I'll have to take you home, but right now you sit up and listen. What I told dear Mary as a joke is true. My ancestors, those highly revered ship-owners and captains, surely had commissions to raid commerce in the Revolution and again in 1812. Very patriotic and virtuous. But to the British they were pirates, and what they took they kept. That's how the family fortune started that was lost by my father. That's where the money that makes money came from. We can be proud of it."

I brought in a carton of tomato paste, slashed it open, and stacked the charming slender little cans on their depleted shelf. "Maybe you don't know, because you're kind of foreigners. Money not only has no heart but no honor nor any memory. Money is respectable automatically if you keep it a while. You must not think I am denouncing money. I admire it very much. Gentlemen, may I introduce some newcomers to our community. Let's see, I'll put them here beside you catsups. Make these bread-and-butter pickles welcome in their new home. New Yorkers, born and sliced and bottled. I was discussing money with my friends here. One of your finest families—oh, you'd know the name! Everybody in the world does, I guess. Well, they got their big start selling beef to the British when our country was at war with the British, and their money is as admired as any and so is the family. And another dynasty, probably the greatest bankers of them all. The founder bought three hundred rifles from the Army. The Army had rejected them as dangerously defective and so he got them very cheap, maybe fifty cents apiece. Pretty soon General Frémont was ready to start his heroic trek to the West, and he bought the rifles, sight unseen, for twenty dollars apiece. No one ever heard whether they blew up in the troopers' hands. And that was the money that makes money. It doesn't matter how you get it just as long as you get it and use it to make more. I'm not being cynical. Our lord and master, Marullo of the ancient Roman name, is quite right. Where money is concerned, the ordinary rules of conduct take a holiday. Why do I talk to groceries? Perhaps because you are discreet. You do not repeat my words, or gossip. Money is a crass and ungracious subject only when you have it. The poor find it fascinating. But don't you agree that if one becomes actively interested in money, he should know something of its nature and character and tendencies? I'm afraid that very few men, and they great artists or misers, are interested in money for itself. And you can kick out those misers who are conditioned by fear."

By now there was a large pile of empty cartons on the floor. I carried them to the storeroom to be trimmed and kept. Lots of people carry supplies home in them and, as Marullo would say, "It saves bags, kid."

There's that "kid" again. I don't mind it any more. I want him to call me "kid," even to think of me as "kid." While I was stacking the cartons, there came a battering on the front door. I looked at my big old silver railroad watch, and do you know for the first time in my life I had not opened on the moment of nine. Here it was plainly quarter after nine. All that discussion with the groceries had thrown me. Through the glass-and-iron screen of the door I could see it was Margie Young-Hunt. I had never really looked at her, had never inspected her. Maybe that's why she did the fortune—just to make sure I knew she existed. I shouldn't change too quickly.

I threw open the doors.

"Didn't mean to rout you out."

"But I'm late."

"Are you?"

"Sure. It's after nine."

She sauntered in. Her behind stuck out nice and round and bounced slowly, one up and one down with each step. She was well enough stacked in front so she didn't have to emphasize them. They were there. Margie is what Joey-boy would call a "dish," and my own son Allen too, maybe. Perhaps I was seeing her for the first time. Her features regular, nose a little long, lips outlined fuller than they were, the lower particularly. Her hair dyed a rich chestnut brown that doesn't occur in nature, but pretty. Her chin was fragile and deep-cut but there was plenty of muscle in the cheeks and very wide cheekbones. Margie's eyes had had care. They were that hazel to blue to steel color that changes with the light. It was a durable face that had taken it and could take it, even violence, even punching. Her eyes flicked about, to me, to the groceries, and back to me. I imagined she was a very close observer and a good rememberer too.

"I hope you don't have the same problem as yesterday."

She laughed. "No—no. I don't get a drummer every day. This time I really ran out of coffee."

"Most people do."

"What do you mean?"

"Well, the first ten people every morning ran out of coffee."

"Is that true?"

"Sure. Say, I want to thank you for sending your drummer in."

"It was his idea."

"But you did it. What kind of coffee?"

"Doesn't matter. I make lousy coffee no matter what kind I get."

"Do you measure?"

"Sure, and it's still lousy. Coffee just isn't—I nearly said 'my cup of tea.' "

"You did say it. Try this blend." I picked a can from the shelf and as she reached to take it from me—just that little gesture—every part of her body moved, shifted, announced itself quietly. I'm here, the leg. Me, the thigh. Not better than me, the soft belly. Everything was new, newly seen. I caught my breath. Mary says a woman can put out signals or not, just as she wishes. And if that's so, Margie had a communications system that ran from her pointed patent-leather toe to her curving soft chestnut hair.

"You seem to have got over your mullygrabs."

"I had 'em bad yesterday. Don't know where they come from."

"Don't I know! Sometimes with me not for the usual reason."

"You did quite a job with that fortune."

"Sore about it?"

"No. I'd just like to know how you did it."

"You don't believe in that stuff."

"It's not belief. You hit some things right on the nose. Things I'd been thinking and things I've been doing."

"Like what?"

"Like it's time for a change."

"You think I rigged the cards, don't you?"

"Doesn't matter. If you did—what made you? Have you thought of that?"

She looked me full in the eyes, suspicious, probing, questioning. "Yeah!" she said softly. "I mean no, I never thought of that. If I rigged them, what made me? That would be like unrigging the rig."

Mr. Baker looked in the door. "Morning, Margie," he said. "Ethan, have you given any thought to my suggestion?"

"I sure have. And I'd like to talk to you."

"Any time at all, Ethan."

"Well, I can't get out during the week. You know, Marullo's hardly ever here. Going to be home tomorrow?"

"After church, sure. That's an idea. You bring Mary about four. While the ladies jaw about Easter hats, we'll slip off and—"

"I've got a hundred things I want to ask. Guess I better write them down."

"Anything I know, you're welcome to. See you then. Morning, Margie."

When he went out, Margie said, "You're beginning fast."

"Maybe just limbering up. Say—know what would be interesting? How about if you turned the cards blindfolded or something and see how close they come to yesterday."

"No!" she said. "That wouldn't work. You kidding me, or do you really go for it?"

"Way I look at it, it doesn't matter about believing. I don't believe in extrasensory perception, or lightning or the hydrogen bomb, or even violets or schools of fish—but I know they exist. I don't believe in ghosts but I've seen them."

"Now you're kidding."

"I'm not."

"You don't seem like the same man."

"I'm not. Maybe nobody is, for long."

"What caused it, Eth?"

"I don't know. Maybe I'm sick of being a grocery clerk."

"It's about time."

"Do you really like Mary?"

"Sure I do. Why would you ask that?"

"You just don't seem to be the same kind of—well, you're so different from her."

"I see what you mean. But I do like her. I love her."

"So do I."

"Lucky."

"I know I am."

"I meant her. Well, I'll go make my lousy coffee. I'll think about that card deal."

"Sooner the better, before it cools."

She tapped out, her neat buttocks jumping like live rubber. I had never seen her before. I wonder how many people I've looked at all my life and never seen. It's scary to think about. Point of reference again. When two people meet, each one is changed by the other so you've got two new people. Maybe that means—hell, it's complicated. I agreed with myself to think about such things at night when I couldn't sleep. Forgetting to open on time scared me. That's like dropping your handkerchief at the scene of the murder, or your glasses like those what-you-callems in Chicago. What does that mean? What crime? What murder?

At noon I made four sandwiches, cheese and ham, with lettuce and mayonnaise. Ham and cheese, ham and cheese—when a man marries, he lives in the trees. I took two of the sandwiches and a bottle of Coke to the back door of the bank and handed them in to Joey-boy. "Find the mistake?"

"Not yet. You know, I'm so close to it, I'm blind."

"Why not lay off till Monday?"

"Can't. Banks are a screwy lot."

"Sometimes if you don't think about something, it comes to you."

"I know. Thanks for the sandwiches." He looked inside to make sure there was lettuce and mayonnaise.

Saturday afternoon before Easter in the grocery business is what my august and illiterate son would call "for the birds." But two things did happen that proved to me at least that some deep-down underwater change was going on in me. I mean that yesterday, or any yesterday before that, I wouldn't have done what I did. It's like looking at wallpaper samples. I guess I had unrolled a new pattern.

The first thing was Marullo coming in. His arthritis was hurting him pretty bad. He kept flexing his arms like a weight-lifter.

"How it goes?"

"Slow, Alfio." I had never called him by his first name before.

"Nobody in town—"

"I like it better when you call me 'kid.' "

"I thought you don't like it."

"I find I do, Alfio."

"Everybody gone away." His shoulders must have been burning as though there were hot sand in the joints.

"How long ago did you come from Sicily?"

"Forty-seven years. Long time."

"Ever been back?"

"No."

"Why don't you go on a visit?"

"What for? Everything changed."

"Don't you get curious about it?"

"Not much."

"Any relatives alive?"

"Sure, my brother and his kids and they got kids."

"I'd think you'd want to see them."

He looked at me, I guess, as I'd looked at Margie, saw me for the first time.

"What you got on your mind, kid?"

"Hurts me to see your arthritis. I thought how its warm in Sicily. Might knock the pain out."

He looked at me suspiciously. "What's with you?"

"How do you mean?"

"You look different."

"Oh! I got a little bit of good news."

"Not going to quit?"

"Not right away. If you wanted to make a trip to Italy, I could promise I'd be here."

"What's good news?"

"Can't tell you yet. It's like this. . . ." I balanced my palm back and forth.

"Money?"

"Could be. Look, you're rich enough. Why don't you go back to Sicily and show 'em what a rich American looks like? Soak up some sun. I can take care of the store. You know that."

"You ain't quitting?"

"Hell, no. You know me well enough to know I wouldn't run out on you."

"You changed, kid. Why?"

"I told you. Go bounce the bambinos."

"I don't belong there," he said, but I knew I'd planted something—really something. And I knew he'd come in late that night and go over the books. He's a suspicious bastard.

He'd hardly left when—well, it was like yesterday—the B. B. D. and D. drummer came in.

"Not on business," he said. "I'm staying the weekend out at Montauk. Thought I'd drop in."

"I'm glad you did," I said. "I want to give you this." I held out the billfold with the twenty sticking out.

"Hell, that's good will. I told you I'm not on business."

"Take it!"

"What you getting at?"

"It constitutes a contract where I come from."

"What's the matter, you sore?"

"Certainly not."

"Then why?"

"Take it! The bids aren't all in."

"Jesus—did Waylands make a better offer?"

"No."

"Who, then—them damn discount houses?"

I pushed the twenty-dollar bill into his breast pocket behind his peaked handkerchief. "I'll keep the billfold," I said. "It's nice."

"Look I can't make an offer without I talk to the head office. Don't close till maybe Tuesday. I'll telephone you. If I say it's Hugh, you'll know who it is."

"It's your money in the pay phone."

"Well, hold it open, will you?"

"It's open," I said. "Doing any fishing?"

"Only for dames. I tried to take that dish Margie out there. She wouldn't go. Damn near snapped my head off. I don't get dames."

"They're curiouser and curiouser."

"You can say that again," he said, and I haven't heard that expression in fifteen years. He looked worried. "Don't do anything till you hear from me," he said. "Jesus, I thought I was conning a country boy."

"I will not sell my master short."

"Nuts. You just raised the ante."

"I just refused a bribe if you feel the urge to talk about it."

I guess that proves I was different. The guy began to look at me with respect and I liked it. I loved it. The bugger thought I was like him, only better at it.

Just before I was ready to close up Mary telephoned. "Ethan," she said, "now don't get mad—"

"At what, flower feet?"

"Well, she's so lonely and I thought—well, I asked Margie to dinner."

"Why not?"

"You're not mad?"

"Hell, no."

"Don't swear. Tomorrow's Easter."

"That reminds me, press your prettiest. We're going to Baker's at four o'clock."

"At their house?"

"Yes, for tea."

"I'll have to wear my Easter church outfit."

"Good stuff, fern tip."

"You're not mad about Margie?"

"I love you," I said. And I do. I really do. And I remember thinking what a hell of a man a man could become.

CHAPTER V

W<small>HEN</small> I walked up Elm Street and turned in at the walk of buried ballast stones, I stopped and looked at the old place. It felt different. It felt mine. Not Mary's, not Father's, not old Cap'n's, but mine. I could sell it or burn it or keep it.

I'd taken only two of the back steps when the screen door whapped open and Allen boiled out yelling, "Where's the Peeks? Didn't you bring me the Peeks?"

"No," I said. And, wonder layered with wonders, he didn't scream his pain and loss. He didn't appeal to his mother to agree that I had promised.

He said, "Oh!" and went quietly away.

"Good evening," I said to his retreating back and he stopped and said, "Good evening," as though it were a foreign word he'd just learned.

Mary came into the kitchen. "You've had a haircut," she said. She identifies any strangeness in me as a fever or a haircut.

"No, pin curl, I have not."

"Well, I've been going like spit to get the house ready."

"Ready?"

"I told you, Margie's coming for dinner."

"I know, but why all the festive hurly-burly?"

"We haven't had a dinner guest in ages."

"That's true. That's really true."

"Are you going to put on your dark suit?"

"No, Old Dobbin, my decent gray."

"Why not the dark?"

"Don't want to spoil the press for church tomorrow."

"I can press it tomorrow morning."

"I'll wear Old Dobbin, as sweet a suit as you'll find in the county."

"Children," she called, "don't you touch anything! I've put out the nut dishes. You don't want to wear the dark?"

"No."

"Margie will be dressed to the nines."

"Margie likes Old Dobbin."

"How do you know?"

"She told me."

"She did not."

"Wrote a letter to the paper about it."

"Be serious. You *are* going to be nice to her?"

"I'm going to make love to her."

"I'd think you'd like to wear the dark—with her coming."

"Look, flower girl, when I came in, I didn't give a damn what I wore or nothing. In two short moments you have made it impossible for me to wear anything but Old Dobbin."

"Just to be mean?"

"Sure."

"Oh!" she said in the same tone Allen had used.

"What's for dinner? I want to wear a tie to match the meat."

"Roast chicken. Can't you smell it?"

"Guess I can. Mary—I—" But I didn't go on. Why do it? You can't buck a national instinct. She'd been to the Chicken Bargain Day at the Safe Rite Store. Cheaper than Marullo's. Of course I got them wholesale and I have explained to Mary the come-on bargains at the chain stores. The bargain draws you in and you pick up a dozen other things that aren't bargains just because they're under your hand. Everyone knows it and everyone does it.

My lecture to Mary Manyflowers died afoaling. The New Ethan Allen Hawley goes along with the national follies and uses them when he can.

Mary said, "I hope you don't think I was disloyal."

"My darling, what can be virtuous or sinful about a chicken?"

"It was awful cheap."

"I think you did the wise—the wifely thing."

"You're making fun."

Allen was in my bedroom waiting for me. "Can I look at your Knight Templar sword?"

"Sure. It's in the corner of the closet."

He knew perfectly well where it was. While I skinned off my clothes, he got it out of the leather case and unsheathed it and held the shiny plated blade up in the light and looked at his noble posture in the mirror.

"How's the essay going?"

"Huh?"

"Don't you mean, 'I beg your pardon, sir'?"

"Yes, sir."

"I said, how's the essay?"

"Oh! Fine."

"You going to do it?"

"Sure."

"Sure?"

"Sure, sir."

"You can look at the hat, too. In that big leather case on the shelf. Feather's kind of yellowy."

I got in the big old wide-bottomed tub with the lion's feet. They made them big enough to luxuriate in in those days. I scrubbed Marullo and the whole day off my skin with a brush and I shaved in the tub without looking, feeling for the whiskers with my fingertips. Everyone would agree that's pretty Roman and decadent. While I combed my hair, I looked in the mirror. I hadn't seen my face in a long time. It's quite possible to shave every day and never really to see your face, particularly if you don't care much for it. Beauty is only skin deep, and also beauty must come from inside. It better be the second if I was to get anywhere. It isn't that I have an ugly face. To me, it just isn't interesting. I made a few expressions and gave it up. They weren't noble or menacing or proud or funny. It was just the same damn face making faces.

When I came back to the bedroom, Allen had the plumed Knight Templar hat on, and if it makes me look that silly I must resign. The leather hatbox was open on the floor. It has a support made of velvet-covered cardboard like an upside-down porridge bowl.

"I wonder if they can bleach that ostrich plume or do I have to get a new one?"

"If you get a new one, can I have this?"

"Why not? Where's Ellen? I haven't heard her young screechy voice."

"She's writing on her I Love America essay."

"And you?"

"I'm thinking about it. Will you bring some Peeks home?"

"I'll probably forget it. Why don't you drop in at the store and pick it up someday?"

"Okay. Mind if I ask something—sir?"

"I'd be flattered."

"Did we use to own all High Street for two blocks?"

"We did."

"And did we have whaling ships?"

"Yep."

"Well, why don't we now?"

"We lost them."

"How come?"

"Just up and lost them."

"That's a joke."

"It's a pretty darned serious joke, if you dissect it."

"We're dissecting a frog at school."

"Good for you. Not so good for the frog. Which of these beauty-ties shall I wear?"

"The blue one," he said without interest. "Say, when you get dressed can you—have you got time to come up in the attic?"

"I'll make time if it's important."

"Will you come?"

"I will."

"All right. I'll go up now and turn on the light."

"Be with you in a couple of tie-tying moments."

His footsteps sounded hollowly on the uncarpeted attic stairs.

If I think about it while I tie a bow, the tie has a rotating tendency, but if I let my fingers take their own way, they do it perfectly. I commissioned my fingers and thought about the attic of the old Hawley house, my house, my attic. It is not a dark and spidery prison for the broken and the abandoned. It has windows with small panes so old that the light comes through lavender and the outside is wavery—like a world seen through water. The books stored there are not waiting to be thrown out or given to the Seamen's Institute. They sit comfortably on their shelves waiting to be rediscovered. And the chairs, some unfashionable for a time, some rump-sprung, are large and soft. It is not a dusty place either. Housecleaning is attic-cleaning also, and since it is mostly closed away, dust does not enter. I remember as a child scrambling among the brilliants of books or, battered with agonies, or in the spectral half-life that requires loneliness, retiring to the attic, to lie curled in a great body-molded chair in the violet-lavender light from the window. There I could study the big adze-squared beams that support the roof—see how they are mortised one into another and pinned in place with oaken dowels. When it rains from rustling drip to roar on the roof, it is a fine secure place. Then the books, tinted with light, the picture books of children grown, seeded, and gone; *Chatterboxes* and the Rollo series; a thousand acts of God—*Fire, Flood, Tidal Waves, Earthquakes*—all fully illustrated; the Gustave Doré Hell, with Dante's squared cantos like bricks between; and the heartbreaking stories of Hans Christian Andersen, the blood-chilling violence and cruelty of the Grimm Brothers, the Morte d'Arthur of majesty with drawings by Aubrey Beardsley, a sickly, warped creature, a strange choice to illustrate great, manly Malory.

I remember thinking how wise a man was H. C. Andersen. The king told his secrets down a well, and his secrets were safe. A man who tells secrets or stories must think of who is hearing or reading, for a story has as many versions as it has readers. Everyone takes what he wants or can from it and thus changes it to his measure. Some pick out parts and reject the rest, some strain the story through their mesh of prejudice, some paint it with their own delight. A story must have some points of contact with the reader to make him feel at home in it. Only then can he accept wonders. The tale I may tell to Allen must be differently built from the same tale told to my Mary, and that in turn shaped to fit Marullo if Marullo is to join it. But perhaps the Well of Hosay Andersen is best. It only receives, and the echo it gives back is quiet and soon over.

I guess we're all, or most of us, the wards of that nineteenth-century science which denied existence to anything it could not measure or explain. The things we couldn't explain went right on but surely not with our blessing. We did not see what we couldn't explain, and meanwhile a great part of the world was abandoned to children, insane people, fools, and mystics, who were more interested in what is than in why it is. So many old and lovely things are stored in the world's attic, because we don't want them around us and we don't dare throw them out.

A single unshaded light hung from a roof beam. The attic is floored with hand-hewn pine planks twenty inches wide and two inches thick, ample support for the neat stacks of trunks and boxes, of paper-wrapped lamps and vases and all manner of exiled finery. And the light glowed softly on the generations of books in open bookcases—all clean and dustless. My Mary is a stern and uncompromising dust harrier and she is neat as a top sergeant. The books are arranged by size and color.

Allen rested his forehead on the top of a bookcase and glared down at the books. His right hand was on the pommel of the Knight Templar sword, point downward like a cane.

"You make a symbolic picture, my son. Call it 'Youth, War, and Learning.' "

"I want to ask you—you said there was books to look up stuff."

"What kind of stuff?"

"Patriotic jazz, for the essay."

"I see. Patriotic jazz. How's this for beat? 'Is life so dear or peace so sweet as to be purchased at the price of chains and slavery? Forbid it, Almighty God! I know not what course others may take, but as for me, give me liberty or give me death!' "

"Great! That's the berries."

"Sure is. There were giants on the earth in those days."

"I wisht I lived then. Pirate ships. Oh boy! Bang-bang! Strike your colors! Pots of gold and ladies in silk dresses and jewels. I sure wisht I lived then. Some of our folks done— did it. You said so yourself."

"Kind of genteel piracy—they called them privateers. I guess it wasn't as sweet as it sounds from a distance. Salt beef and biscuit. There was scurvy on the earth in those days too."

"I wouldn't mind that. I'd get the gold and bring it home. I guess they won't let you do it any more."

"No—it's bigger and better organized now. They call it diplomacy."

"There's a boy in our school that won two television prizes—fifty dollars and two hundred dollars. How's that?"

"He must be smart."

"Him? Course not. It's a trick, he says. You got to learn the trick and then you get a gimmick."

"Gimmick?"

"Sure—like you're a cripple or you support your old mother raising frogs. That gives you audience interest so they choose you. He's got a magazine with every contest in the whole country in it. Can I get one of those magazines, Pop?"

"Well, piracy is out, but I guess the impulse lingers."

"How do you mean?"

"Something for nothing. Wealth without effort."

"Can I get that magazine?"

"I thought such things were in disrepute since the payola scandals."

"Hell, no. I mean no, sir. They just changed it around a little. I'd sure like to cut in on some of that loot."

"It is loot, isn't it?"

"It's all dough, no matter how you get it."

"I don't believe that. It doesn't hurt the money to get it that way but it hurts the one who gets it."

"I don't see how. It's not against the law. Why, some of the biggest people in this country—"

"Charles, my son, my son."

"How do you mean, Charles?"

"Do you have to be rich, Allen? Do you have to?"

"Do you think I like to live without no motorbike? Must be twenty kids with motorbikes. And how you think it is if your family hasn't even got a car, leave alone no television?"

"I'm deeply shocked."

"You don't know how it is, Dad. One day in class I did a theme how my great-granddad was a whaling captain."

"He was."

"Whole class bust out laughing. Know what they call me? Whaley. How'd you like that?"

"Pretty bad."

"It wouldn't be so bad if you were a lawyer or in a bank or like that. Know what I'm going to do with the first chunk of loot I win?"

"No, what?"

"I'm going to buy you an automobile so you won't feel so lousy when other people all got one."

I said, "Thank you, Allen." My throat was dry.

"Oh, that's all right. I can't get a license yet anyway."

"You'll find all the great speeches of our nation in that case, Allen. I hope you'll read some of them."

"I will. I need to."

"You surely do. Good hunting." I went quietly down the stairs and moistened my lips as I went. And Allen was right. I felt lousy.

When I sat down in my big chair under the reading light, Mary brought the paper to me.

"What a comfort you are, wiggles."

"That suit looks real nice."

"You're a good loser and a good cook."

"The tie matches your eyes."

"You're up to something. I can tell. I'll trade you a secret for a secret."

"But I don't have one," she said.

"Make one up!"

"I can't. Come on, Ethan, tell me."

"Any eary children listening in?"

"No."

"Well, Margie Young-Hunt came in today. Out of coffee, so she said. I think she's carrying a torch for me."

"Come on, tell."

"Well, we were talking about the fortune and I said it would be interesting to do it again and see if it was the same."

"You didn't!"

"I did so. And she said it would be interesting."

"But you don't like things like that."

"I do when they're good."

"Think she'll do it tonight?"

"If you care to offer me a penny for my thoughts, I think that's why she's coming."

"Oh, no! I asked her."

"After she set you up for it."

"You don't like her."

"On the contrary—I'm beginning to like her very much, and to respect her."

"I wish I could tell when you're joking."

Ellen came in then quietly so that you couldn't tell whether she had been listening but I suspect she had. Ellen is a girl-girl-girl and thirteen to boot, sweet and sad, gay and delicate, sickly when she needs it. She is in that stage like dough beginning to set. She may be pretty, or not. She is a leaner, leans on me, breathes on me too, but her breath is sweet like a cow's breath. She's a toucher, too.

Ellen leaned on the arm of my chair and her thin little shoulder touched mine. She ran one pink finger down my coat sleeve and onto the hairs on my wrist and it tickled. The blond hairs on her arm shone like gold dust under the lamp. A devious one, she is, but then I guess all girl-girl-girls are.

"Nail polish," I said.

"Mama lets me if it's only pink. Your nails are rough."

"Aren't they?"

"But they're clean."

"I scrubbed them."

"I hate dirty nails like Allen's."

"Maybe you just hate Allen lock, stock, and bobtail."

"I do."

"Good for you. Why don't you kill him?"

"You're silly." She crawled her fingers behind my ear. She's probably making some boy kids very nervous already.

"I hear you are working on your essay."

"Stinker told you."

"Is it good?"

"Oh, yes! Very good. I'll let you read it when it's done."

"Honored. I see you're dressed for the occasion."

"This old thing? I'm saving my new dress for tomorrow."

"Good idea. There'll be boys."

"I hate boys. I do hate boys."

"I know you do. Hostility is your motto. I don't like 'em much myself. Now lean off me a minute. I want to read the paper."

She flounced like a 1920 movie star and instantly took her revenge. "When are you going to be rich?"

Yes, she'll give some man a bad time. My instinct was to grab her and paddle her but that's exactly what she wanted. I do believe she had eye shadow on. There was as little pity in her eyes as you'll find in a panther's eyes.

"Next Friday," I said.

"Well, I wish you'd hurry up. I'm sick of being poor." And she slipped quickly out. A listener at doors too. I do love her, and that's odd because she is everything I destest in anyone else—and I adore her.

No newspaper for me. I hadn't even unfolded it when Margie Young-Hunt arrived. She was done up—hairdresser done up. I guess Mary would know how it's done, but I don't.

In the morning the out-of-coffee Margie was set for me like a bear trap. The same evening she drew a bead on Mary. If her behind bounced, I couldn't see it. If anything was under her neat suit, it was hiding. She was a perfect guest —for another woman—helpful, charming, complimentary, thoughtful, modest. She treated me as though I had taken on forty years since the morning. What a wonderful thing a woman is. I can admire what they do even if I don't understand why.

While Margie and Mary went through their pleasant litany, "What have you done with your hair?" . . . "I like it" . . . "That's your color. You should always wear it"—the harmless recognition signals of women—I thought of the most feminine story I ever heard. Two women meet. One cries, "What have you done with your hair? It looks like a wig." "It is a wig." "Well, you'd never know it."

Maybe these are deeper responses than we know or have any right to know.

Dinner was a series of exclamations about the excellence of the roast chicken and denials that it was edible. Ellen studied our guest with a recording eye, every detail of hairdress and make-up. And I knew then how young they start the minute examination on which they base what is called their intuition. Ellen avoided my eyes. She knew she had shot to kill and she expected revenge. Very well, my savage daughter. I shall revenge myself in the cruelest way you can imagine. I shall forget it.

And it was a good dinner, over-rich and too much of it, as company dinners must be, and a mountain of dishes not ordinarily used. And coffee afterward, which we do not ordinarily have.

"Doesn't it keep you awake?"

"Nothing keeps me awake."

"Not even me?"

"Ethan!"

And then the silent, deadly war of the dishes. "Let me help."

"Not at all. You're the guest."

"Well, let me carry them."

Mary's eyes sought out the children and her spirit moved on them with fixed bayonet. They knew what was coming, but they were helpless.

Mary said, "The children always do it. They love to. And they do it so well. I'm proud of them."

"Well, isn't that nice? You don't see it much any more."

"I know. We feel very fortunate that they want to help."

I could read their ferrety little minds, looking for an escape, thinking of making a fuss, getting sick, dropping the beautiful old dishes. Mary must have read their evil little minds also. She said, "The remarkable thing is that they never break anything, don't even chip a glass."

"Well, you are blessed!" Margie said. "How did you teach them?"

"I didn't. It's just natural with them. You know, some people are just naturally clumsy; well, Allen and Ellen are just naturally clever with their hands."

I glanced at the kids to see how they were handling it. They knew they were being taken. I think they wondered whether Margie Young-Hunt knew it. They were still looking for an escape. I dropped the beam full on them.

"Of course they like to hear compliments," I said, "but we're holding them up. They'll miss the movie if we don't let them get to it."

Margie had the grace not to laugh and Mary gave me a quick and startled look of admiration. They hadn't even asked to go to the movie.

Even if teen-age children aren't making a sound, it's quieter when they're gone. They put a boiling in the air around them. As they left, the whole house seemed to sigh and settle. No wonder poltergeists infest only houses with adolescent children.

The three of us circled warily around the subject each one knew was coming. I went to the glass-fronted cabinet and took out three long-stemmed, lily-shaped glasses, cotton twist, brought home from England, heaven knows how long ago. And I poured from a basket-covered gallon jug, dark and discolored with age.

"Jamaica rum," I said. "Hawleys were seamen."

"Must be very old," said Margie Young-Hunt.

"Older than you or me or my father."

"It'll take the top of your head off," Mary said. "Well, this must be a party. Ethan only gets it out for weddings and funerals. Do you think it's all right, dear? Just before Easter, I mean?"

"The Sacrament isn't Coca-Cola, my darling."

"Mary, I've never seen your husband so gay."

"It's the fortune you read," said Mary. "It's changed him overnight."

What a frightening thing is the human, a mass of gauges and dials and registers, and we can read only a few and those perhaps not accurately. A flare of searing red pain formed in my bowels and moved upward until it speared and tore at the place just under my ribs. A great wind roared in my ears and drove me like a helpless ship, dismasted before it could shorten sail. I tasted bitter salt and I saw a pulsing, heaving room. Every warning signal screamed danger, screamed havoc, screamed shock. It caught me as I passed behind my ladies' chairs and doubled me over in quaking agony, and just as suddenly it was gone. I straightened up and moved on and they didn't even know it had happened. I understand how people once believed the devil could take possession. I'm not sure I don't believe it. Possession! The seething birth of something foreign with every nerve resisting and losing the fight and settling back beaten to make peace with the invader. Violation—that's the word, if you can think of the sound of a word edged with blue flame like a blowtorch.

My dear's voice came through. "It doesn't really harm to hear nice things," she said.

I tried my voice and it was strong and good. "A little hope, even hopeless hope, never hurt anybody," I said, and I put the jug away in its cabinet, and went back to my chair and drank half the glass of ancient, fragrant rum and sat down and crossed my knees and locked my fingers in my lap.

"I don't understand him," Mary said. "He's always hated fortune-telling, made jokes about it. I just don't understand."

My nerve ends were rustling like dry, windblown winter grass and my laced fingers had whitened from pressure.

"I'll try to explain it to Mrs. Young—to Margie," I said. "Mary comes from a noble but poor Irish family."

"We weren't all that poor."

"Can't you hear it in her speech?"

"Well, now that you mention it—"

"Well, Mary's sainted, or should be, grandmother was a good Christian, wasn't she, Mary?"

It seemed to me a little hostility was growing in my dear. I went on. "But she had no trouble believing in fairy people, although in strict, unbending Christian theology the two don't mix."

"But that's different."

"Of course it is, darling. Nearly everything's different. Can you disbelieve in something you don't know about?"

"Look out for him," Mary said. "He'll catch you in a word trap."

"I will not. I don't know about fortunes or fortune-telling. How can I not believe in it? I believe it exists because it happens."

"But you don't believe it's true."

"What's true is that people get it done, millions of them, and pay for it. That's enough to know to be interested, isn't it?"

"But you don't—"

"Wait! It isn't that I don't believe but that I don't know. They're not the same thing. I don't know which comes first —the fortune or the fortune-telling."

"I think I know what he means."

"You do?" Mary was not pleased.

"Suppose the fortune-teller was sensitive to things that are going to happen anyway. Is that what you mean?"

"That's different. But how can cards know?"

I said, "The cards can't even move without someone turning them."

Margie did not look at me but I knew she sensed Mary's growing unease and she wanted instructions.

"Couldn't we work out a test?" I asked.

"Well, that's a funny thing. These things seem to resent a test and go away, but there's no harm trying. Can you think of a test?"

"You haven't touched your rum." They lifted their glasses together and sipped and put them down. I finished mine and got out the bottle.

"Ethan, do you think you should?"

"Yes, dearling." I filled my glass. "Why can't you turn the cards blindfolded?"

"They have to be read."

"How would it be if Mary turned them or I did, and you read them?"

"There's supposed to be a closeness between the reader and the cards, but I don't know—we could try."

Mary said, "I think if we do it at all, we ought to do it the right way." She's always that way. She doesn't like change —little change, I mean. The big ones she can handle better than anyone, blows up at a cut finger but would be calm and efficient with a cut throat. I had a throb of unease because I had told Mary we discussed this, and here we were seeming to think of it for the first time.

"We talked about it this morning."

"Yes, when I came in for coffee. I've been thinking about it all day. I brought the cards."

It is Mary's tendency to confuse intentness with anger and anger with violence and she is terrified of violence. Some drinking uncles put that fear on her, and it's a shame. I could feel her fear rising.

"Let's not fool with it," I said. "Let's play some cassino instead."

Margie saw the tactic, knew it, had probably used it. "All right with me."

"My fortune's set. I'm going to be rich. Let it go at that."

"You see, I told you he didn't believe in it. He leads you all around the bush and then he won't play. He makes me so mad sometimes."

"I do? You never show it. You are always my darling wife."

Isn't it strange how sometimes you can feel currents and cross-currents—not always, but sometimes. Mary doesn't use her mind for organized thought and maybe this makes her more receptive of impressions. A tension was growing in the room. It crossed my mind that she might not be best friends with Margie any more—might never feel easy with her.

"I'd really like to know about the cards," I said. "I'm ignorant. I always heard that gypsies do it. Are you a gypsy? I don't think I ever knew one."

Mary said, "Her maiden name was Russian but she's from Alaska."

Then that accounted for the wide cheekbones.

Margie said, "I have a guilty secret I've never told you, Mary, how we came to be in Alaska."

"The Russians owned it," I said. "We bought it from them."

"Yes, but did you know it was a prison, like Siberia, only for worse crimes?"

"What kind of crimes?"

"The worst. My great-grandmother was sentenced to Alaska for witchcraft."

"What did she do?"

"She raised storms."

I laughed. "I see you come by it naturally."

"Raising storms?"

"Reading cards—same thing, maybe."

Mary said, "You're joking. That isn't true."

"It may be joking, Mary, but it's true. That was the worst crime, worse than murder. I've still got her papers—only of course they're in Russian."

"Can you speak Russian?"

"Only a little now."

I said, "Maybe witchcraft still is the worst crime."

"See what I mean?" said Mary. "He jumps this side and that side. You never know what he's thinking. Last night he —he got up before daylight this morning. Went for a walk."

"I'm a scoundrel," I said. "An unmitigated, unredeemable rascal."

"Well, I would like to see Margie turn the cards—but her own way without you mixing in. If we keep talking, the children will be home and then we can't."

"Excuse me a moment," I said. I climbed the stairs to our bedroom. The sword was on the bed and the hatbox open on the floor. I went to the bathroom and flushed the toilet. You can hear the water rushing all over the house. I wet a cloth in cold water and pressed it against my forehead and particularly against my eyes. They seemed to bulge from inside pressure. The cold water felt good. I sat on the toilet seat and put my face down against the damp washcloth and when it warmed up I wet it again. Going through the bedroom, I picked the plumed Knight Templar's hat from its box and marched down the stairs wearing it.

"Oh, you fool," said Mary. And she looked glad and relieved. The ache went out of the air.

"Can they bleach ostrich feathers?" I asked. "It's turned yellow."

"I think so. Ask Mr. Schultz."

"I'll take it down Monday."

"I wish Margie would turn the cards," said Mary. "I would dearly love that."

I put the hat on the newel post of the banister, and it looked like a drunken admiral if there is such a thing.

"Get the card table, Eth. It takes lots of room."

I brought it from the hall closet and snapped the legs open.

"Margie likes a straight chair."

I set a dining chair. "Do we have to do anything?"

"Concentrate," said Margie.

"On what?"

"As near as possible on nothing. The cards are in my purse over on the couch."

I'd always thought of fortune-telling cards as greasy and thick and bent, but these were clean and shining, as though they were coated with plastic. They were longer and narrower than playing cards and many more than fifty-two. Margie sat straight at the table and fanned them—bright-colored pictures and intricate suits. The names were in French: *l'empereur, l'ermite, le chariot, la justice, le mat, le diable*—earth, sun, moon, and stars, and suits of swords, cups, batons, and money, I guess, if *deniero* means money, but the symbol was shaped like a heraldic rose, and each suit with its *roi, reine,* and *chevalier.* Then I saw strange cards—disturbing cards—a tower riven by lightning, a wheel of fortune, a man hanging by his feet from a gallows, called *le pendu,* and Death—*la mort,* a skeleton with a scythe.

"Kind of gloomy," I said. "Do the pictures mean what they seem to?"

"It's how they fall in relation. If they fall upside down they reverse their meaning."

"Is there a variation in meaning?"

"Yes. That's the interpretation."

The moment she had the cards Margie became formal. Under the lights her hands showed what I had seen before, that she was older than she looked.

"Where did you learn it?" I asked.

"I used to watch my grandmother and later I took it up as a trick for parties—I suppose a way of getting attention."

"Do you believe in it?"

"I don't know. Sometimes remarkable things come out. I don't know."

"Could the cards be a concentration ritual—psychic exercise?"

"Sometimes I think that's true. When I find I give a value to a card it didn't have before, that's when it is usually accurate." Her hands were like living things as they shuffled and cut and shuffled and cut again and passed them to me to cut.

"Who am I doing?"

"Read Ethan," Mary cried. "See if it matches yesterday's."

Margie looked at me. "Light hair," she said, "blue eyes. Are you under forty?"

"Just."

"The king of batons." She found it in the deck. "This is you"—a picture of a crowned and robed king holding a huge red and blue scepter and *Roi de Bâton* printed under him. She laid it out face up and reshuffled the deck. Then she turned the cards rapidly, speaking in a singsong voice as she did. A card on top of my card—"This covers you." Crosswise on top—"This crosses you." One above—"This crowns you." One below—"This is your foundation. This before, this behind you." She had formed a cross of cards on the table. Then rapidly she turned up four in a line to the left of the cross, saying, "Yourself, your house, your hopes, your future." The last card was the man hanged upside down, le pendu, but from where I sat across the table he was right side up.

"So much for my future."

"It can mean salvation," she said. Her forefinger traced the line of her lower lip.

Mary demanded, "Is the money there?"

"Yes—it's there," she said absently. And suddenly she gathered the cards, shuffled them over and over, and laid them out again, muttering her ritual under her breath. She didn't seem to study individual cards but to see the whole group at once, and her eyes were misty and remote.

A good trick, I thought, a killer at ladies' clubs—or anywhere else. So must the Pythoness have looked, cool and composed and confusing. If you can hold people tense, hardly breathing, expectant for a long time, they'll believe anything—not acting, so much as technique, timing. This woman was wasting her talent on traveling salesmen. But what did she want of us or of me? Suddenly she gathered the cards, patted them square, and put them in the red box, which said: *I. Muller & Cie, Fabrique de Cartes.*

"Can't do it," she said. "Happens sometimes."

Mary said breathlessly, "Did you see something you don't want to tell?"

"Oh, I'll tell all right! Once when I was a little girl I saw a snake change its skin, a Rocky Mountain rattler. I watched the whole thing. Well, looking at the cards, they disappeared and I saw that snake changing its skin, part dusty and ragged and part fresh and new. You figure it out."

I said, "Sounds like a trance state. Ever have it happen before?"

"Three times before."

"Make any sense the other times?"

"Not that I know of."

"Always the snake?"

"Oh, no! Other things, but just as crazy."

Mary said enthusiastically, "Maybe it's a symbol of the change in fortune that's coming to Ethan."

"Is he a rattlesnake?"

"Oh! I see what you mean."

"Makes me feel crawly," Margie said. "Once I kind of liked snakes and then when I grew up I hated them. They give me the willies. I'd better be going."

"Ethan can see you home."

"Wouldn't think of it."

"I'd be glad to."

Margie smiled at Mary. "You keep him right here with you," she said. "You don't know what it's like to be without one."

"Nonsense," said Mary. "You could get a husband by crooking your finger."

"That's what I did before. It's no good. If they come that easy, they're not worth having. Keep him home. Someone might grab him." She got into her coat as she talked—a fast scrammer. "Lovely dinner. I hope you'll ask me back. Sorry about the fortune, Ethan."

"Will we see you in church tomorrow?"

"No. I'm going up to Montauk tonight."

"But it's too cold and wet."

"I love the mornings on the sea up there. Good night." She was out before I could even hold the door for her, out as though something was after her.

Mary said, "I didn't know she was going up there tonight."

And I couldn't tell her: Neither did she.

"Ethan—what do you make of that fortune tonight?"

"She didn't tell one."

"You forget, she said there would be money. But what do you make of it? I think she saw something she didn't want to tell. Something that scared her."

"Maybe she once saw the snake and it stayed in her mind."

"You don't think it had a—meaning?"

"Honey roll, you're the fortune expert. How would I know?"

"Well, anyway, I'm glad you don't hate her. I thought you did."

"I'm tricky," I said. "I conceal my thoughts."

"Not from me you don't. They'll stay right through the second show."

"Come again?"

"The children. They always do. I thought you were wonderful about the dishes."

"I'm devious," I said. "And, in due course, I have designs on your honor."

CHAPTER VI

I T HAS been my experience to put aside a decision for future pondering. Then one day, fencing a piece of time to face the problem, I have found it already completed, solved, and the verdict taken. This must happen to everyone, but I have no way of knowing that. It's as though, in the dark and desolate caves of the mind, a faceless jury had met and decided. This secret and sleepless area in me I have always thought of as black, deep, waveless water, a spawning place from which only a few forms ever rise to the surface. Or maybe it's a great library where is recorded everything that has ever happened to living matter back to the first moment when it began to live.

I think some people have closer access to this place than others—poets, for example. Once, when I had a paper route and no alarm clock, I worked out a way to send a signal and to get a reply. Lying in bed at night, I would see myself standing on the edge of the black water. I pictured a white stone held in my hand, a circular stone. I would write on its surface in very black letters "4 o'clock," then drop the stone and watch it sink, turning over and over, until it disappeared. It worked for me. On the second of four I awakened. Later I could use it to arouse me at ten minutes of four or quarter after. And it never failed me.

And then sometimes a strange, sometimes hideous thing thrusts up to the surface as though a sea serpent or a kraken emerged from the great depths.

Only a year ago Mary's brother Dennis died in our house, died dreadfully, of an infection of the thyroid that forced the juices of fear through him so that he was violent and terrified and fierce. His kindly Irish horse-face grew bestial. I helped to hold him down, to pacify and reassure him in his death-dreaming, and it went on for a week before his lungs began to fill. I didn't want Mary to see him die. She had never seen death, and this one, I knew, might wipe out her sweet memory of a kindly man who was her brother. Then, as I sat waiting by his bed, a monster swam up out of my dark water. I hated him. I wanted to kill him, to bite out his throat. My jaw muscles tightened and I think my lips fleered back like a wolf's at the kill.

When it was over, in panic guilt I confessed what I had felt to old Doc Peele, who signed the death certificate.

"I don't think it's unusual," he said. "I've seen it on people's faces, but few admit it."

"But what causes it? I liked him."

"Maybe an old memory," he said. "Maybe a return to the time of the pack when a sick or hurt member was a danger. Some animals and most fish tear down and eat a weakened brother."

"But I'm not an animal—or a fish."

"No, you're not. And perhaps that's why you find it foreign. But it's there. It's all there."

He's a good old man, Doc Peele, a tired old man. He's birthed and buried us for fifty years.

Back to that Congress in the Dark—it must have been working overtime. Sometimes a man seems to reverse himself so that you would say, "He can't do that. It's out of character." Maybe it's not. It could be just another angle, or it might be that the pressures above or below have changed his shape. You see it in war a lot—a coward turning hero and a brave man crashing in flames. Or you read in the morning paper about a nice, kind family man who cuts down wife and children with an ax. I think I believe that a man is changing all the time. But there are certain moments when the change becomes noticeable. If I wanted to dig deep enough, I could probably trace the seeds of my change right back to my birth or before. Recently many little things had begun to form a pattern of larger things. It's as though events and experiences nudged and jostled me in a direction contrary to my normal one or the one I had come to think was normal—the direction of the grocery clerk, the failure, the man without real hope or drive, barred in by responsibilities for filling the bellies and clothing the bodies of his family, caged by habits and attitudes I thought of as being moral, even virtuous. And it may be that I had a smugness about being what I called a "Good Man."

And surely I knew what was going on around me. Marullo didn't have to tell me. You can't live in a town the size of New Baytown and not know. I didn't think about it much. Judge Dorcas fixed traffic tickets for favors. It wasn't even secret. And favors call for favors. The Town Manager, who was also Budd Building Supplies, sold equipment to the township at a high price, and some of it not needed. If a new paved street went in, it usually turned out that Mr. Baker and Marullo and half a dozen other business leaders had bought up the lots before the plan was announced. These were just facts of nature, but I had always believed they weren't facts of my nature. Marullo and Mr. Baker and the drummer and Margie Young-Hunt and Joey Morphy in a concentration had been nudging me and altogether it amounted to a push, so that "I've got to put aside a little time to think it out."

My darling was purring in her sleep, with the archaic smile on her lips, and she had the extra glow of comfort and solace she gets after love, a calm fulfilledness.

I should have been sleepy after wandering around the night before, but I wasn't. I've noticed that I am rarely sleepy if I know I can sleep long in the morning. The red dots were swimming on my eyes, and the street light threw the shadows of naked elm branches on the ceiling, where they made slow and stately cats' cradles because the spring wind was blowing. The window was open halfway and the white curtains swelled and filled like sails on an anchored boat. Mary must have white curtains and often washed. They give her a sense of decency and security. She pretends a little anger when I tell her it's her lace-curtain Irish soul.

I felt good and fulfilled too, but whereas Mary dives for sleep, I didn't want to go to sleep. I wanted to go on fully

tasting how good I felt. I wanted to think about the I Love
America Essay Contest my offspring were entering. But behind these and others, I wanted to consider what was happening to me and what to do about it, so naturally I got
out the last thing first and I found that the dark jury of the
deep had already decided for me. There it was, laid out and
certain. It was like training for a race and preparing and
finally being down at start with your spikes set in their holes.
No choice then. You go when the pistol cracks. I found I
was ready with my spikes set, waiting only for the shot. And
apparently I was the last to know. All day people had remarked that I looked well, by that meaning I looked different, more confident, changed. That drummer had a look of
shock in the afternoon. Marullo had inspected me uneasily.
And Joey-boy felt the need to apologize for something I had
done. Then Margie Young-Hunt—maybe she was the sharp-
est with her rattlesnake dream. Some way she had penetrated and discovered a certainty about me before I was
certain of it. And the symbol was a rattlesnake. I found I
was grinning in the dark. And afterward, confused, she used
the oldest trick—the threat of infidelity, a bait cast in a flowing tide to find what fish are feeding there. I didn't remember the secret whisper of her hidden body—no, the picture
was of her clawed hands that showed age and nervousness
and the cruelty that comes to one when control of a situation is lost.

Sometimes I wish I knew the nature of night thoughts.
They're close kin to dreams. Sometimes I can direct them,
and other times they take their head and come rushing over
me like strong, unmanaged horses.

Danny Taylor came in. I didn't want to think about him
and be sad but he came anyway. I had to use a trick a tough
old sergeant taught me once, and it works. There was a day
and a night and a day in the war that was all one piece, one
unit of which the parts were just about all the dirty dread-
fulness that can happen in that sick business. While it was
going on I'm not sure I knew its agony because I was busy
and unutterably tired, but afterward that unit of a day and
a night and a day came back to me over and over **again in**

my night thoughts until it was like that insanity they call battle fatigue and once named shell-shock. I used every trick I could not to think of it, but it crept back in spite of me. It waited through the day to get at me in the dark. Once mawkish with whisky I told it to my top sergeant, an old pro who had been in wars we have forgotten ever happened. If he had worn his ribbons, there'd have been no room for buttons—Mike Pulaski, a polack from Chicago, no relation to the hero. By good fortune, he was decently drunk or he might have clammed up out of a conditioned conviction about fraternizing with an officer.

Mike heard me out, staring at a spot between my eyes. "Yeah!" he said. "I know about that. Trouble is, a guy tries to shove it out of his head. That don't work. What you got to do is kind of welcome it."

"How do you mean, Mike?"

"Take it's something kind of long—you start at the beginning and remember everything you can, right to the end. Every time it comes back you do that, from the first right through the finish. Pretty soon it'll get tired and pieces of it will go, and before long the whole thing will go."

I tried it and it worked. I don't know whether the head-shrinkers know this but they should.

When Danny Taylor came into my night I gave him Sergeant Mike's treatment.

When we were kids together, same age, same size, same weight, we used to go to the grain and feed store on High Street and get on the scales. One week I'd be half a pound heavier and the next Danny would catch up with me. We used to fish and hunt and swim together and go out with the same girls. Danny's family was well fixed like most of the old families of New Baytown. The Taylor house is that white one with the tall fluted columns on Porlock Street. Once the Taylors had a country house too—about three miles from town.

The country all around us is rolling hills covered with trees, some scrub pine and some with second-growth oak, and hickory and some cedars. Once, long before I was born, the oaks were monsters, so big that the local-built ships

had cut their keels and ribs and planking within a short distance of the shipyards until it was all gone. In this roly-
poly country the Taylors once had a house set in the middle of a big meadow, the only level place for miles around.
It must once have been a lake bottom because it was flat
as a table and surrounded by low hills. Maybe sixty years
ago, the Taylor house burned down and was never rebuilt.
As kids Danny and I used to ride out there on bicycles. We
played in the stone cellar and built a hunting lodge of bricks
from the old foundation. The gardens must have been wonderful. We could see avenues of trees and a suggestion of
formal hedges and borders among the scrabble of the returned forest. Here and there would be a stretch of stone
balustrade, and once we found a bust of Pan on a tapering
stand. It had fallen on its face and buried its horns and
beard in the sandy loam. We stood it up and cleaned it
and celebrated it for a time, but greed and girls got the better of us. We finally carted it into Floodhampton and sold it
to a junk man for five dollars. It must have been a good
piece, maybe an old one.

Danny and I were friends as all boys must have friends.
Then his appointment to the Naval Academy came through.
I saw him once in uniform and not again for years. New
Baytown was and is a tight, close-made town. Everyone
knew Danny was expelled and no one discussed it. Taylors
died out, well, just as Hawleys died out. I'm the only one
left, and, of course, Allen, my son. Danny didn't come back
until they were all dead, and he came back a drunk. At
first I tried to help but he didn't want me. He didn't want
anybody. But, in spite of it, we were close—very close.

I went over everything I could remember right up to that
very morning when I gave him the dollar to let him find
his local oblivion.

The structure of my change was feeling, pressures from
without, Mary's wish, Allen's desires, Ellen's anger, Mr.
Baker's help. Only at the last when the move is mounted
and prepared does thought place a roof on the building and
bring in words to explain and to justify. Suppose my humble
and interminable clerkship was not virtue at all but a moral

laziness? For any success, boldness is required. Perhaps I was simply timid, fearful of consequences—in a word, lazy. Successful business in our town is not complicated or obscure and it is not widely successful either, because its practicers have set artificial limits for their activities. Their crimes are little crimes and so their success is small success. If the town government and the business complex of New Baytown were ever deeply investigated it would be found that a hundred legal and a thousand moral rules were broken, but they were small violations—petty larceny. They abolished part of the Decalogue and kept the rest. And when one of our successful men had what he needed or wanted, he reassumed his virtue as easily as changing his shirt, and for all one could see, he took no hurt from his derelictions, always assuming that he didn't get caught. Did any of them think about this? I don't know. And if small crimes could be condoned by self, why not a quick, harsh, brave one? Is murder by slow, steady pressure any less murder than a quick and merciful knife-thrust? I don't feel guilt for the German lives I took. Suppose for a limited time I abolished all the rules, not just some of them. Once the objective was reached, could they not all be reassumed? There is no doubt that business is a kind of war. Why not, then, make it all-out war in pursuit of peace? Mr. Baker and his friends did not shoot my father, but they advised him and when his structure collapsed they inherited. And isn't that a kind of murder? Have any of the great fortunes we admire been put together without ruthlessness? I can't think of any.

And if I should put the rules aside for a time, I knew I would wear scars but would they be worse than the scars of failure I was wearing? To be alive at all is to have scars.

All this wondering was the weather vane on top of the building of unrest and of discontent. It could be done because it had been done. But if I opened up that door, could I ever get it closed again? I did not know. I could not know until I had opened it. . . . Did Mr. Baker know? Had Mr. Baker even thought of it? . . . Old Cap'n thought the Bakers burned the *Belle-Adair* for the insurance. Could that and my father's misfortune be the reason Mr. Baker wanted to help me? Were these his scars?

What was happening could be described as a great ship being turned and bunted and shoved about and pulled around by many small tugs. Once turned by tide and tugs, it must set a new course and start its engines turning. On the bridge which is the planning center, the question must be asked: All right, I know now where I want to go. How do I get there, and where are lurking rocks and what will the weather be?

One fatal reef I knew was talk. So many betray themselves before they are betrayed, with a kind of wistful hunger for glory, even the glory of punishment. Andersen's Well is the only confidant to trust—Andersen's Well.

I called out to old Cap'n. "Shall I set the course, sir? Is it a good course? Will it get me there?"

And for the first time he denied me his command. "You'll have to work it out yourself. What's good for one is bad for another, and you won't know till after."

The old bastard might have helped me then, but perhaps it wouldn't have made any difference. No one wants advice —only corroboration.

CHAPTER VII

Wʜᴇɴ I awakened, old sleepy Mary was up and gone and coffee and bacon were afoot. I could smell them. And you'd have to search for a better day for a resurrection, a green and blue and yellow day. From the bedroom window I could see that everything was resurrecting, grass, trees. They chose a proper season for it. I put on my Christmas dressing gown and my birthday slippers. In the bathroom I found some of Allen's hair goo and slicked it on, so that my combed and brushed scalp felt tight like a cap.

Easter Sunday breakfast is an orgy of eggs and pancakes, and bacon curling about everything. I crept up on Mary and patted her silk-covered fanny and said, "*Kyrie eleison!*"

"Oh!" she said. "I didn't hear you coming." She regarded my dressing gown, paisley pattern. "Nice," she said. "You don't wear it enough."

"I haven't time. I haven't had time."

"Well, it's nice," she said.

"Ought to be. You picked it. Are the kids sleeping through these wonderful smells?"

"Oh, no. They're out back, hiding eggs. I wonder what Mr. Baker wants."

The quick jump never fails to startle me. "Mr. Baker, Mr. Baker. Oh! He probably wants to help me start my fortune."

"Did you tell him? About the cards?"

"Course not, darling. But maybe he guessed." Then I said seriously, "Look, cheesecake, you do think I have a great business brain, don't you?"

"What do you mean?" She had a pancake up for turning, and it stayed up.

"Mr. Baker thinks I should invest your brother's legacy."

"Well, if Mr. Baker—"

"Now wait. I don't want to do it. That's your money and your safety."

"Doesn't Mr. Baker know more about that than you do, dear?"

"I'm not sure. All I know is my father thought he knew. That's why I'm working for Marullo."

"Still, I think Mr. Baker—"

"Will you be guided by me, sweetheart?"

"Well, of course—"

"In everything?"

"Are you being silly?"

"I'm dead serious—dead!"

"I believe you are. But you can't go around doubting Mr. Baker. Why, he's—he's—"

"He's Mr. Baker. We'll listen to what he has to say and then—I still will want that money right in the bank where it is."

Allen shot through the back door as though fired by a slingshot. "Marullo," he said. "Mr. Marullo's outside. He wants to see you."

"Now what?" Mary demanded.

"Well, ask him in."

"I did. He wants to see you outside."

"Ethan, what is it? You can't go out in your robe. It's Easter Sunday."

"Allen," I said, "you tell Mr. Marullo I'm not dressed. Tell him he can come back later. But if he's in a hurry, he can come in the front door if he wants to see me alone." He dashed.

"I don't know what he wants. Maybe the store's been robbed."

Allen shot back. "He's going around front."

"Now, dear, don't you let him spoil your breakfast, you hear me?"

I went through the house and opened the front door.

Marullo was on the porch, dressed in his best for Easter mass, and his best was black broadcloth and big gold watch chain. He held his black hat in his hand and he smiled at me nervously like a dog out of bounds.

"Come in."

"No," he said. "I just got one word to say. I heard how that fella offered you a kickback."

"Yes?"

"I heard how you threw him out."

"Who told you?"

"I can't tell." He smiled again.

"Well, what about it? You trying to say I should have taken it?"

He stepped forward and shook my hand, pumped it up and down twice very formally. "You're a good fella," he said.

"Maybe he didn't offer enough."

"You kidding? You're a good fella. That's all. You're a good fella." He reached in his bulging side pocket and brought out a bag. "You take this." He patted my shoulder and then in a welter of embarrassment turned and fled; his short legs pumped him away and his fat neck flamed where it bulged over his stiff white collar.

"What was it?"

I looked in the bag—colored candy Easter eggs. We had a big square glass jar of them at the store. "He brought a present for the kids," I said.

"Marullo? Brought a present. I can't believe it."

"Well, he did."

"Why? He never did anything like that."

"I guess he just plain loves me."

"Is there something I don't know?"

"Duck blossom, there are eight million things none of us know." The children were staring in from the open back door. I held out the bag to them. "A present from an admirer. Don't get into them until after breakfast."

As we were getting dressed for church, Mary said, "I wish I knew what that was all about."

"Marullo? I'll have to admit, darling, I wish I knew what it was all about too."

"But a bag of cheap candy—"

"Do you suppose it might be a grave simplicity?"

"I don't understand."

"His wife is dead. He has neither chick nor child. He's getting old. Maybe—well, maybe he's lonely."

"He never has been here before. While he's lonesome, you should ask him for a raise. He doesn't drop in on Mr. Baker. It makes me nervous."

I gauded myself like the flowers of the field, decent dark suit, my burying black, shirt and collar so starchly white they threw the sun's light back in the sun's face, cerulean tie with cautious polka dots.

Was Mrs. Margie Young-Hunt whomping up ancestral storms? Where did Marullo get his information? It could only be Mr. Bugger to Mrs. Young-Hunt to Mr. Marullo. I do not trust thee Margie Young, the reason why I cannot tongue. But this I know and know right spung, I do not trust thee Mrs. Young. And with that singing in my head I delved in the garden for a white flower for my Easter buttonhole. In the angle made by the foundation and the sloping cellar door there is a protected place, the earth warmed by the furnace and exposed to every scrap of winter sunlight. There white violets grow, brought from the cemetery where they grow wild over the graves of my ancestors. I picked three tiny lion-faced blossoms for my buttonhole and gathered a round dozen for my darling, set their own pale leaves about them for a nosegay, and bound them tight with a bit of aluminum foil from the kitchen.

"Why, they're lovely," Mary said. "Wait till I get a pin, I'll wear them."

"They're the first—the very first, my creamy fowl. I am your slave. Christ is risen. All's right with the world."

"Please don't be silly about sacred things, dear."

"What in the world have you done with your hair?"

"Do you like it?"

"I love it. Always wear it that way."

"I wasn't sure you'd like it. Margie said you'd never notice. Wait till I tell her you did." She set a bowl of flowers on her head, the yearly vernal offering to Eostre. "Like it?"

"I love it."

Now the young got their inspection, ears, nostrils, shoe-shines, every detail, and they resisted every moment of it. Allen's hair was so plastered that he could hardly blink. The heels of his shoes were unpolished but with infinite care he had trained a line of hair to roll on his crested brow like a summer wave.

Ellen was girl of a girlness. All in sight was in order. I tried my luck again. "Ellen," I said, "you're doing something different with your hair. It becomes you. Mary, darling, don't you like it?"

"Oh! She's beginning to take pride," Mary said.

We formed a procession down our path to Elm Street, then left to Porlock, where our church is, our old white-steepled church, stolen intact from Christopher Wren. And we were part of a growing stream, and every woman in passing had delight of other women's hats.

"I have designed an Easter hat," I said. "A simple, off-the-face crown of thorns in gold with real ruby droplets on the forehead."

"Ethan!" said Mary sternly. "Suppose someone should hear you."

"No, I guess it couldn't be popular."

"I think you're horrid," Mary said, and so did I, worse than horrid. But I did wonder how Mr. Baker would respond to comment on his hair.

Our family rivulet joined other streams and passed stately greetings and the stream was a river pouring into St. Thomas's Episcopal Church, a medium-high church, maybe a little higher than center.

When the time comes that I must impart the mysteries of life to my son, which I have no doubt he knows, I must remember to inform him about hair. Armed with a kindly word for hair, he will go as far as his concupiscent little heart desires. I must warn him, however. He may kick, beat, drop, tousle, or bump them, but he must never—never —mess their hair. With this knowledge he can be king.

The Bakers were just ahead of us going up the steps, and we passed decorous greetings. "I believe we're seeing you at tea."

"Yes, indeed. A very happy Easter to you."

"Can that be Allen? How he's grown. And Mary Ellen. Well, I can't keep track—they shoot up so."

There's something very dear about a church you grew in. I know every secret corner, secret odor of St. Thomas's. In that font I was christened, at that rail confirmed, in that pew Hawleys have sat for God knows how long, and that is no figure of speech. I must have been deeply printed with the sacredness because I remember every desecration, and there were plenty of them. I think I can go to every place where my initials are scratched with a nail. When Danny Taylor and I punched the letters of a singularly dirty word with a pin in the Book of Common Prayer, Mr. Wheeler caught us and we were punished, but they had to go through all the prayerbooks and the hymnals to make sure there weren't more.

Once, in that chair stall under the lectern, a dreadful thing happened. I wore the lace and carried the cross and sang a beefy soprano. Once the bishop was officiating, a nice old man, hairless as a boiled onion, but to me glowing with rays of holiness. So it was that, stunned with inspiration, I set the cross in its socket at the end of processional and forgot to throw the brass latch that held it in. At the reading of the second lesson I saw with horror the heavy brass cross sway and crash on that holy hairless head. The bishop went down like a pole-axed cow and I lost the lace to a boy who couldn't sing as well, a boy named Skunkfoot Hill. He's an anthropologist now, somewhere in the West. The incident seemed to prove to me that intentions, good or bad, are not enough. There's luck or fate or something else that takes over accidents.

We sat the service through and heard the news announced that Christ was risen indeed. It ran shivers up my spine as always. I took communion with a good heart. Allen and Mary Ellen weren't yet confirmed and they got pretty restless and had to be given the iron eye to stop their jittering. When Mary's eyes are hostile, they can pierce even the armor plate of adolescence.

Then in the drenching sunshine we shook hands and greeted and shook hands and wished the season's best to the community of our neighbors. All those we had spoken to coming in, we regreeted going out—a continuation of the litany, of a continuous litany in the form of decorous good manners, a quiet supplication to be noticed and to be respected.

"Good morning. And how are you this fine day?"

"Very well, thank you. How is your mother?"

"She's getting old—getting old—the aches and daggers of getting old. I'll tell her you asked for her."

The words are meaningless except in terms of feeling. Does anyone act as the result of thought or does feeling stimulate action and sometimes thought implement it? Ahead of our small parade in the sun went Mr. Baker, avoiding stepping on cracks; his mother, dead these twenty years, was safe from a broken back. And Mrs. Baker, Amelia, tripping along beside him, trying to match his uneven stride with her fluttering feet, a small, bright-eyed bird of a woman, but a seed-eating bird.

Allen, my son, walked beside his sister, but each of them tried to give the impression that they were total strangers. I think she despises him and he detests her. This may last all their lives while they learn to conceal it in a rose cloud of loving words. Give them their lunches, my sister, my wife —their hard-boiled eggs and pickles, their jelly-and-peanut-butter sandwiches, their red barrel-smelling apples, and turn them free in the world to spawn.

And that's just what she did. They walked away, carrying their paper bags, each one to a separate private world.

"Did you enjoy the service, my darling?"

"Oh, yes! I always do. But you—sometimes I wonder if you believe—no, I mean it. Well, your jokes—sometimes—"

"Pull up your chair, my dimpsy darling."

"I have to get lunch on."

"Bugger lunch."

"That's what I mean. Your jokes."

"Lunch is not sacred. If it were warmer, I could carry you to a rowboat and we would go out past the breakwater and fish for porgies."

"We're going to the Bakers'. Do you know whether you believe in the church or not, Ethan? Why do you call me silly names? You hardly ever use my name."

"To avoid being repetitious and tiresome, but in my heart your name rings like a bell. Do I believe? What a question! Do I lift out each shining phrase from the Nicene creed, loaded like a shotgun shell, and inspect it? No. It isn't necessary. It's a singular thing, Mary. If my mind and soul and body were as dry of faith as a navy bean, the words, 'The Lord is my Shepherd, I shall not want. He maketh me to lie down in green pastures,' would still make my stomach turn over and put a flutter in my chest and light a fire in my brain."

"I don't understand."

"Good girl. Neither do I. Let's say that when I was a little baby, and all my bones soft and malleable, I was put in a small Episcopal cruciform box and so took my shape. Then, when I broke out of the box, the way a baby chick escapes an egg, is it strange that I had the shape of a cross? Have you ever noticed that chickens are roughly egg-shaped?"

"You say such dreadful things, even to the children."

"And they to me. Ellen, only last night, asked, 'Daddy, when will we be rich?' But I did not say to her what I know: 'We will be rich soon, and you who handle poverty badly will handle riches equally badly.' And that is true. In poverty she is envious. In riches she may be a snob. Money does not change the sickness, only the symptoms."

"You talk this way about your own children. What must you say of me?"

"I say you are a blessing, a dearling, the brightness in a foggy life."

"You sound drunk—anyway intoxicated."

"I am."

"You aren't. I could smell it."

"You are smelling it, sweetheart."

"What's come over you?"

"Ah! you do know, don't you? A change—a bloody big storm of a change. You are only feeling the outmost waves."

"You worry me, Ethan. You really do. You're wild."

"Do you remember my decorations?"

"Your medals—from the war?"

"They were awarded for wildness—for wilderness. No man on earth ever had less murder in his heart than I. But they made another box and crammed me in it. The times, the moment, demanded that I slaughter human beings and I did."

"That was wartime and for your country."

"It's always some kind of time. So far I have avoided my own time. I was a goddam good soldier, potkin—clever and quick and merciless, an effective unit for wartime. Maybe I could be an equally efficient unit in this time."

"You're trying to tell me something."

"Sadly enough, I am. And it sounds in my ears like an apology. I hope it is not."

"I'm going to set out lunch."

"Not hungry after that nor'easter of a breakfast."

"Well, you can nibble something. Did you see Mrs. Baker's hat? She must have got it in New York."

"What has she done with her hair?"

"You noticed that? It's almost strawberry."

" 'To be a light to lighten the gentiles, and to be the glory of thy peo-ple Israel.' "

"Why would Margie want to go to Montauk this time of year?"

"She loves the early morning."

"She's not an early riser. I joke with her about that. And don't you think it was queer, Marullo bringing candy eggs?"

"Do you connect the two events? Margie gets up early and Marullo brings eggs."

"Don't be silly."

"I'm not. For once I'm not. If I tell you a secret, will you promise not to tell?"

"It's a joke!"

"No."

"Well, I promise."

"I think Marullo is going to make a trip to Italy."

"How do you know? Did he tell you?"

"Not exactly. I put things together. I *put* things together."

"But that'll leave you alone in the store. You'll have to get someone to help you."

"I can handle it."

"You do practically everything now. You'll have to get someone in to help."

"Remember—it isn't sure and it's a secret."

"Oh, I never forget a promise."

"But you'll hint."

"Ethan, I will not."

"Do you know what you are? A dear little baby rabbit with flowers on your head."

"You help yourself in the kitchen. I'm going to freshen up."

When she was gone, I sprawled out in my chair and I heard in my secret ears, "Lord, now lettest Thou Thy servant de-part in pee-ace, according to Thy word." And darned if I didn't go to sleep. Dropped off a cliff into the dark, right there in the living room. I don't do that often. And because I had been thinking of Danny Taylor, I dreamed of Danny Taylor. We were not small or great but grown, and we were at the flat dry lake-bottom with the old house foundations and cellar hole. And it was early summer, for I remarked the fatness of the leaves and the grass so heavy that it bent of its weight, the kind of day that makes you feel fat and crazy too. Danny went behind a young juniper straight and slender as a column. I heard his voice, distorted and thick like words spoken under water. Then I was with him and he was melting and running down over his frame. With my palms I tried to smooth him up-ward, back in place, the way you try to smooth wet cement when it runs out of the form, but I couldn't. His essence ran between my fingers. They say a dream is a moment.

This one went on and on and the more I tried, the more he melted.

When Mary awakened me I was panting with effort.

"Spring fever," she said. "That's the first sign. When I was a growing girl, I slept so much my mother sent for Doctor Grady. She thought I had sleeping sickness, but I was only growing in the spring."

"I had a daymare. I wouldn't wish a dream like that on anyone."

"It's all the confusion. Go up and comb your hair and wash your face. You look tired, dear. Are you all right? It's nearly time to go. You slept two hours. You must have needed it. I wish I knew what's on Mr. Baker's mind."

"You will, darling. And promise me you will listen to every word."

"But he might want a word alone with you. Businessmen don't like ladies listening."

"Well, he can't have it that way. I want you there."

"You know I have no experience in business."

"I know—but it's your money he'll be talking about."

You can't know people like the Bakers unless you are born knowing them. Acquaintance, even friendship, is a different matter. I know them because Hawleys and Bakers were alike in blood, place of origin, experience, and past fortune. This makes for a kind of nucleus walled and moated against outsiders. When my father lost our money, I was not edged completely out. I am still acceptable as a Hawley to Bakers for perhaps my lifetime because they feel related to me. But I am a poor relation. Gentry without money gradually cease to be gentry. Without money, Allen, my son, will not know Bakers and his son will be an outsider, no matter what his name and antecedents. We have become ranchers without land, commanders without troops, horsemen on foot. We can't survive. Perhaps that is one reason why the change was taking place in me. I do not want, never have wanted, money for itself. But money is necessary to keep my place in a category I am used to and comfortable in. All this must have worked itself out in the dark place below my thinking level. It emerged not as a thought but as a conviction.

"Good afternoon," Mrs. Baker said. "So glad you could come. You've neglected us, Mary. Hasn't it been a glorious day? Did you enjoy the service? For a clergyman I think he's such an interesting man."

"We don't see you nearly often enough," Mr. Baker said. "I remember your grandfather sitting in that very chair and reporting that the dirty Spaniards had sunk the *Maine*. He spilled his tea, only it wasn't tea. Old Cap'n Hawley used to lace his rum with a little tea. He was a truculent man, some thought a quarrelsome man."

I could see that Mary was first shaken and then pleased at this warmth. Of course she didn't know I had promoted her to be an heiress. A reputation for money is almost as negotiable as money itself.

Mrs. Baker, her head jerking with some nervous disorder, poured tea into cups as thin and fragile as magnolia petals, and her pouring hand was the only steady part of her.

Mr. Baker stirred with a thoughtful spoon. "I don't know whether I love tea or the ceremony of it," he said. "I like all ceremonies—even the silly ones."

"I think I understand," I said. "This morning I felt comfortable in the service because it had no surprises. I knew the words before they were said."

"During the war, Ethan—listen to this, ladies, and see if you can remember anything like it—during the war I served as a consultant to the Secretary of War. I spent some time in Washington."

"I hated it," said Mrs. Baker.

"Well, there was a big military tea, a real doozer, maybe five hundred guests. The ranking lady was the wife of a five-star general and next in importance was the lady of a lieutenant general. Mrs. Secretary, the hostess, asked the five-star lady to pour the tea and Mrs. Three-Stars to pour coffee. Well, the top lady refused because, and I quote her, 'Everyone knows coffee outranks tea.' Now, did you ever hear that?" He chuckled. "As it turned out, whisky outranked everybody."

"It was such a restless place," Mrs. Baker said. "People moved before they had time to gather a set of habits, or manners."

Mary told her story of an Irish tea in Boston with the water boiling in round tubs over an open fire and served with tin ladles. "And they don't steep. They boil," she said. "That tea will unsettle varnish on a table."

There must be ritual preliminaries to a serious discussion or action, and the sharper the matter is, the longer and lighter must the singing be. Each person must add a bit of feather or a colored patch. If Mary and Mrs. Baker were not to be a part of the serious matter, they would long since have set up their own pattern of exchange. Mr. Baker had poured wine on the earth of conversation and so had my Mary, and she was pleased and excited by their attentiveness. It remained for Mrs. Baker and for me to contribute and I felt it only decent to be last.

She took her turn and drew her source from the teapot as the others had. "I remember when there were dozens of kinds of tea," she offered brightly. "Why, everyone had recipes for nearly everything. I guess there wasn't a weed or a leaf or a flower that wasn't made into some kind of tea. Now there are only two, India and China, and not much China. Remember tansy and camomile and orange-leaf and flower—and—and cambric?"

"What's cambric?" Mary asked.

"Equal parts hot water and hot milk. Children love it. It doesn't taste like milk and water." That accounted for Mrs. Baker.

It was my turn, and I intended to make a few carefully meaningless remarks about the Boston Tea Party, but you can't always do what you intended. Surprises slip out, not waiting for permission.

"I went to sleep after service," I heard me say. "I dreamed of Danny Taylor, a dreadful dream. You remember Danny."

"Poor chap," said Mr. Baker.

"Once we were closer than brothers. I had no brother. I guess we were brothers in a way. I don't carry it out, of course, but I feel I should be my brother Danny's keeper."

Mary was annoyed with me for breaking the pattern of the conversation. She took a small revenge. "Ethan gives him money. I don't think it's right. He just uses it to get drunk."

"Wellll!" said Mr. Baker.

"I wonder—anyway the dream was a noonmare. I give him so little—a dollar now and then. What else can he do with a dollar but get drunk? Maybe with a decent amount he could get well."

"No one would dare do that," Mary cried. "That would be after killing him. Isn't that so, Mr. Baker?"

"Poor chap," Mr. Baker said. "A fine family the Taylors were. It makes me sick to see him this way. But Mary's right. He'd probably drink himself to death."

"He is anyway. But he's safe from me. I don't have a decent amount to give him."

"It's the principle," Mr. Baker said.

Mrs. Baker contributed a feminine savagery: "He should be in an institution where they could look after him."

All three were annoyed with me. I should have stayed with the Boston Tea Party.

Strange how the mind goes romping, playing blindman's buff or pin-the-tail-on-the-donkey when it should be using every observation to find a path through the minefield of secret plans and submerged obstacles. I understood the house of Baker and the house of Hawley, the dark walls and curtains, the funereal rubber plants unacquainted with sun; the portraits and prints and remembrances of other times in pottery and scrimshaw, in fabrics and wood which bolt it to reality and to permanence. Chairs change with style and comfort but chests and tables, bookcases and desks, relate to a solid past. Hawley was more than a family. It was a house. And that was why poor Danny held onto Taylor Meadow. Without it, no family—and soon not even a name. By tone and inflection and desire, the three sitting there had canceled him. It may be that some men require a house and a history to reassure themselves that they exist—it's a slim enough connection, at most. In the store I was a failure and a clerk, in my house I was Hawley, so I too must be unsure. Baker could offer a hand to Hawley. Without my house, I too would have been canceled. It was not man to man but house to house. I resented the removal from real of Danny Taylor, but I couldn't stop it. And this thought sharpened and tempered me. Baker was going to try to refurbish Hawley for Baker's participation in Mary's fancied inheritance. Now I was on the edge of the minefield. My heart hardened against my selfless benefactor. I felt it harden and grow wary and dangerous. And with its direction came the feeling of combat, and the laws of controlled savagery, and the first law is: Let even your defense have the appearance of attack.

I said, "Mr. Baker, we don't need to go over the background. You know better than I do the slow, precise way in which my father lost the Hawley substance. I was away at war. How did it happen?"

"It wasn't his intention, but his judgment—"

"I know he was unworldly—but how did it happen?"

"Well, it was a time of wild investment. He invested wildly."

"Did he have any advice?"

"He put money in munitions that were already obsolete. Then when the contracts were canceled, he lost."

"You were in Washington. Did you know about the contracts?"

"Only in a general way."

"But enough so you didn't invest."

"No, I didn't."

"Did you advise my father about investments?"

"I was in Washington."

"But you knew he had borrowed the money on the Hawley property, the money to invest?"

"Yes, I knew that."

"Did you advise against it?"

"I was in Washington."

"But your bank foreclosed."

"A bank doesn't have any choice, Ethan. You know that."

"Yes, I know. Only it's a shame you couldn't have advised him."

"You shouldn't blame him, Ethan."

"Now that I understand it, I don't. I didn't mean to blame him, but I never quite knew what happened."

I think Mr. Baker had prepared an opening. Having lost his chance, he had to grope about for his next move. He coughed, blew his nose and wiped it with a paper handkerchief from a flat pocket package, wiped his eyes with a second sheet, polished his glasses with a third. Everyone has his own method for gaining time. I've known a man to take five minutes to fill and light a pipe.

When he was ready again, I said, "I know I have no right in myself to ask you for help. But you yourself brought up the long partnership of our families."

"Good people," he said. "And usually men of excellent judgment, conservative—"

"But not blindly so, sir. I believe that once they decided on a course they drove through."

"That they did."

"Even if it came to sinking an enemy—or burning a ship?"

"They were commissioned, of course."

"In 1801, I believe, sir, they were questioned about what constituted an enemy."

"There's always some readjustment after a war."

"Surely. But I'm not taking up old scores for talk. Frankly, Mr. Baker, I want to—to rehabilitate my fortunes."

"That's the spirit, Ethan. For a time I thought you'd lost the old Hawley touch."

"I had; or maybe I'd not developed it. You've offered help. Where do I start?"

"The trouble is, you need capital to start."

"I know that. But if I had some capital, where would I start?"

"This must be tiresome for the ladies," he said. "Maybe we should go into the library. Business is dull to ladies."

Mrs. Baker stood up. "I was just about to ask Mary to

help me select some wallpaper for the big bedroom. The samples are upstairs, Mary."

"I'd like Mary to hear—"

But she went along with them, as I knew she would. "I don't know a thing about business," she said. "But I do know about wallpaper."

"But you're concerned, darling."

"I just get mixed up, Ethan. You know I do."

"Maybe I'll get more mixed up without you, darling."

Mr. Baker had probably suggested the wallpaper bit. I think his wife does not choose the paper. Surely no woman picked the dark and geometric paper in the room where we sat.

"Now," he said when they were gone, "your problem is capital, Ethan. Your house is clear. You can mortgage it."

"I won't do that."

"Well, I can respect that, but it's the only collateral you have. There is also Mary's money. It's not much, but with some money you can get more money."

"I don't want to touch her money. That's her safety."

"It's in a joint account and it's not earning anything."

"Let's say I overcame my scruples. What have you in mind?"

"Have you any idea what her mother's worth?"

"No—but it seems substantial."

He cleaned his glasses with great care. "What I say is bound to be in confidence."

"Of course."

"Fortunately I know you are not a talker. No Hawley ever was, except perhaps your father. Now, I know as a businessman that New Baytown is going to grow. It has everything to make it grow—a harbor, beaches, inland waters. Once it starts, nothing can stop it. A good businessman owes it to his town to help it develop."

"And take a profit."

"Naturally."

"Why hasn't it developed?"

"I think you know that—the mossbacks on the council. They're living in the past. They hold back progress."

It always interested me to hear how philanthropic the taking of a profit can be. Stripped of its forward-looking, good-of-the-community clothing, Mr. Baker's place was just what it had to be. He and a few others, a very few, would support the town's present administrations until they had bought or controlled all the future facilities. Then they would turn the council and the Town Manager out and let progress reign, and only then would it be discovered that they owned every avenue through which it could come. From pure sentiment, he was willing to cut me in for a small share. I don't know whether or not he had intended to let me know the timetable, or whether his enthusiasm got the better of him, but it did come through the generalities. The town election is July seventh. By that time, the forward-looking group must have the wheels of progress under control.

I don't suppose there is a man in the world who doesn't love to give advice. As I maintained a small reluctance, my teacher grew more vehement and more specific.

"I'll have to think about it, sir," I said. "What's easy for you is a mystery to me. And of course I'll have to discuss it with Mary."

"Now that's where I think you're wrong," he said. "There's too much petticoat in business today."

"But it's her inheritance."

"Best thing you can do for her is make her some money for a surprise. They like it better that way."

"I hope I don't sound ungrateful, Mr. Baker. I think slowly. I'll just have to mull it over. Did you hear Marullo is going to Italy?"

His eyes sharpened. "For good?"

"No, just a visit."

"Well, I hope he makes some arrangement to protect you in case something happened to him. He's not a young man. Has he made a will?"

"I don't know."

"If a bunch of his wop relations moved in, you might find yourself out of a job."

I retired into a protective vagueness. "You've given me a lot to chew on," I said. "But I wonder if you can give me some little idea of when you will start."

"I can tell you this: Development is pretty much dependent on transportation."

"Well, the big thruways are moving out."

"Still a long way to come. The kind of men with the kind of money we want to attract will want to come by air."

"And we have no airport?"

"That's right."

"Furthermore, we have no place for an airport without pushing hills around."

"An expensive operation. The cost of labor would be prohibitive."

"Then what is your plan?"

"Ethan, you'll have to trust me and forgive me. I can't tell you that at this time. But I do promise that if you can raise some capital, I'll see that you get in on the ground floor. And I can tell you that there is a very definite situation, but it has to be solved."

"Well, I guess that's better than I deserve."

"The old families must stick together."

"Is Marullo part of the group?"

"Certainly not. He goes his own way with his own crowd."

"They do pretty well, don't they?"

"Better than I think is healthy. I don't like to see these foreigners creeping in."

"And July seventh is the sound-off."

"Did I say that?"

"No, I guess I just imagined it."

"You must have."

And with that Mary came back from the wallpaper. We did our courteous duties and walked slowly toward home.

"They just couldn't have been nicer. What did he say?"

"Same old thing. I should use your money to get a start, and I won't do it."

"I know you're thinking of me, dear. But I say if you don't take his advice you're a fool."

"I don't like it, Mary. Suppose he's wrong. You'd be without protection."

"I tell you this, Ethan, if you don't do it, I'll take the money and hand it over to him. I promise you I will."

"Let me think about it. I don't want to involve you in business."

"You don't have to. That money's in a joint account. You know what the fortune said."

"Oh, Lord—the fortune again."

"Well, I believe it."

"If I lost your money, you'd hate me."

"I wouldn't. You are my fortune! That's what Margie said."

"What Margie said, is in my head, in letters red, until I'm dead."

"Don't make a joke."

"Maybe I'm not. Don't let fortune spoil the sweetness of our failure."

"I don't see how a little money could spoil anything. Not a lot of money—just enough." I didn't answer. "Well —do you?"

I said, "O prince's daughter, there is no such thing as just enough money. Only two measures: No Money and Not Enough Money."

"Why, that's not true."

"That *is* true. Remember the Texas billionaire who died recently? He lived in a hotel room and out of a suitcase. He left no will, no heirs, but he didn't have enough money. The more you have, the less enough it is."

She said sarcastically, "I suppose you find it sinful for me to want new living-room curtains and a water heater big enough so four people can bathe the same day and I can wash dishes too."

"I was not reporting on sin, you juggins. I was stating a fact, a law of nature."

"You seem to have no respect for human nature."

"Not human nature, my Mary—nature. Squirrels bank

ten times as many hickory nuts as they can ever use. The pocket gopher, with a stomach full to bursting, still loads his cheeks like sacks. And how much of the honey the clever bees collect do the clever bees eat?"

When Mary is confused or perplexed, she spurts anger the way an octopus spurts ink, and hides in the dark cloud of it.

"You make me sick," she said. "You can't let anyone have a little happiness."

"My darling, it isn't that. It's a despairing unhappiness I'm afraid of, the panic money brings, the protectiveness and the envy."

She must have been unconsciously fearful of the same thing. She struck at me, probed for a hurting place, and found it and twisted the jagged words. "Here's a grocery clerk without a bean worried about how bad it will be when he's rich. You act as though you could pick up a fortune any time you want to."

"I think I can."

"How?"

"That's the worry."

"You don't know how or you'd have done it before. You're just bluffing. You always bluff."

The intent to wound raises rage. I could feel the fever rise in me. Ugly, desperate words moved up like venom. I felt a sour hatefulness.

Mary said, "Look! There it goes! Did you see it?"

"Where? What?"

"Went right past the tree there and into our yard."

"What was it, Mary? Tell me! What did you see?"

In the dusk I saw her smile, that incredible female smile. It is called wisdom but it isn't that but rather an understanding that makes wisdom unnecessary.

"You didn't see anything, Mary."

"I saw a quarrel—but it got away."

I put my arm about her and turned her. "Let's go around the block before we go in."

We strolled in the tunnel of the night and we didn't speak again, or need to.

CHAPTER VIII

As a child I hunted and killed small creatures with energy and joy. Rabbits and squirrels, small birds, and later ducks and wild geese came crashing down, rumpled distortions of bone and blood and fur and feathers. There was a savage creativeness about it without hatred or rancor or guilt. The war retired my appetite for destruction; perhaps I was like a child overindulged in sweets. A shotgun's blast was no longer a shout of fierce happiness.

In this first spring a bouncing pair of rabbits paid daily visits to our garden. They loved best my Mary's carnations, ate them down to raw crowns.

"You'll have to get rid of them," Mary said.

I brought out my 12-bore, sticky with grease, and found some old thickened shells with number five shot. In the evening I sat on the back steps and when the rabbits were in line I blasted both of them with one shot. Then I buried the furry ruins under the big lilac and I was miserable in the stomach.

It was simply that I had grown unused to killing things. A man can get used to anything. Slaughtering or undertaking or even execution; rack and pincers must be just a job when one gets used to it.

When the children had gone to bed I said, "I'm going out for a while."

Mary didn't ask where or why, as she would have a few days ago. "Shall you be late?"

"No, not late."

"I won't wait up, I'm sleepy," she said. And it seemed that, having accepted a direction, she was farther along than I. I still had the rabbit misery. Perhaps it is natural for a man who has destroyed something to try to restore a balance by creating something. But was that my impulse?

I fumbled my way into the stinking kennel where Danny Taylor lived. A lighted candle burned in a saucer beside his Army cot.

Danny was in bad shape, blue and gaunt and sick. His skin had a pewter sheen. It was hard not to be sick at the smell of the dirty place and the dirty man, under a filthy comforter. His eyes were open and glazed. I expected him to babble in delirium. It was a shock when he spoke clearly and in the tone and manner of Danny Taylor.

"What do you want here, Eth?"

"I want to help you."

"You know better than that."

"You're sick."

"Think I don't know it? I know it better than anyone." He groped behind his cot and brought out a bottle of Old Forester one-third full. "Have a shot?"

"No, Danny. That's expensive whisky."

"I have friends."

"Who gave it to you?"

"That's none of your business, Eth." He took a drink and kept it down, but for a moment it was not easy. And then his color came back. He laughed. "My friend wanted to talk business but I fooled him. I passed out before he could get it said. He didn't know how little it takes. Do you want to talk business Eth? 'Cause I can pass out again quick."

"Do you have any feeling about me, Danny? Any trust? Any—well, feeling?"

"Sure I do, but when it comes right down to it I am a drunk, and a drunk feels strongest about liquor."

"If I could raise the money, would you go for a cure?"

The frightening thing was how quickly he had become normal and easy and—like himself. "I might say I would, Eth. But you don't know drunks. I'd take the money and drink it up."

"Well, suppose I paid it right to the hospital, or wherever."

"I'm trying to tell you. I'd go with the best intentions, and in a few days I'd get out. You can't trust a drunk, Eth. That's what you can't understand. No matter what I did or said—I'd still get out."

"Don't you want to come out of it, Danny?"

"I guess I don't. I guess you know what I want." He hoisted the bottle again, and again I was astonished at the speed of the reaction. Not only did he become the old Danny I knew but his senses and perceptions were sharpened, so clear in fact that he read my thought. "Don't trust it," he said. "It's only for a little time. Alcohol stimulates and then depresses. I hope you won't stay around to see that. Right now, I don't believe it will happen. I never do when I'm up." Then his eyes, wet and shining in the candlelight, looked into me. "Ethan," he said. "You offered to pay for a cure for me. You haven't the money, Ethan."

"I could get it. Mary inherited some from her brother."

"And you would give me that?"

"Yes."

"Even though I tell you never to trust a drunk? Even if I assure you I would take your money and break your heart?"

"You're breaking my heart now, Danny. I had a dream about you. We were out at the old place—remember?"

He raised the bottle and then put it down, saying, "No, not yet—not yet. Eth—never—never trust a drunk. When he —when I'm—horrible—a dead thing—there's still a clever, secret mind at work, and it's not a friendly mind. Right now, right at this moment, I'm a man who was your friend. I lied to you about passing out. Oh, I passed out all right, but I know about the bottle."

"Wait," I said, "before you go any further, else it will look—well, you might suspect me. It was Baker brought the bottle, wasn't it?"

"Yes."

"He wanted you to sign something."

"Yes, but I passed out." He chuckled to himself and

again lifted the bottle to his lips, but in the candlelight I saw the smallest bubble. He had taken only a drop.

"That's one of the things I wanted to tell you, Danny. Was it the old place he wanted?"

"Yes."

"How does it happen you haven't sold it?"

"I thought I told you. It makes me a gentleman, lacking only the conduct of a gentleman."

"Don't sell it, Danny. Hold onto it."

"What's it to you? Why not?"

"For your pride."

"I don't have any pride left, only position."

"Yes, you have. When you asked me for money, you were ashamed. That means pride."

"No, I told you. That was a trick. Drunks are clever, I tell you. It embarrassed you, and you gave me a buck because you thought I was ashamed. I wasn't ashamed. I just wanted a drink."

"Don't sell it, Danny. It's valuable. Baker knows it. He doesn't buy anything without value."

"What's valuable about it?"

"It's the only place nearby level enough for an airfield."

"I see."

"If you'll hold out, it can be a whole new start for you, Danny. Hold onto it. You could take the cure and when you came out you'd have a nest egg."

"But no nest. Maybe I'd rather sell it and drink it up and —'When the bough breaks the cradle will fall, and down will come baby, cradle and all.'" He sang shrilly and laughed. "Do you want the place, Eth? Is that why you came here?"

"I want you to be well."

"I am well."

"I want to explain, Danny. If you were a bum, you could be free to do whatever you want. But you have something a group of forward-looking citizens want and need."

"Taylor Meadow. And I'm going to hold onto it. I'm forward-looking too." He glanced affectionately at the bottle.

"Danny, I told you, it's the only place for an airport. It's a key place. They have to have it—either that or level the hills, and they can't afford that."

"Then I have them by the ying-yang and I'm going to twist."

"You've forgotten, Danny. A man of property is a precious vessel. Already I've heard that the kindest thing would be to put you in an institution where you would get the care you need."

"They wouldn't dare."

"Oh, yes they would—and feel virtuous about it. You know the process. The judge, you know him, would rule you incompetent to handle property. He would appoint a guardian, and I can guess which one. And all this would be expensive, so of course your property would have to be sold to pay the costs, and guess who would be there to buy it."

His eyes were shiny and he listened with his mouth parted. Now he looked away.

"You're trying to scare me, Eth. You picked the wrong time. Catch me in the morning when I'm cold and the world is green vomit. Right now—my strength it is the strength of ten because the bottle's here." He waved it like a sword and his eyes went to slits gleaming in the candlelight. "Did I tell you, Eth? I think I did—a drunk has a special evil kind of intelligence."

"But I've told you what will happen."

"I agree with you. I know it's true. You've made your point. But instead of scaring me, you're roused my imp. Whoever thinks a drunk is helpless is crazy. A drunk is a very special vehicle with special abilities. I can fight back, and right now I seem to want to."

"Good boy! That's what I want to hear."

He sighted at me over the neck of the whisky bottle as though it were the bead on the end of a rifle. "You'd loan me Mary's money?"

"Yes."

"Without security?"

"Yes."

"Knowing the chance of getting it back is a thousand to one against?"

"Yes."

"There's an ugly thing in a drunk, Eth. I don't believe you." He licked his dry lips. "Would you put the money in my hands?"

"Whenever you say."

"I've told you not to."

"But I will."

This time he tipped the bottle back and the big bubble rose inside the glass. When he stopped drinking, his eyes were even shinier but they were cold and impersonal as a snake's eyes. "Can you get the money this week, Eth?"

"Yes."

"Wednesday?"

"Yes."

"Have you got a couple of bucks now?"

I had just that—a dollar bill, a half, a quarter, two dimes and a nickel, and three pennies. I poured them into his outstretched hand.

He finished the bottle and dropped it on the floor. "Somehow I never put you down for clever, Eth. Do you know even a basic cure would cost about a thousand dollars?"

"All right."

"This is fun, Eth. This isn't chess, it's poker. I used to be pretty good at poker—too good. You're betting I'll put up my meadow as collateral. And you're betting that a thousand dollars' worth of booze will kill me, and there you'll be with an airport in your lap."

"That's a nasty thing, Danny."

"I warned you I was nasty."

"Couldn't you think I meant it the way I said it?"

"No. But I've got a way to—keep it the way you said it. You remember me in the old days, Eth. Do you think I don't remember you? You're the kid with the built-in judge. Okay. I'm getting dry. The bottle's empty. I'm going out. My price is one thousand bucks."

"All right."

"In cash on Wednesday."

"I'll bring it."

"No note, no signature, no nothing. And don't think you remember me, Ethan, from the old days. My friend here has changed all that. I have no loyalty, no fairness. What you'll get is nothing but hearty laughter."

"I would only ask you to try."

"Sure, I'll promise, Eth. But I hope I've convinced you what a drunk's promise is worth. Just bring the cash. Stay as long as you like. My house is your house. I'm going out. See you Wednesday, Eth." He eased himself up out of the old Army cot, flung the comforter behind it, and walked out with a rolling gait. His pants were not zipped up.

I sat for a while, watching the candle gutter down into the grease of the saucer. Everything he had said was true, except one thing on which I placed my bet. He hadn't changed that much. Somewhere in the wreckage was Danny Taylor. I didn't believe he could amputate Danny. I loved Danny and I was prepared to—do just what he said. I was. From a distance I heard him singing in a clear, high falsetto:

> "Speed, bonnie boat, like a bird on the wing.
> 'Onward!' the sailors cry!
> Carry the lad that's born to be king
> Over the sea to Skye."

After a lonely while I blew out the candle and walked home by way of High Street. Willie wasn't asleep yet in the police car.

"Seems to me you're out a lot, Eth," he said.

"You know how it is."

"Sure. Spring. Young man's fancy."

Mary was asleep, smiling, but when I slipped in beside her, she half awakened. The misery was in my stomach—the cold, hurting misery. Mary turned on her side and gathered me into her warm grass-smelling body and I needed her. I knew the misery would get less, but right now I needed her. I don't know whether she really awakened but even sleeping she knew my need.

And afterward she was awake and she said, "I suppose you're hungry."

"Yes, Helen."

"What do you want?"

"Onion sandwich—no, two onion sandwiches on rye bread."

"I'll have to have one to stand you."

"Don't you want one?"

"Of course."

She padded down the stairs and came back in a little while with sandwiches and a carton of milk and two glasses.

It was a pretty hot onion. "Mary, muldoon," I began.

"Wait till you swallow."

"Did you mean that about not wanting to know about business?"

"Why—yes."

"Well, I have a lead. I want a thousand dollars."

"Was it something Mr. Baker told you?"

"In a way. But private too."

"Well, you just write a check."

"No, darling, I want you to get it in cash. And you might pass the word at the bank that you're getting new furniture or rugs or something."

"But I'm not."

"You will."

"Is it a secret?"

"You said you wanted it that way."

"Yes—well—I do. Yes. It's better that way. This is a burny onion. Would Mr. Baker approve?"

"He would if he did it."

"When do you want it?"

"Tomorrow."

"I can't eat this onion. I guess I smell bad enough now, though."

"You're my darling."

"I can't get over Marullo."

"How do you mean?"

"Coming to the house. Bringing candy."

"God works in a mysterious way."

"Now don't be sacrilegious. Easter isn't over."

"Yes 'tis. It's one-fifteen."

"Good Lord! We better get to sleep."

"Ah! There's the rub—Shakespeare."

"You'd make a joke about anything."

But it was no joke. The misery stayed, not thought about but aching away, and sometimes I would have to ask myself, Why do I ache? Men can get used to anything, but it takes time. Once long ago I took a job wheeling nitroglycerin in a dynamite plant. The pay was high because the stuff is tricky. At first I worried with every step I took, but in a week or so it was only a job. Why, I'd even got used to being a grocery clerk. There's something desirable about anything you're used to as opposed to something you're not.

In the dark with the red spots swimming in my eyes, I inquired of myself concerning what they used to call matters of conscience, and I could find no wound. I asked whether, having set my course, I could change direction or even reverse the compass ninety degrees and I thought I could but I didn't want to.

I had a new dimension, and I was fascinated with it. It was like discovering an unused set of muscles or having come true the child's dream that I could fly. Often I can replay events, scenes, conversations, and pick up from the repeat details which escaped me at first showing.

Mary found strangeness in Marullo's coming to the house with candy eggs, and I trust Mary's sense of strangeness. I had thought of it as a thank offering because I had not cheated him. But Mary's question made me reinspect for something I knew but had passed by. Marullo did not reward for things past; he bribed for things to come. He was not interested in me except in so far as I could be of use to him. I went back over his business instruction and the talk about Sicily. Somewhere he had lost his certainty. In some way he wanted something of me or needed something. There was a way to find out. If I should ask for something he would ordinarily refuse and get it from him, then I would know that he was off balance and deeply troubled. I put Marullo aside and went to Margie. Margie—that gives you an idea of her age. "Margie, I'm always dreaming of you, Margie. I'd give the world to . . ."

I replayed the Margie scenes against the swimming spots on the ceiling, trying to add no more than was really there. For a long time, maybe two years, there had been a Mrs. Young-Hunt who was a friend of my wife, part of the conversations I did not listen to. Then suddenly Margie Young-Hunt had emerged, and then Margie. She must have come to the store before Good Friday, but I could not remember it. On that day it was as though she announced herself. Before that it is possible that she didn't see me any more than I saw her. But from that time on she was present—a mover and a shaker. What did she want? Could it be pure mischief of a woman with too little to do? Or did she move to a plan? It did seem to me that she had announced herself to me—made me conscious of her and kept me aware of her. It seemed to me that she started the second fortune-telling in good faith, intending it to be the usual performance, polished and professional. Then something happened, something that tore it up. Mary had said nothing to cause her tension, nor had I. Had she really seen the vision of the snake? That would be the simplest explanation and probably the true one. Maybe she was truly intuitive, an intruder into the minds of others. The fact that she had caught me midway in a metamorphosis made me likely to believe this, but it could have been an accident. But what made her run to Montauk when she had not intended to go, join up with the drummer, spill the beans to Marullo? Somehow I didn't believe she spilled things she didn't intend to spill. Somewhere in the attic bookcases there was an account of the life of—was it Bering? No, Baranov, Alexander Baranov, the Russian governor somewhere near 1800. Maybe there would be some reference to Alaska as a prison for witches. It was too unlikely a story to be made up. I must look. I thought maybe I could creep up there now without waking Mary.

Then I heard a creak of the old oak stair treads, then a second and a third, so I knew it was not a settling of the house from a change of temperature. It had to be Ellen walking in her sleep.

Of course I love my daughter, but sometimes she

frightens me for she seems to have been born clever, at once jealous and loving. She was always jealous of her brother and often I feel she is jealous of me. It seemed to me that her preoccupation with sex began very early. Maybe fathers always feel this. When she was a very little girl, her uninhibited interest in male genitalia was embarrassing. Then she went into the secrecy of change. Here was no angelic innocent girlhood of the magazines. The house boiled with nervousness, the walls vibrated with unease. I've read that in the Middle Ages pubescent girls were thought to be susceptible to witchcraft and I'm not sure it is not so. For a time we had what we called as a joke a poltergeist. Pictures fell from their hangings, dishes crashed to the floor. There were poundings in the attic and thumpings in the cellar. I don't know what caused it, but I was interested enough to keep my eye on Ellen, on her secret comings and goings. She was like a night cat. I satisfied myself that she was not responsible for the fallings and crashings and thumpings, but also I found they never happened when she was out of the house. She might be sitting staring into space when the poltergeist came, but she was always there.

As a child I remember hearing that the old Hawley house was haunted long ago by the ghost of one of the puritan-pirate ancestors but, according to accounts, he was a decent ghost who walked and wandered and groaned as he should. The stairs creaked under his invisible weight and he rapped on the wall when a death was imminent, all proper and in good taste. The poltergeist was something quite different— malicious, malignant, and mischievous and vengeful. He never broke a valueless thing. Then he went away. I never really believed in him. He was a family joke, except that there he was and there were the broken pictures and shattered china.

When he left, Ellen began walking in her sleep as she was now. I could hear her slow but certain footsteps going downstairs. And at the same time my Mary sighed deeply and murmured beside me. And a breeze sprang up and moved the shadows of leafing limbs on the ceiling.

I slipped quietly from bed and slid into my bathrobe,

for I, like everyone else, believed that a sleepwalker should not be startled awake.

This sounds as though I didn't like my daughter, but I do. I love her, but I am somewhat in fear of her because I don't understand her.

If you use our stairs near the edge on the side of the wall, they do not creak. I discovered that as a tomcatting boy coming home from the back fences of the town. I still use the knowledge if I do not want to disturb Mary. I used it now—moved silently down the staircase, trailing my fingers against the wall for guidance. A dim and lacy sublight penetrated from the street-lamp side and dissipated to semidarkness away from the window. But I could see Ellen. She seemed to have a glow, perhaps her white nightgown. Her face was shadowed but her arms and hands picked up light. She was standing at the glass-fronted cabinet where the worthless family treasures are kept, the carved scrimshaw, the sperm whales and boats complete with oars and irons and crews, harpooner in the bow—all carved from whales' bone—like teeth and the curved tusks of walrus; a small model of the *Belle-Adair*, shiny with varnish, her furled sails and cordage brown and dusty. There were bits of the *chinoiserie* the old captains brought from the Orient after they had stripped the China area of sperm whales, bits and pieces, ebony and ivory, laughing and serious gods, Buddhas, serene and dirty, carved flowers in rose quartz and soapstone and some jade—yes, some good jade—and thin cups, translucent and lovely. Some of the things might be valuable—like the small shapeless horses which yet had life—but if they were valuable it was an accident, must have been. How would those sailing, whale-killing men know good from bad —or would they? Or did they?

The cabinet had always been the holy place of the *parenti* to me—Roman masks of the ancestors, or the lares and penates back to a stone fallen from the moon. We even had a mandrake root—a perfect little man, sprouted from the death-ejected sperm of a hanged man, and also we had a veritable mermaid, pretty ratty by now, but cleverly made by sewing the front end of a monkey and the after end of a fish together. It had shrunk with the years and the stitches showed, but its little teeth still showed in a ferocious smile.

I presume that every family has a magic thing, a continuity thing that inflames and comforts and inspires from generation to generation. Ours was a—how shall I say?— a kind of mound of translucent stone, perhaps quartz or jadeite or even soapstone. It was circular, four inches in diameter and an inch and a half at its rounded peak. And carved on its surface was an endless interweaving shape that seemed to move and yet went no place. It was living but had no head or tail, nor beginning or end. The polished stone was not slick to the touch but slightly tacky like flesh, and it was always warm to the touch. You could see into it and yet not through it. I guess some old seaman of my blood had brought it back from China. It was magic—good to see, to touch, to rub against your cheek or to caress with your fingers. This strange and magic mound lived in the glass cabinet. As child and boy and man I was allowed to touch it, to handle it, but never to carry it away. And its color and convolutions and texture changed as my needs changed. Once I supposed it was a breast, to me as a boy it became yoni, inflamed and aching. Perhaps later it evolved to brain or even enigma, the headless, endless, moving thing—the question which is whole within itself, needing no answer to destroy it, no beginning or end to limit it.

The glass case had a brass lock from colonial times and a square brass key, always in the lock.

My sleeping daughter had the magic mound in her hands, caressing it with her fingers, petting it as though it were alive. She pressed it against her unformed breast, placed it on her cheek below her ear, nuzzled it like a suckling puppy, and she hummed a low song like a moan of pleasure and of longing. There was destruction in her. I had been afraid at first that she might want to crash it to bits or hide it away, but now I saw that it was mother, lover, child, in her hands.

I wondered how I might awaken her without fright. But why are sleepwalkers awakened? Is it for fear that they may hurt themselves? I've never heard of injury in this state, except through awakening. Why should I interfere? This was no nightmare full of pain or fear but rather pleasure and association beyond waking understanding. What call had I to spoil it? I moved quietly back and sat down in my big chair to wait.

The dim room seemed swarming with particles of brilliant light moving and whirling like clouds of gnats. I guess they were not really there but only prickles of weariness swimming in the fluid of my eyes, but they were very convincing. And it did seem true that a glow came from my daughter Ellen, not only from the white of her gown but from her skin as well. I could see her face and I should not have been able to in the darkened room. It seemed to me that it was not a little girl's face at all—nor was it old, but it was mature and complete and formed. Her lips closed firmly, which they did not normally do.

After a time Ellen put the talisman firmly and precisely back in its place and she closed the glass-fronted case and twisted the brass key that kept it closed. Then she turned and walked past my chair and up the stairs. Two things I may have imagined—one, that she did not walk like a child but like a fulfilled woman, and second, that as she went the luminescence drained away from her. These may be impressions, children of my mind, but a third thing is not. As she ascended the stairs, there was no creak of wood. She must have been walking near to the wall, where the treads do not complain.

In a few moments I followed her and found her in her bed, asleep and properly covered. She breathed through her mouth and her face was a sleeping child's face.

On compulsion I went down the stairs again and opened the glass case. I took the mound in my hands. It was warm from Ellen's body. As I had done in childhood, I traced the endless flowing form with my forefingertip and I took comfort in it. I felt close to Ellen because of it.

I wonder, did the stone bring her somehow close to me—to the Hawleys?

CHAPTER IX

O N MONDAY perfidious spring dodged back toward winter with cold rain and raw gusty wind that shredded the tender leaves of too trusting trees. The bold and concupiscent bull sparrows on the lawns, intent on lechery, got blown about like rags, off course and off target, and they chattered wrathfully against the inconstant weather.

I greeted Mr. Red Baker on his tour, his tail blown sideways like a battle flag. He was an old acquaintance, squinting his eyes against the rain. I said, "From now on you and I can be friends on the surface, but I feel it only right to tell you that our smiles conceal a savage contest, a conflict of interests." I could have said more but he was anxious to finish his chores and get under cover.

The Morph was on time. He may have been waiting for me—probably was. "Hell of a day," he said, and his oiled-silk raincoat flapped and billowed around his legs. "I hear you did a social turn with my boss."

"I needed some advice. He gave me tea too."

"He'll do that."

"You know how advice is. You only want it if it agrees with what you wanted to do anyway."

"Sounds like investment."

"My Mary wants some new furniture. When a woman wants something she first dresses it up as a good investment."

"Not only women, either," said Morph. "I do it myself."

"Well, it's her money. She wants to shop around for bargains."

At the corner of High Street we watched a tin sign tear

loose from Rapp's Toy Store and go skidding and screeching along, sounding like a traffic accident.

"Say, I heard your boss is going to make a trip home to Italy."

"I don't know. Seems odd to me he never went before. Those families are awful close."

"Got time for a cup of coffee?"

"I ought to get swept out. Should be a busy morning after the holiday."

"Oh, come on! Live big. The personal friend of Mr. Baker can afford time for a cup of coffee." He didn't say it meanly the way it looks in print. He could make anything sound innocent and well-intentioned.

In all the years I had never gone into the Foremaster Grill for a cup of coffee in the morning and I was probably the only man in town who didn't. It was a custom, a habit, and a club. We climbed on stools at the counter and Miss Lynch, I went to school with her, slid coffee to us without spilling any in the saucer. A tiny bottle of cream leaned against the cup but she rolled two paper-wrapped cubes of sugar like dice so that Morph cried out, "Snake eyes."

Miss Lynch—Miss Lynch. The "miss' was part of her name by now, and part of herself. I guess she will never be able to excise it. Her nose gets redder every year, but it's sinus, not booze.

"Morning, Ethan," she said. "You celebrating something?"

"He dragged me in," I said, and then as an experiment in kindness, "Annie."

Her head snapped around as though at a pistol shot and then, as the idea got through, she smiled and, do you know, she looked exactly as she had in the fifth grade, red nose and all.

"It's good to see you, Ethan," she said and wiped her nose on a paper napkin.

"When I heard it, I was surprised," Morph said. He picked at the paper on the sugar cube. His nails were polished. "You get an idea and then it's fixed and you think it's true. Gives you a turn when it's not."

"I don't know what you're talking about."

"I guess I don't either. Goddam these wrappers. Why can't they just put it loose in a bowl?"

"Maybe because people might use more."

"I guess so. I knew a guy once lived on sugar for a while. He'd go in the Automat. Ten cents for a cup of coffee, drink half, fill it up with sugar. At least he didn't starve to death."

As usual, I wondered if that guy wasn't Morph—a strange one, tough, ageless man with a manicure. I think he was a fairly well-educated man, but only because of his processes, his technique of thinking. His erudition hid in a demi-world dialect, a language of the bright, hard, brassy illiterate. "Is that why you use one lump of sugar?" I asked.

He grinned. "Everybody's got a theory," he said. "I don't care how beat a guy is, he'll have a theory why he's beat. A theory can lead you down the garden path 'cause you'll follow it in spite of road signs. I guess that's what fooled me about your boss."

I hadn't had coffee away from home in a long time. It wasn't very good. It didn't taste like coffee at all but it was hot, and I spilled some on my shirt, so I know it was also brown.

"I guess I don't know what you mean."

"I been trying to track where I got the idea. I guess it's because he says he's been here forty years. Thirty-five years or thirty-seven years, okay, but not forty years."

"I guess I'm not too bright."

"That would make it 1920. You still don't dig it? Well, in a bank you've got to case people quick, check hustlers, you know. Pretty soon you get a built-in set of rules. You don't even think about it. It just clicks into place—and you can be wrong. Maybe he did come in 1920. I could be wrong."

I finished my coffee. "Time to sweep out," I said.

"You fool me too," Morph said. "If you asked questions I'd be hard to get. But you don't, so I got to tell you. Nineteen twenty-one was the first emergency immigration law."

"And?"

"In 1920 he could come in. In 1921 he probably couldn't."

"And?"

"So—anyway my weasel brain says—he came in after 1921 by the back door. So he can't go home because he can't get a passport to get back."

"God, I'm glad I'm not a banker."

"You'd probably be better than I am. I talk too much. If he's going back, I'm real wrong. Wait up—I'm coming. Coffee's on me."

" 'By, Annie," I said.

"Come in again, Eth. You never come in."

"I will."

As we crossed the street Morph said, "Don't let on to his guinea eminence that I pulled a blooper about him being deportation bait, will you?"

"Why should I?"

"Why did I? What's in that jewel case?"

"Knight Templar's hat. Feather's yellow. Going to see if it can be whited up."

"You belong to that?"

"It's in the family. We been Masons since before George Washington was Grand Master."

"He was? Does Mr. Baker belong?"

"It's in his family too."

We were in the alley now. Morph fished for the key to the bank's back door. "Maybe that's why we open the safe like a lodge meeting. Might as well be holding candles. It's kind of holy."

"Morph," I said. "you're full of bull this morning. Easter didn't clean you up at all."

"I'll know in eight days," he said. "No, I mean it. Comes nine o'clock on the nose we stand uncovered in front of the holy of holies. Then the time lock springs and Father Baker genuflects and opens the safe and we all bow down to the Great God Currency."

"You're nuts, Morph."

"Maybe so. Goddam this old lock. You could open it with an ice pick but not with the key." He jiggled the key and kicked at the door until it finally burst open. He took a piece of Kleenex from his pocket and jammed it into the spring lock's seat.

I caught myself about to ask, Isn't that dangerous?

He answered without the question. "Damn thing won't lock itself open. Course Baker checks to see it's locked after the safe's open. Don't blow my dirty suspicions to Marullo, will you? He's too solvent."

"Okay, Morph," I said and turned to my own door on my own side of the alley, and looked around for the cat that always tried to get in, but he wasn't there.

Inside, the store looked changed and new to me. I saw things I had never seen before and didn't see things that had worried and irritated me. And why not? Bring new eyes to a world or even new lenses, and presto—new world.

The leaky valve of the old box toilet hissed softly. Marullo wouldn't get a new valve because the water wasn't metered and who cared. I went to the front of the store and lifted a slotted two-pound weight from the old-fashioned balance scale. In the toilet I hung the weight on the chain above the oaken tassel. The toilet flushed and kept on flushing. I went back to the front of the store to listen and could hear it bubbling and scolding in the bowl. It's a sound you can't mistake for anything else. Then I returned the weight to its bar on the scale and took my place in my pulpit behind the counter. My congregation in the shelves stood waiting. Poor devils, they couldn't get away. I particularly noticed the Mickey Mouse mask smiling down from its box in the pew of breakfast foods. That reminded me of my promise to Allen. I found the extension hand for grabbing things from top shelves and took a box down and stood it under my coat in the storeroom. When I was back in the pulpit, the next Mickey Mouse in line smiled down at me.

I reached behind the canned goods and brought out the gray linen sack of small change for the cash register, then, remembering something, reached farther until my hand found the old greasy .38-caliber revolver that had been there ever since I can remember. It was a silvered Iver Johnson with most of the silver peeled off. I broke it and saw the cartridges green with verdigris. The cylinder was so sluggish with ancient grease that it turned with difficulty. I put the disreputable and probably dangerous piece in the drawer below the cash register, pulled out a clean apron, and wrapped it around my middle, folding the top over neatly to conceal the strings.

Is there anyone who has not wondered about the decisions and acts and campaigns of the mighty of the earth? Are they born in reasoning and dictated by virtue or can some of them be the products of accidents, of daydreaming, of imagining, of the stories we tell ourselves? I know exactly how long I had been playing a game of imagining because I know it started with the Morph's rules for successful bank robbery. I had gone over his words with a childish pleasure adults ordinarily will not admit. It was a play game that ran parallel with the store's life and everything that happened seemed to fall into place in the game. The leaking toilet, the Mickey Mouse mask Allen wanted, the account of the opening of the safe. New curves and angles dropped into place, the Kleenex nudged in the door lock in the alley. Little by little the game grew, but entirely in the mind until this morning. Putting the scale weight on the toilet chain was the first physical contribution I had made to the mental ballet. Getting the old pistol out was the second. And now I began to wonder about the timing. The game was growing in precision.

I still carry my father's big silver Hamilton railroad watch with thick hands and big black numbers, a wonderful watch for time-telling, if not for beauty. This morning I put it in my shirt pocket before I swept out the store. And I checked the time so that at five minutes to nine I had the front doors open and had just taken the first deliberate broom strokes at the sidewalk. It's amazing how much dirt accumulates over a weekend, and what with the rain, the dirt was slush.

What a wonderful precision instrument is our bank—like my father's railroad watch. At five minutes of nine Mr. Baker came into the wind from Elm Street. Harry Robbit and Edith Alden must have been watching. They backed out of the Foremaster Grill and joined him midstreet.

"Morning, Mr. Baker," I called. "Morning, Edith. Morning, Harry."

"Good morning, Ethan. You're going to need a hose for that!" They entered the bank.

I leaned my broom in the store entrance, took the weight from the scale, went behind the cash register, opened the drawer, and went through fast but deliberate pantomime. I walked to the storeroom, hung the weight on the toilet chain. Hooked the skirt of my apron over the belly band, put on my raincoat, and stepped to the back door and opened it a crack. As the black minute hand of my watch crossed twelve the clock bell of the firehouse began bonging. I counted eight steps across the alley and then in my mind twenty steps. I moved my hand but not my lips—allowed ten seconds, moved my hand again. All this I saw in my mind—I counted while my hands made certain movements —twenty steps, quick but deliberate, then eight more steps. I closed the alley door, took off my raincoat, unhooked my apron, went into the toilet, took the weight off the chain and stopped the flushing, moved back of the counter, opened the drawer, opened my hatbox and closed and strapped it, went back to the entrance, took up my broom, and looked at the watch. It was two minutes and twenty seconds past nine o'clock; pretty good, but with a little practice it could be cut under two minutes.

I was only half finished with the sidewalk when Stoney, the chief constable, came across from the Foremaster Grill.

"Morning, Eth. Gimme a quick half-pound of butter, pound of bacon, bottle of milk, and a dozen eggs. My wife run out of everything."

"Sure thing, Chief. How's everything?" I got the things together and snapped open a bag.

"Okay," he said. "I come by a minute ago but I heard you was in the can."

"It'll take me a week to get over all those hard-boiled eggs."

"That's the truth," said Stoney. "Man's got to go, he's got to go."

So that was all right.

As he was about to leave, he said, "What's with your friend, Danny Taylor?"

"I don't know—is he on one?"

"No, he looked pretty good, fairly clean. I was sitting in the car. He had me witness his signature."

"For what?"

"I don't know. Had two papers but turned back so I couldn't see."

"Two papers?"

"Yeah, two. He signed twice and I witnessed twice."

"Was he sober?"

"Seemed like. Had his hair cut and a necktie on."

"I wish I could believe it, Chief."

"So do I. Poor fella. I guess they never stop trying. I got to get home." And he galloped away. Stoney's wife is twenty years younger than he is. I went back and brushed the larger pieces of filth off the sidewalk.

I felt lousy. Maybe the first time is always hard.

I was right about the heavy custom. It seemed to me that everybody in town had run out of everything. And since our deliveries of fruits and vegetables didn't come in until about noon, the pickings were pretty slim. But even with what we had, the customers kept me jumping.

Marullo came in about ten o'clock and for a wonder he gave me a hand, weighing and wrapping and ringing up money on the cash register. He hadn't helped around the store for a long time. Mostly he just wandered in and looked around and went out—like an absentee landlord. But this morning he helped to open the crates and boxes of fresh stuff when it came in. It seemed to me that he was uneasy and that he studied me when I wasn't looking. We didn't have time to talk but I could feel his eyes on me. I thought it must be hearing that I had refused the bribe. Maybe Morph was right. A certain kind of man, if he hears you have been honest, probes for the dishonesty that prompted it. The what's-he-getting-out-of-it? attitude must be particularly strong in men who play their own lives like a poker hand. The thought gave me a little chuckle but a deep one that didn't even raise a bubble to the surface.

About eleven o'clock, my Mary came in, shining in a new cotton print. She looked pretty and happy and a little breathless, as though she had done a pleasant but dangerous thing—and she had. She gave me a brown manila envelope.

"I thought you might be wanting this," she said. She smiled at Marullo the bright birdlike way she does when she doesn't really like someone. And she didn't like or trust Marullo—never had. I always put it down to the fact that a wife never likes her husband's boss or his secretary.

I said, "Thank you, dear. You're very thoughtful. Sorry I can't take you for a boat ride on the Nile right now."

"You *are* busy," she said.

"Well, didn't you run out of everything?"

"Sure I did. Here, I've got a list. Will you bring things home tonight? I know you're too rushed to put them up now."

"But no hard-boiled eggs—"

"No, darling. Not for a whole year."

"Those Easter bunnies were sure busy."

"Margie wants to take us to dinner at the Foremaster tonight. She says she never gets to entertain us."

"Fine," I said.

"She says her place is too small."

"Is it?"

"I'm keeping you from your work," she said.

Marullo's eyes were on the brown envelope in my hand. I put it up under my apron and stuffed it in my pocket. He knew it was a bank envelope. And I could feel his mind hunting like a terrier after rats in a city dump.

Mary said, "I didn't get a chance to thank you for the candy, Mr. Marullo. The children loved it."

"Just good wishes of the Easter," he said. "You dress like springtime."

"Why, thank you. I got wet too. I thought the rain was over, but it came back."

"Take my raincoat, Mary."

"I wouldn't think of it. It's just a shower now. You get back to your customers."

The pace got worse. Mr. Baker looked in and saw the line

of people waiting and went out. "I'll come back later," he called.

And still they came, right up until noon, and then, as usually happens, all custom stopped. People were eating lunch. The traffic died out in the street. For the first time all morning no one was wanting something. I drank more milk from the carton I had opened. Anything I took from the store I marked down and just deducted it from my pay. Marullo let me have things wholesale. It makes a big difference. I don't think we could have lived on my pay if he hadn't.

He leaned back against the counter and folded his arms and that hurt, so he shoved his hands in his pockets until that hurt.

I said, "I'm sure glad you helped out. Never saw such a rush. But I guess they can't go on living on left-over potato salad."

"You do a nice job, kid."

"I do a job."

"No, they come back. They like you."

"They're just used to me. I've been here forever." And then I tried a little tiny probe. "I'll bet you're looking forward to that hot Sicilian sun. It is hot in Sicily. I was there in the war."

Marullo looked away. "I don't make my mind yet."

"Why not?"

"Well, I been away so long time—forty years. I don't know nobody there."

"But you have relatives."

"They don't know me neither."

"I sure wish I could take a vacation in Italy—without a rifle and a field pack. Forty years is a long time, though. What year did you come over?"

"Nineteen twenty—long time ago."

Morph seemed to have hit it on the nose. Maybe bankers and cops and customs men get an instinct. Then another, maybe a little deeper probe came to my mind. I opened the drawer and took out the old revolver and tossed it on the counter. Marullo put his hands behind him. "What you got there, kid?"

"I just thought you ought to get a permit for it if you haven't got one. The Sullivan Act is a tough one."

"Where'd it come from?"

"It's been here all along."

"I never saw it. It don't belong to me. It's yours."

"Not mine. I never saw it before either. It's got to belong to somebody. Long as it's here don't you think you better apply for a permit? You sure it's not yours?"

"I tell you I never saw it. I don't like guns."

"That's funny. I thought all big Mafia men loved 'em."

"How you mean, Mafia? You trying to say I'm Mafia?"

I made a big innocent joke about it. "The way I heard it, all Sicilians belong to Mafia."

"That's crazy. I don't even know no Mafia."

I tossed the gun into the drawer. "Live and learn!" I said. "Well, I sure don't want it. Maybe I better turn it over to Stoney. Tell him I just came on it behind something, because that's what I did."

"You do that," said Marullo. "I never saw it in my life. I don't want it. It's not mine."

"Okay," I said. "Out it goes."

It takes quite a few documents to get a Sullivan Act permit—almost as many as to get a passport.

My boss had ants. Maybe too many small things had happened too close together.

The elderly Miss Elgar, the princess royal of New Baytown, came in close-hauled, with a set jib. Between Miss Elgar and the world were two plates of safety glass, a space between. She negotiated for a dozen eggs. Having known me as a little boy, she never thought of me as anything else. I could see that she was amazed and pleased that I could make change.

"I thank you, Ethan," she said. Her eyes slid over the coffee-grinder and over Marullo and gave equal attention to each. "How's your father, Ethan?"

"Fine, Miss Elgar," I said.

"Give him my greetings, that's a good boy."

"Yes, ma'am. I surely will, ma'am." I wasn't about to reregulate her time sense. They say she still winds the grandfather clock every Sunday night and it has been electrified for years. It wouldn't be bad to be that way, suspended in time—not bad at all, an endless afternoon of now. She nodded gravely to the coffee-grinder before she left.

"Crazy in the head," Marullo said and screwed his forefinger into his temple.

"Nobody changes. Nobody gets hurt."

"Your father is dead. Why don't you tell her he's dead?"

"If she'd believed me, she'd forget it. She always asks after him. It's not so long ago she stopped inquiring after my grandfather. She was his friend, they say, the old goat."

"Crazy in the head," Marullo observed. But for some reason having to do with Miss Elgar's unusual feeling about time, he had got hold of himself. It's hard to know how simple or complicated a man is. When you become too sure, you're usually wrong. I think, from habit and practice, Marullo had reduced his approaches to men to three: command, flattery, and purchase. And the three must have worked often enough to allow him to depend on them. Somewhere in his dealing with me he had lost the first.

"You're a good kid," he said. "You're a good friend too."

"Old Cap'n, he was my grandfather, used to say, 'If you want to keep a friend never test him.' "

"That's smart."

"He was smart."

"All over Sunday I been thinking, kid—even in church I was thinking."

I knew he had been worried about the kickback, at least I thought he had, so I jumped it out to save him time.

"About that fine present, huh?"

"Yeah." He looked at me with admiration. "You're smart too."

"Not smart enough to be working for myself."

"You been here how long—twelve years?"

"That's it—too long. 'Bout time for a change, don't you think?"

"And you never took none of the petty cash and you never took nothing home without you wrote it down."

"Honesty is a racket with me."

"Don't make no joke. What I say is true. I check. I know."

"You may pin the medal on my left lapel."

"Everybody steals—some more, some less—but not you. I know!"

"Maybe I'm waiting to steal the whole thing."

"Don't make jokes. What I say is true."

"Alfio, you've got a jewel. Don't polish me too much. The paste may show through."

"Why don't you be partners with me?"

"On what? My salary?"

"We work it out some way."

"Then I couldn't steal from you without robbing myself."

He laughed appreciatively. "You're smart, kid. But you don't steal."

"You didn't listen. Maybe I plan to take it all."

"You're honest, kid."

"That's what I'm telling you. When I'm most honest, nobody believes me. I tell you, Alfio, to conceal your motives, tell the truth."

"What kind of talk you do?"

"*Ars est celare artem.*"

He moved his lips over that and then broke into a laugh. "Ho," he cried. "Ho! Ho! *Hic erat demonstrandum.*"

"Want a cold Coke?"

"No good for here!" He flung his arms across his abdomen.

"You aren't old enough for a bad stomach, not over fifty."

"Fifty-two, and I got a bad stomach."

"Okay," I said. "Then you came over at twelve if it was 1920. I guess they start Latin early in Sicily."

"I was choirboy," he said.

"I used to carry the cross in the choir myself. I'm going to have a Coke. Alfio," I said, "you work out a way for me to buy in here and I'll look at it. But I warn you, I don't have money."

"We work it out."

"But I'm going to have money."

His eyes were on my face and couldn't seem to remove themselves. And Marullo said softly, "*Io lo credo.*"

Power but not of glory surged through me. I opened a Coke and, tipping it back, looked down its brown barrel at Marullo's eyes.

"You're a good kid," he said and he shook my hand and wandered away, out of the store.

On an impulse I called after him, "How does your arm feel?"

He turned with a look of astonishment. "It don't hurt no more," he said. And he went on and repeated the words to himself, "It don't hurt no more."

He came back excitedly. "You got to take that dough."

"What dough?"

"That five per cent."

"Why?"

"You got to take it. You can buy in with me a little and a little, only hold out for six per cent."

"No."

"What you mean no, if I say yes?"

"I won't need it, Alfio. I'd taken it if I needed to, but I don't need it."

He sighed deeply.

The afternoon wasn't as busy as the morning, but it wasn't light either. There's always a slack time between three and four—usually twenty minutes to half an hour, I don't know why. Then it picks up again, but that's people going home from work and wives whomping up a last-ditch dinner.

In the slack period Mr. Baker came in. He waited, regarding the cheese and sausage in the cold chamber, until the store was clear of two customers, both sloppy shoppers, the kind who don't know what they want, the kind who pick up and put down, hoping that something will jump into their arms and demand to be bought.

At last the shoppers were finished and gone.

"Ethan," he said, "did you know Mary drew out a thousand dollars?"

"Yes, sir. She told me she was going to."

"Do you know what she wants it for?"

"Sure, sir. She's been talking about it for months. You know how women are. The furniture gets a little worn, but just the minute they decide to get new, the old stuff is just impossible."

"Don't you think it's foolish to spend it now on that kind of stuff? I told you yesterday there was going to be an opening."

"It's her money, sir."

"I wasn't talking about gambling, Ethan. I was talking about sure-fire investment. I believe with that thousand she could get her furniture in a year and still have a thousand."

"Mr. Baker, I can't very well forbid her to spend her own money."

"Couldn't you persuade her, couldn't you reason with her?"

"It never occurred to me."

"That sounds like your father, Ethan. That sounds wishy-washy. If I'm going to help you get on your feet I can't have you wishy-washy."

"Well, sir."

"And it isn't like she was going to spend it locally. No, she's going to wander around the discount houses and pay cash. There's no telling what she'll pick up. Local man might charge more but he'd be here if she got a lemon. You should put your foot down, Ethan. Try to get her to redeposit it! Or you tell her to put the money in my hands She'll never regret it."

"It's money her brother left her, sir."

"I know that. I tried to reason with her when she drew it. She just turned blue-eyed vague—said she wanted to look around. Can't she look around without a thousand dollars in her pocket? You ought to know better, if she doesn't."

"I guess I'm out of practice, Mr. Baker. We haven't **had** any money since we were married."

"Well, you'd better learn and learn quick or you won't have any very long. The spending habit is like a dope with some women."

"Mary hasn't had a chance to develop the habit, sir."

"Well, she will. Just let her taste blood and she'll turn killer."

"Mr. Baker, I don't think you mean that."

"I do too."

"There's never been a more careful wife with money. She's had to be."

For some reason he had worked up a storm. "It's you I'm disappointed in, Ethan. If you're going to get any place you've got to be the boss in your own house. You could hold off new furniture another little while."

"I could, but she can't." The thought came to me that maybe bankers develop X-ray eyes for money, that maybe he could see the envelope through my clothes. "I'll try to reason with her, Mr. Baker."

"If she hasn't spent it already. Is she home now?"

"She said she was going to get a bus to Ridgehampton."

"Good God! There goes a thousand bucks."

"Well, she still has some capital."

"That's not the point. Your only entrance is money."

"Money gets money," I said softly.

"That's right. Lose sight of that and you're a gone goose, a clerk for the rest of your life."

"I'm sorry it happened."

"Well, you better lay down the law."

"Women are funny, sir. Maybe your talking about making money yesterday gave her the idea it was easy to get."

"Well, you disabuse her, because without it you can't get any."

"Would you like a cold Coke, sir?"

"Yes, I would."

He couldn't drink it out of the bottle. I had to open a package of paper picnic cups, but it cooled him a little. He muttered like retreating thunder.

Two Negro ladies from the crossing came in and he had to swallow his Coke and his rage. "You talk to her," he said savagely and he strode out and crossed the street to go home. I wondered if he was mad because he was suspicious, but I didn't think so. No, I think he was mad because he felt he'd lost his habit of command. You can get furious at someone who doesn't take your advice.

The Negro ladies were pleasant. There's a community of colored at the crossing, very nice people. They don't trade with us much because they have their own store, only now and then they do some comparative shopping to see if their racial loyalty isn't costing them too much. They did more pricing than buying and I understand why—pretty women, too, such long, straight, slender legs. It's a wonder what a lack of malnutrition in childhood can do for the human body, or the human spirit, for that matter.

Just before closing time I telephoned Mary. "Pigeon-flake, I'm going to be a little late."

"Don't forget we're having dinner with Margie at the Foremaster."

"I remember."

"How late are you going to be?"

"Ten or fifteen minutes. I want to walk down and look at the dredger in the harbor."

"Why?"

"I'm thinking of buying it."

"Oh!"

"Want me to pick up some fish?"

"Well, if you see some nice flounder. That's about all that's running."

"All right—I'm running."

"Now don't dawdle. You'll have to bathe and change. The Foremaster, you know."

"I won't, my fair, my lovely. Mr. Baker gave me hell for letting you spend a thousand dollars."

"Why, that old goat!"

"Mary—Mary! The walls have ears."

"You tell him what he can do."

"But he can't. Besides, he thinks you're a nitwit."

"What?"

"And I'm a wishy-washy, a washy-wishy—a you know how I am."

She was laughing her lovely trill, something that raises goose lumps of pleasure on my soul.

"Hurry home, darling," she said. "Hurry home." And how's that for a man to have! When I hung up, I stood by the phone all weak and leaky and happy if there is such a condition. I tried to think how it had been before Mary, and I couldn't remember, or how it would be without her, and I could not imagine it except that it would be a condition bordered in black. I guess everyone at some time or other writes his epitaph. Mine would be "Good-by Charley."

The sun was below the western hills but a great powdery cloud scooped its light and threw it on the harbor and the breakwater and the sea beyond so that the whitecaps were pink as roses. The piles in the water by the city pier are triple logs iron-banded at the top and sloping like pylons to shear the winter ice. On top of each one a gull stood motionless, usually a male with white immaculate vest and clean gray wings. I wonder if each one owns his place and can sell or rent it at will.

A few fishing boats were in. I know all the fishermen, have known them all my life. And Mary was right. They only had flounder. I bought four nice ones from Joe Logan and stood by while he filleted them for me, his knife slipping along the spine as easily as it would through water. In the spring there is one sure subject—when will the weakfish come? We used to say, "When lilacs bloom the weakfish coome," but you can't depend on it. Seems to me that all my life the weaks have not arrived or have just left. And what beautiful fish they are when you get one, slender as trout, clean, silver as—silver. They smell good. Well, they weren't running. Joe Logan hadn't taken a single one.

"Me, I like blowfish," Joe said. "Funny thing, when you call them blowfish nobody will touch them, but call them sea chicken and customers fight for them."

"How's your daughter, Joe?"

"Oh, she seems to get better and then she fades off. It's killing me."

"Too bad. I'm sorry."

"If there was anything to do—"

"I know—poor kid. Here's a bag. Just drop the flounders in it. Give her my love, Joe."

He looked me long in the eyes as though he hoped to draw something out of me, some medicine. "I'll do that, Eth," he said. "I'll tell her."

Back of the breakwater the county dredger was working, its giant screw augering up mud and shells and the pumps pushing the junk through pipe on pontoons and flinging it behind the black-tarred bulkheads on the shore. Its running lights were on and its riding lights too and two red balls were hoisted to show that it was working. A pale cook in white cap and apron leaned his bare arms on the rail and looked down into the troubled water and occasionally he spat into the roil. The wind was inshore. It brought from the dredger the stink of mud and long-dead shells and tarnished weed together with the sweet smell of baking cinnamon in apple pie. The great auger turned with majesty, boring out the channel.

Then with a flash of pink the sails of a lithe yacht caught the afterglow and came about and lost the light. I wandered back and turned left past the new mariana and the old yacht club and the American Legion Hall with brown-painted machine guns mounted beside its steps.

At the boat yard they were working late trying to get the stored craft painted and ready against the coming summer. The unusual cold of the early spring had set them back with the painting and varnishing.

I walked well past the boat works and then down through the weed-grown lot to the harbor's edge and then slowly back toward Danny's lean-to shack. And I whistled an old tune against his wishing me to.

And it seemed he did. His shack was empty but I knew as surely as if I saw him that Danny was lying hidden in the weeds, perhaps between the huge square timbers that were scattered about. And since I knew he would come back as soon as I was gone, I took the brown envelope from my pocket and propped it on his dirty bed and I went away, still whistling, except for one moment when I called softly, "Good-by, Danny. Good luck." And I went on whistling back to the street and over to Porlock and past the great houses to Elm and so to my own—the Hawley house.

I found my Mary in the eye of a storm, quiet and slowly rotating herself with debris and great winds surging around her. She directed the devastation in her white nylon slip and slippers; her new-washed hair clustered on curlers on her head like a large litter of suckling sausages. I can't remember when we had been out to dinner at a restaurant. We couldn't afford it and had lost the habit. Mary's wild excitement fluttered the children on the edges of her personal hurricane. She fed them, washed them, issued orders, rescinded orders. The ironing board was standing in the kitchen with my dear and valued clothing pressed and hanging on the backs of chairs. Mary would pause in her gallop to swipe the iron at a dress she was pressing. The children were almost too excited to eat, but they had their orders.

I have five suits called best—a good number for a grocery clerk to have. I fingered them on the chair backs. They were called Old Blue, Sweet George Brown, Dorian Grey, Burying Black, and Dobbin.

"Which one shall I wear, cuddles?"

"Cuddles? Oh! Well, it's not formal and it's Monday night. I'd say it would be Sweet George or Dorian, yes, Dorian, that's formal enough without being formal."

"And my polka-dot bow tie?"

"Of course."

Ellen broke in. "Papa! You're not going to wear a bow tie! You're too old."

"I am not. I'm young and gay and giddy."

"You'll be a laughing stork. I'm glad I'm not going."

"I am too. Where do you get the idea that I'm an old stork?"

"Well you aren't old, but you're too old for a bow tie."

"You're a nasty little conformist."

"Well, if you want to be a laughing stork."

"That's what I want to be. Mary, don't you want me to be a laughing stork?"

"Let your father alone, he has to bathe. I laid a shirt out on the bed."

Allen said, "I'm halfway through my I Love America essay."

"That's good, because come summer I'm going to put you to work."

"Work?"

"In the store."

"Oh!" He didn't seem too enthusiastic.

Ellen gave an opening gasp but when she had our attention she didn't say anything. Mary repeated the eighty-five things the children were to do and not to do while we were gone and I went upstairs for my tub.

I was tying my dear blue polka-dot, my only blue polka-dot tie when Ellen leaned in against the door. "It wouldn't be so bad if you were younger," she said with dreadful femininity.

"You're going to give some happy husband a rough time, my dear."

"Even the seniors in high school wouldn't wear it."

"Prime Minister Macmillan does."

"That's different. Daddy, is it cheating to copy something out of a book?"

"Explain!"

"Well, if a person, if I was writing my essay and I took stuff out of a book—how about that?"

"It would depend on how you did it."

"Like you said—explain."

"Don't you mean 'as I said'?"

"Yes."

"Well, if you put quotation marks around it and a footnote telling who wrote it, it could add dignity and authority. I guess half the writing in America is quotations if it isn't anthologies. Now do you like my tie?"

"S'pose you didn't put those marks . . ."

"Then it would be stealing like any other kind of stealing. You didn't do that, did you?"

"No."

"Then what is your problem?"

"Could they put you in jail?"

"Might—if you got money for it. Don't do it, my girl. Now what do you think about my tie?"

"I guess you're just impossible," she said.

"If you plan to join the others, you might tell your blinking brother that I brought him his bleeding Mickey Mouse mask and shame on him."

"You never listen, really listen."

"I do too."

"No, you don't. You'll be sorry."

"Good-by, Leda. Say hello to the swan."

She lounged away, a baby-fatted volupt. Girls kill me. They turn out to be girls.

My Mary was just beautiful, just beautiful and shining. A light from inside her oozed out of her pores. She took my arm as we walked down Elm Street under the arching trees with the street lights playing on us and I swear our legs moved with the proud and tender steps of thoroughbreds coming to the barrier.

"You must come to Rome! Egypt isn't big enough for you. The great world calls."

She giggled. I swear she giggled as would have done honor to our daughter.

"We're going to go out more often, my darling."

"When?"

"When we are rich."

"When is that?"

"Soon. I'm going to teach you to wear shoes."

"Will you light your cigars with ten-dollar bills?"

"Twenties."

"I like you."

"Shucks, ma'am. You oughten to say that. You plumb embarrass me."

Not long ago the owners of the Foremaster installed bow windows on the street, with small square panes of bottle glass, designed to make the place look old and authentic—and it did so look—but people sitting inside at the tables had their faces altered by the warping glass. One face would be all jaw, another one big vacant eye, but it all added to the age and the authenticity of the old Foremaster and so did the geraniums and lobelias in the window boxes.

Margie was waiting for us, hostess to her fingertips. She introduced her companion, a Mr. Hartog of New York, sun-lamp tanned and set with teeth like an ear of Country Gentleman. Mr. Hartog looked wrapped and shellacked, but he answered all sentences with an appreciative laugh. That was his contribution and it wasn't a bad one.

"How d'you do?" said Mary.

Mr. Hartog laughed.

I said, "I hope you know your companion is a witch."

Mr. Hartog laughed. We all felt good.

Margie said, "I've asked for a table by the window. That one there."

"You also had them put special flowers, Margie."

"Mary, I have to do something to repay all your kindness."

They went on like this during and after Margie had seated us, and Mr. Hartog laughed at every period, clearly a brilliant man. I made a plan to get a word from him, but later.

The set table seemed fine and very white and the silver which wasn't silver looked extra silvery.

Margie said, "I'm the hostess and that means I'm the boss and I say martinis whether you want them or not." Mr. Hartog laughed.

The martinis came, not in little glasses but big as bird baths with twists of lemon peel. The first taste bit like a vampire bat, made its little anesthesia, and after that the drink mellowed and toward the bottom turned downright good.

"We're going to have two," said Margie. "The food's pretty good here but not that good."

Then I told how I had always planned to open a bar where you could only get your second martini. I would make a fortune.

Mr. Hartog laughed and four more bird baths appeared at our table while I was still chewing the first lemon peel.

With the first taste of his second drink, Mr. Hartog developed the power of speech. He had a low, vibrant voice, like that of an actor or a singer or a salesman of some product people don't want. You might even call it a bedside voice.

"Mrs. Young-Hunt tells me you're in business here," he said. "It's a fascinating town—unspoiled."

I was about to tell him exactly what my business consisted in when Margie took the ball. "Mr. Hawley is the coming power of this county," she said.

"So? What line are you in, Mr. Hawley?"

"Everything," said Margie. "Absolutely everything, but not openly, you understand." Her eyes had a liquor shine. I looked at Mary's eyes and they were just beginning to surface, so I judged the others had had a couple before we came, or at least Margie had.

"Well, that saves me from denying it," I said.

Mr. Hartog came back to his laugh. "You have a lovely wife. That's half the battle."

"That's the whole battle."

"Ethan, you'll make him think we fight."

"Oh, we do!" I gulped half the glass and felt the warmth spring up behind my eyes. And I was looking at the bottle end of one of the tiny window panes. It caught the candlelight and seemed to revolve slowly. Maybe it was self-hypnosis, for I heard my own voice go on, listened to myself from outside myself. "Mrs. Margie is the Witch of the East. A martini is not a drink. It's a potion." The gleaming glass still held me.

"Oh, dear! I always thought of myself as Ozma. Wasn't the Witch of the East a wicked witch?"

"She was indeed."

"And didn't she melt?"

Through the crooked glass I saw a man's figure walking past on the sidewalk. He was all misshaped by the distortion, but he carried his head a little to the left and walked curiously on the outsides of his feet. Danny did that. I saw myself leap up and run after him. I saw myself run to the corner of Elm Street but he had disappeared, perhaps in the back garden of the second house. I called, "Danny! Danny! Give me back the money. Please, Danny, give it to me. Don't take it. It's poisoned. I poisoned it!"

I heard a laugh. It was Mr. Hartog's laugh. Margie said, "Well, I would rather be Ozma."

I wiped the tears from my eyes with my napkin and explained, "I should drink it, not bathe my eyes in it. It burns."

"Your eyes are all red," Mary said.

I couldn't get back to the party but I heard myself talk and tell stories and I heard my Mary laugh like golden glory so I guess I was funny, and even charming, but I couldn't ever get back to the table. And I think Margie knew it. She kept looking at me with a concealed question, damn her. She was a witch.

I don't know what we had to eat. I remember white wine so perhaps it was fish. The brittle glass revolved like a propeller. And there was brandy, so I must have had coffee—and then it was over.

Going out, when Mary and Mr. Hartog had gone ahead, Margie asked, "Where did you go?"

"I don't know what you mean."

"You went away. You were only part here."

"Aroint ye, witch!"

"Okay, bud," she said.

On our way home I searched the shadows of the gardens. Mary clung to my arm and her footsteps were a little jerky. "What a nice time," she said. "I never had a better time."

"It was nice."

"Margie's a perfect hostess. I don't know how I'll match that dinner."

"She surely is."

"And you, Ethan. I knew you could be funny but you had us laughing all the time. Mr. Hartog said he was weak from laughing about Mr. Red Baker."

Had I told that? Which one? I must have. Oh, Danny—give back the money! Please!

"You're better than a show," my Mary said. And in our own doorway I grabbed her so tight that she whimpered. "You're tipped, darling. You're hurting. Please don't let's wake the children."

It was my intention to wait until she slept and then to creep out, to go to his shack, to look for him, even to put the police on him. But I knew better. Danny was gone. I knew Danny was gone. And I lay in the darkness and watched the little red and yellow spots swimming in the water of my eyes. I knew what I had done, and Danny knew it too. I thought of my small rabbit slaughter. Maybe it's only the first time that's miserable. It has to be faced. In business and in politics a man must carve and maul his way through men to get to be King of the Mountain. Once there, he can be great and kind—but he must get there first.

CHAPTER X

THE Templeton Airfield is only about forty miles from New Baytown, and that's about five minutes' flying time for the jets. They come over with increasing regularity, swarms of deadly gnats. I wish I could admire them, even love them the way my son Allen does. If they had more than one purpose, maybe I could, but their only function is killing and I've had a bellyful of that. I haven't learned, as Allen has, to locate them by looking ahead of the sound they make. They go through the sound barrier with a boom that makes me think the furnace has exploded. When they go over at night they get into my dreams and I awaken with a sad sick feeling as though my soul had an ulcer.

Early in the morning a flight of them boomed through and I jumped awake, a little trembly. They must have made me dream of those German 88-millimeter all-purpose rifles we used to admire and fear so much.

My body was prickly with fear sweat as I lay in the gathering morning light and listened to the slender spindles of malice whining away in the distance. I thought how that shudder was under the skin of everybody in the world, not in the mind, deep under the skin. It's not the jets so much as what their purpose is.

When a condition or a problem becomes too great, humans have the protection of not thinking about it. But it goes inward and minces up with a lot of other things already there and what comes out is discontent and uneasiness, guilt and a compulsion to get something—anything—before it is all gone. Maybe the assembly-line psychoanalysts aren't dealing with complexes at all but with those warheads that may one day be mushroom clouds. It does seem to me that nearly everyone I see is nervous and restless and a little loud and gaily crazy like people getting drunk on New Year's Eve. Should auld acquaintance be forgot and kiss your neighbor's wife.

I turned my head toward mine. She was not smiling in her sleep. Her mouth was drawn down and there were lines of weariness around her squinched-shut eyes and so she was sick, because that's the way she looks when she is sick. She is the wellest wife in the world until she is sick, which isn't often, and then she is the sickest wife in the world.

Another flight of jets exploded through sound. We had maybe a half-million years to get used to fire and less than fifteen to build thinking about this force so extravagantly more fierce than fire. Would we ever have the chance to make a tool of this? If the laws of thinking are the laws of things, can fission be happening in the soul? Is that what is happening to me, to us?

I remember a story Aunt Deborah told me long ago. Early in the last century some of my people were Cambellites. Aunt Deborah was a child then, but she remembered how the end of the world was coming at a certain time. Her parents gave everything away, everything they owned but the bed sheets. Those they put on and at the predicted time they went to the hills to meet the End of the World. Dressed in sheets, hundreds of people prayed and sang. The night came and they sang louder and danced and as it got near time there was a shooting star, she said, and everybody screamed. She could still remember the screaming. Like wolves, she said, like hyenas, although she had never heard a hyena. Then the moment came. White-dressed men and women and children held their breaths. The moment went on and on. The children got blue in the face—and then it passed. It was done and they were cheated out of their destruction. In the dawn they crept down the hill and tried to get back the clothes they had given away, and the pots and pans and their ox and their ass. And I remember knowing how bad they must have felt.

I think what brought that back was the jets—all that enormous effort and time and money to stockpile all that death. Would we feel cheated if we never used it? We can shoot rockets into space but we can't cure anger or discontent.

My Mary opened her eyes. "Ethan," she said, "you're talking in your mind. I don't know what it's about but it's loud. Stop thinking, Ethan."

I was going to suggest that she give up drink but she looked too miserable. I don't always know when not to joke, but this time I said, "Head?"

"Yes."

"Stomach?"

"Yes."

"All over?"

"All over."

"I'll get you something."

"Get me a grave."

"Stay down."

"I can't. I've got to get the children off to school."

"I'll do it."

"You've got to go to work."

"I'll do it, I tell you."

After a moment she said, "Ethan, I don't think I can get up. I feel too bad."

"Doctor?"

"No."

"I can't leave you alone. Can Ellen stay with you?"

"No, she has examinations."

"Could I call up Margie Young-Hunt to come over?"

"Her phone is out. She's getting a new thingamabob."

"I can go by and ask her."

"She'd kill anybody that waked her this early."

"I could slip a note under her door."

"No, I don't want you to."

"Nothing to it."

"No, no. I don't want you to. I don't want you to."

"I can't leave you alone."

"That's funny. I feel better. I guess it was shouting at you that did it. Well, it's true," she said, and to prove it she got up and put on her dressing gown. She did look better.

"You're wonderful, my darling."

I cut myself shaving and went down to breakfast with a red tatter of toilet paper sticking to my face.

No Morph standing on the porch picking his teeth when I went by. I was glad. I didn't want to see him. I hurried just in case he might try to catch up with me.

When I opened the alley door I saw the brown bank envelope that had been pushed under it. It was sealed and bank envelopes are tough. I had to get out my pocket knife to slit it open.

Three sheets of paper from a five-cent lined school pad, written on with a soft lead pencil. A will: "I, being in my right mind . . ." and "In consideration I . . ." A note of hand: "I agree to repay and pledge my . . ." Both papers signed, the writing neat and precise. "Dear Eth: This is what you want."

The skin on my face felt as hard as a crab's back. I closed the alley door slowly as you'd close a vault. The first two sheets of paper I folded carefully and placed in my wallet, and the other—I crumpled it and put it in the toilet and pulled the chain. It's a high box toilet with a kind of step in the bowl. The balled paper resisted going over the edge, but finally it did.

The alley door was a little open when I emerged from the cubicle. I thought I had closed it. Going toward it, I heard a small sound and, looking up, I saw that damn cat on one of the top storage shelves hooking out with its claws for a hanging side of bacon. It took a long-handled broom and quite a chase to drive it out into the alley. As it streaked past me, I swiped at it and missed and broke the broom handle against the doorjamb.

There was no sermon for the canned goods that morning. I couldn't raise a text. But I did get out a hose to wash down the front sidewalk and the gutter too. Afterward I cleaned the whole store, even corners long neglected and choked with flug. And I sang too:

"Now is the winter of our discontent
Made glorious summer by this sun of York."

I know it's not a song, but I sang it.

PART TWO

CHAPTER XI

NEW Baytown is a lovely place. Its harbor, once a great
one, is sheltered from the northeast screamers by an offshore
island. The village is strewn about a complex of inland waters fed by the tides, which at ebb and flow drive wild races
through narrow channels from the harbor and the sea. It is
not a crowded or an urban town. Except for the great houses
of the long-gone whalers, the dwellings are small and neat,
distributed among fine old trees, oaks of several kinds,
maples and elms, hickory and some cypresses, but except
for the old planted elms on the original streets, the native
timber is largely oak. Once the virgin oaks were so many and
so large that several shipyards drew planks and knees, keels
and keelsons, from nearby.

Communities, like people, have periods of health and
times of sickness—even youth and age, hope and despondency. There was a time when a few towns like New Baytown furnished the whale oil that lighted the Western
World. Student lamps of Oxford and Cambridge drew
fuel from this American outpost. And then petroleum,
rock oil gushed out in Pennsylvania and cheap kerosene,
called coal oil, took the place of whale oil and retired
most of the sea hunters. Sickness or the despair fell on
New Baytown—perhaps an attitude from which it did not
recover. Other towns not too far away grew and prospered
on other products and energies, but New Baytown, whose
whole living force had been in square-rigged ships and
whales, sank into torpor. The snake of population crawling
out from New York passed New Baytown by, leaving it to
its memories. And, as usually happens, New Baytown peo-

ple persuaded themselves that they liked it that way. They were spared the noise and litter of summer people, the garish glow of neon signs, the spending of tourist money and tourist razzle-dazzle. Only a few new houses were built around the fine inland waters. But the snake of population continued to writhe out and everyone knew that sooner or later it would engulf the village of New Baytown. The local people longed for that and hated the idea of it at the same time. The neighboring towns were rich, spilled over with loot from tourists, puffed with spoils, gleamed with the great houses of the new rich. Old Baytown spawned art and ceramics and pansies, and the damn broadfooted brood of Lesbos wove handmade fabrics and small domestic intrigues. New Baytown talked of the old days and of flounder and when the weakfish would start running.

In the reedy edges of the inner waters, the mallards nested and brought out their young flotillas, muskrats dug communities and swam lithely in the early morning. The ospreys hung, aimed, and plummeted on fish, and sea gulls carried clams and scallops high in the air and dropped them to break them open for eating. Some otters still clove the water like secret furry whispers; rabbits poached in the gardens and gray squirrels moved like little waves in the streets of the village. Cock pheasants flapped and coughed their crowing. Blue herons poised in the shallow water like leggy rapiers and at night the bitterns cried out like lonesome ghosts.

Spring is late and summer late at New Baytown, but when it comes it has a soft, wild, and special sound and smell and feeling. In early June the world of leaf and blade and flowers explodes, and every sunset is different. Then in the evening the bobwhites state their crisp names and after dark there is a wall of sound of whippoorwill. The oaks grow fat with leaf and fling their long-tasseled blossoms in the grass. Then dogs from various houses meet and go on picnics, wandering bemused and happy in the woods, and sometimes they do not come home for days.

In June man, hustled by instinct, mows grass, riffles the earth with seeds, and locks in combat with mole and rabbit, ant, beetle, bird, and all others who gather to take his garden from him. Woman looks at the curling-edge petals of a rose and melts a little and sighs, and her skin becomes a petal and her eyes are stamens.

June is gay—cool and warm, wet and shouting with growth and reproduction of the sweet and the noxious, the builder and the spoiler. The girls in body-form slacks wander the High Street with locked hands while small transistor radios sit on their shoulders and whine love songs in their ears. The young boys, bleeding with sap, sit on the stools of Tanger's Drugstore ingesting future pimples through straws. They watch the girls with level goat-eyes and make disparaging remarks to one another while their insides whimper with longing.

In June businessmen drop by Al 'n' Sue's or the Foremaster for a beer and stay for whisky and get sweatily drunk in the afternoon. Even in the afternoon the dusty cars creep to the desolate dooryard of the remote and paintless house with every blind drawn, at the end of Mill Street, where Alice, the village whore, receives the afternoon problems of June-bitten men. And all day long the rowboats anchor off the breakwater and happy men and women coax up their dinners from the sea.

June is painting and clipping, plans and projects. It's a rare man who doesn't bring home cement blocks and two-by-fours and on the backs of envelopes rough out drawings of Taj Mahals. A hundred little boats lie belly down and keel up on the shore, their bottoms gleaming with copper paint, and their owners straighten up and smile at the slow, unmoving windrows. Still school grips the intransigent children until near to the end of the month and, when examination time comes, rebellion foams up and the common cold becomes epidemic, a plague which disappears on closing day.

In June the happy seed of summer germinates. "Where shall we go over the glorious Fourth of July? . . . It's getting on time we should be planning our vacation." June is the mother of potentials, ducklings swim bravely perhaps to the submarine jaws of snapping turtles, lettuces lunge toward drought, tomatoes rear defiant stems toward cut-worms, and families match the merits of sand and sunburn over fretful mountain nights loud with mosquito symphonies. "This year I'm going to rest. I won't get so tired. This year I won't allow the kids to make my free two weeks a hell on wheels. I work all year. This is my time. I work all year." Vacation planning triumphs over memory and all's right with the world.

New Baytown had slept for a long time. The men who governed it, politically, morally, economically, had so long continued that their ways were set. The Town Manager, the council, the judges, the police were eternal. The Town Manager sold equipment to the township, and the judges fixed traffic tickets as they had for so long that they did not remember it as illegal practice—at least the books said it was. Being normal men, they surely did not consider it immoral. All men are moral. Only their neighbors are not.

The yellow afternoon had the warm breath of summer. A few early season people, those without children to hold them glued until school was out, were moving in the streets, strangers. Some cars came through, towing small boats and big outboard motors on trailers. Ethan would have known with his eyes closed that they were summer people by what they bought—cold cuts and process cheese, crackers and tinned sardines.

Joey Morphy came in for his afternoon refreshment as he did every day now that the weather was warming. He waved the bottle toward the cold counter. "You should put in a soda fountain," he said.

"And grow four new arms, or split into two clerks like a *puendo* pod? You forget, neighbor Joey, I don't own the store."

"You should."

"Must I tell you my sad story of the death of kings?"

"I know your story. You didn't know your asparagus from a hole in the double-entry bookkeeping. You had to learn the hard way. Now wait—but you learned."

"Small good it does me."

"If it was your store now, you'd make money."

"But it isn't."

"If you opened up next door, you'd take all the customers with you."

"What makes you think so?"

"Because people buy from people they know. It's called good will and it works."

"Didn't work before. Everybody in town knew me. I went broke."

"That was technical. You didn't know how to buy."

"Maybe I still don't."

"You do. You don't even know you've learned. But you've still got a broke state of mind. Junk it, Mr. Hawley. Junk it, Ethan."

"Thanks."

"I like you. When is Marullo going to Italy?"

"He hasn't said. Tell me, Joey—how rich is he? No, don't. I know you're not supposed to talk about clients."

"I can rupture a rule for a friend, Ethan. I don't know all his affairs, but if our account means anything, I'd say he is. He's got his fingers in all kinds of things—piece of property here, vacant lot there, some beach-front houses, and a bundle of first mortgages big around as your waist."

"How do you know?"

"Safe-deposit box. He rents one of our big ones. When he opens it, he has one key and I have the other. I'll admit I've peeked. Guess I'm a peeping Tom at heart."

"But it's all on the level, isn't it? I mean—well you read all the time about—well, drugs and rackets and things like that."

"I wouldn't know about that. He don't tell his business around. Draws some out, puts some back. And I don't know where else he banks. You notice I don't tell his balance."

"I didn't ask."

"Could you let me have a beer?"

"Only to take out. I can put it in a paper cup."

"I wouldn't ask you to break the law."

"Nuts!" Ethan punched holes in a can. "Just hold it down beside you if anybody comes in."

"Thanks. I've put a lot of thought on you, Ethan."

"Why?"

"Maybe because I'm a Nosy Parker. Failure is a state of mind. It's like one of those sand traps an ant lion digs. You keep sliding back. Takes one hell of a jump to get out of it. You've got to make that jump, Eth. Once you get out, you'll find success is a state of mind too."

"Is it a trap too?"

"If it is—it's a better kind."

"Suppose a man makes the jump, and someone else gets tromped."

"Only God sees the sparrow fall, but even God doesn't do anything about it."

"I wish I knew what you're trying to tell me to do."

"I wish I did too. If I did, I might do it myself. Bank tellers don't get to be president. A man with a fistful of stock does. I guess I'm trying to say, Grab anything that goes by. It may not come around again."

"You're a philosopher, Joey, a financial philosopher."

"Don't rub it in. If you don't have it, you think about it. Man being alone thinks about things. You know most people live ninety per cent in the past, seven per cent in the present, and that only leaves them three per cent for the future. Old Satchel Paige said the wisest thing about that I ever heard. He said, 'Don't look behind. Something may be gaining on you.' I got to get back. Mr. Baker's going to New York tomorrow for a few days. He's busy as a bug."

"What about?"

"How do I know? But I separate the mail. He's been getting a lot from Albany."

"Politics?"

"I only separate it. I don't read it. Is business always this slow?"

"Around four o'clock, yes. It'll pick up in ten minutes or so."

"You see? You've learned. I bet you didn't know that before you went broke. Be seeing you. Grab the gold ring for a free ride."

The little buying spurt between five and six came on schedule. The sun, held back by daylight-saving, was still high and the streets light as midafternoon when he brought in the fruit bins and closed the front doors and drew the green shades. Then, reading from a list, he gathered the supplies to carry home and put them all in one big bag. With his apron off and his coat and hat on, he boosted up and sat on the counter and stared at the shelves of the congregation. "No message!" he said. "Only remember the words of Satchel Paige. I guess I have to learn about not looking back."

He took the folded lined pages from his wallet, made a little envelope for them of waxed paper. Then, opening the enamel door to the works of the cold counter, he slipped the waxy envelope in a corner behind the compressor and closed the metal door on it.

Under the cash register on a shelf he found the dusty and dog-eared Manhattan telephone book, kept there for emergency orders to the supply house. Under U, under United States, under Justice, Dept of . . . His finger moved down the column past "Antitrust Div US Court House, Customs Div, Detention Hdqtrs, Fed Bur of Investgatn," and under it, "Immigration & Naturalization Svce, 20 W Bway, BA 7-0300, Nights Sat Sun & Holidays OL 6-5888."

He said aloud, "OL 6-5888—OL 6-5888 because it's late." And then he spoke to his canned goods without looking at them. "If everything's proper and aboveboard, nobody gets hurt."

Ethan went out the alley door and locked it. He carried his bag of groceries across the street to the Foremaster Hotel and Grill. The grill was noisy with cocktailers but the tiny lobby where the public phone booth stood was deserted even by the room clerk. He closed the glass door, put his groceries on the floor, spread his change on the shelf, inserted a dime, and dialed O.

"Operator."

"Oh! Operator—I want to call New York."

"Will you dial the number, please?"

And he did.

Ethan came from work, carrying his bag of groceries.

How good the long afternoons are! The lawn was so tall and lush that it took his footprints. He kissed Mary damply.

"Pollywog," he said, "the lawn is running wild. Do you think I could get Allen to cut it?"

"Well, it's examination time. You know how that is, and school closing and all."

"What's that unearthly squalling sound in the other room?"

"He's practicing with his voice-throwing gadget. He's going to perform at the school closing show."

"Well, I guess I'll have to cut the lawn myself."

"I'm sorry, dear. But you know how they are."

"Yes, I'm beginning to learn how they are."

"Are you in a bad temper? Did you have a hard day?"

"Let's see. No, I guess not. I've been on my feet all day. The thought of pushing the lawnmower doesn't make me jump with joy."

"We should have a power mower. The Johnsons have one you can ride on."

"We should have a gardener and a gardener's boy. My grandfather did. Ride on? Allen might cut the lawn if he could ride."

"Don't be mean to him. He's only fourteen. They're all like that."

"Who do you suppose established the fallacy that children are cute?"

"You *are* in a bad temper."

"Let's see. Yes, I guess I am. And that squalling is driving me crazy."

"He's practicing."

"So you said."

"Now don't take your bad temper out on him."

"All right, but it would help if I could." Ethan pushed through the living room, where Allen was squawking vaguely recognizable words from a vibrating reed held on his tongue. "What in the world is that?"

Allen spat it into his palm. "From that box of Peeks. It's ventriloquism."

"Did you eat the Peeks?"

"No. I don't like it. I've got to practice, Dad."

"Hold up a moment." Ethan sat down. "What do you plan to do with your life?"

"Huh?"

"The future. Haven't they told you in school? The future is in your hands."

Ellen slithered into the room and draped herself on the couch like a knob-kneed cat. She rippled out a steel-cutting giggle.

"He wants to go on television," she said.

"There was a kid only thirteen won a hundred and thirty thousand dollars on a quiz program."

"Turned out it was rigged," said Ellen.

"Well, he still had a hundred and thirty grand."

Ethan said softly, "The moral aspects don't bother you?"

"Well, it's still a lot of dough."

"You don't find it dishonest?"

"Shucks, everybody does it."

"How about the ones who offer themselves on a silver platter and there are no takers? They have neither honesty nor money."

"That's the chance you take—the way the cooky crumbles."

"Yes, it's crumbling, isn't it?" Ethan said. "And so are your manners. Sit up! Have you dropped the word 'sir' from the language?"

The boy looked startled, checked to see if it was meant, then lounged upright, full of resentment. "No, sir," he said.

"How are you doing in school?"

"All right, I guess."

"You were writing an essay about how you love America. Has your determination to destroy her stopped that project?"

"How do you mean, destroy—sir?"

"Can you honestly love a dishonest thing?"

"Heck, Dad, everybody does it."

"Does that make it good?"

"Well, nobody's knocking it except a few eggheads. I finished the essay."

"Good, I'd like to see it."

"I sent it off."

"You must have a copy."

"No, sir."

"Suppose it gets lost?"

"I didn't think of that. Dad, I wish I could go to camp the way all the other kids do."

"We can't afford it. Not all the other kids go—only a few of them."

"I wish we had some money." He stared down at his hands and licked his lips.

Ellen's eyes were narrowed and concentrated.

Ethan studied his son. "I'm going to make that possible," he said.

"Sir?"

"I can get you a job to work in the store this summer."

"How do you mean, work?"

"Isn't your question, 'What do you mean, work?' You will carry and trim shelves and sweep and perhaps, if you do well, you can wait on customers."

"I want to go to camp."

"You also want to win a hundred thousand dollars."

"Maybe I'll win the essay contest. At least that's a trip to Washington anyway. Some kind of vacation after all year in school."

"Allen! There are unchanging rules of conduct, of courtesy, of honesty, yes, even of energy. It's time I taught you to give them lip service at least. You're going to work."

The boy looked up. "You can't."

"I beg your pardon?"

"Child labor laws. I can't even get a work permit before I'm sixteen. You want me to break the law?"

"Do you think all the boys and girls who help their parents are half slave and half criminal?" Ethan's anger was as naked and ruthless as love. Allen looked away.

"I didn't mean that, sir."

"I'm sure you didn't. And you won't again. You stubbed your nose on twenty generations of Hawleys and Allens.

They were honorable men. You may be worthy to be one someday."

"Yes, sir. May I go to my room, sir?"

"You may."

Allen walked up the stairs slowly.

When he had disappeared, Ellen whirled her legs like propellers. She sat up and pulled down her skirt like a young lady.

"I've been reading the speeches of Henry Clay. He sure was good."

"Yes, he was."

"Do you remember them?"

"Not really, I guess. It's been a long time since I read them."

"He's great."

"Somehow it doesn't seem schoolgirl reading."

"He's just great."

Ethan got up from his chair with a whole long and weary day pushing him back.

In the kitchen he found Mary red-eyed and angry.

"I heard you," she said. "I don't know what you think you're doing. He's just a little boy."

"That's the time to start, my darling."

"Don't darling me. I won't stand a tyrant."

"Tyrant? Oh, Lord!"

"He's just a little boy. You went for him."

"I think he feels better now."

"I don't know what you mean. You crushed him like an insect."

"No, darling. I gave him a quick glimpse of the world. He was building a false one."

"Who are you to know what the world is?"

Ethan walked past her and out the back door.

"Where are you going?"

"To cut the lawn."

"I thought you were tired."

"I am—I was." He looked over his shoulder and up at her standing inside the screened door. "A man is a lonely thing," he said, and he smiled at her a moment before he got out the lawnmower.

Mary heard the whirring blades tearing through the soft and supple grass.

The sound stopped by the doorstep. Ethan called, "Mary, Mary, my darling. I love you." And the whirling blades raged on through the overgrown grass.

CHAPTER XII

MARGIE Young-Hunt was an attractive woman, informed, clever; so clever that she knew when and how to mask her cleverness. Her marriages had failed, the men had failed; one by being weak, and the second weaker—he died. Dates did not come to her. She created them, mended her fences by frequent telephone calls, by letters, get-well cards, and arranged accidental meetings. She carried homemade soup to the sick and remembered birthdays. By these means she kept people aware of her existence.

More than any woman in town she kept her stomach flat, her skin clean and glowing, her teeth bright, and her chin-line taut. A goodly part of her income went to hair, nails, massage, creams, and unguents. Other women said, "She must be older than she looks."

When supporting muscles of her breasts no longer responded to creams, massage, and exercise, she placed them in shapely forms that rode high and jauntily. Her make-up took increasing time. Her hair had all the sheen, luster, wave the television products promise. On a date, dining, dancing, laughing, amusing, drawing her escort with a net of small magnets, who could know her cold sense of repetition? After a decent interval and an outlay of money, she usually went to bed with him if she discreetly could. Then back to her fence-mending. Sooner or later the shared bed must be the trap to catch her future security and ease. But the prospective game leaped clear of the quilted jaws. More and more of her dates were the married, the infirm, or the cautious. And Margie knew better than anyone that her time was running out. The tarot cards did not respond when she sought help for herself.

Margie had known many men, most of them guilty, wounded in their vanity, or despairing, so that she had developed a contempt for her quarry as a professional hunter of vermin does. It was easy to move such men through their fears and their vanities. They ached so to be fooled that she no longer felt triumph—only a kind of disgusted pity. These were her friends and associates. She protected them even from the discovery that they were her friends. She gave them the best of herself because they demanded nothing of her. She kept them secret because at the bottom she did not admire herself. Danny Taylor was one of these, and Alfio Marullo another, and Chief Stonewall Jackson Smith a third, and there were others. They trusted her and she them, and their secret existence was the one warm honesty to which she could retire to restore herself. These friends talked freely and without fear to her, for to them she was a kind of Andersen's Well—receptive, unjudging, and silent. As most people have secret vices, Margie Young-Hunt concealed a secret virtue. And because of this quiet thing it is probable that she knew more about New Baytown, and even Wessex County, than anyone, and her knowledge was unwarped because she would not—could not—use it for her own profit. But in other fields, everything that came to her hand was usable.

Her project Ethan Allen Hawley began casually and out of idleness. In a way he was correct in thinking it was mischievous, a testing of her power. Many of the sad men who came to her for comfort and reassurance were hogtied with impotence, bound and helpless in sexual traumas that infected all other areas of their lives. And she found it easy by small flatteries and reassurances to set them free to fight again against their whip-armed wives. She was genuinely fond of Mary Hawley, and through her she gradually became aware of Ethan, bound in another kind of trauma, a social-economic bind that had robbed him of strength and certainty. Having no work, no love, no children, she wondered whether she could release and direct this crippled man toward some new end. It was a game, a kind of puzzle, a test, a product not of kindness but simply of curiosity and idleness. This was a superior man. To direct him would prove her superiority, and this she needed increasingly.

Probably she was the only one who knew the depth of the change in Ethan and it frightened her because she thought it was her doing. The mouse was growing a lion's mane. She saw the muscles under his clothes, felt ruthlessness growing behind his eyes. So must the gentle Einstein have felt when his dreamed concept of the nature of matter flashed over Hiroshima.

Margie liked Mary Hawley very much and she had little sympathy and no pity for her. Misfortune is a fact of nature acceptable to women, especially when it falls on other women.

In her tiny immaculate house set in a large, overgrown garden very near to Old Harbor, she leaned toward the make-up mirror to inspect her tools, and her eyes saw through cream, powder, eye-shadowing, and lashes sheathed in black, saw the hidden wrinkles, the inelasticity of skin. She felt the years creep up like the rising tide about a rock in a calm sea. There is an arsenal of maturity, of middle age, but these require training and technique she did not yet have. She must learn them before her structure of youth and excitement crumbled and left her naked, rotten, ridiculous. Her success had been that she never let down, even alone. Now, as an experiment, she allowed her mouth to droop as it wanted to, her eyelids to fall half-staff. She lowered her high-held chin and a plaited rope came into being. Before her in the mirror she saw twenty years clamber over her and she shuddered as the icy whispering told her what lay waiting. She had delayed too long. A woman must have a showcase in which to grow old, lights, props, black velvet, children, graying and fattening, snickering and pilfering, love, protection, and small change, a serene and undemanding husband or his even more serene and less demanding will and trust fund. A woman growing old alone is useless cast-off trash, a wrinkled obscenity with no hobbled retainers to cluck and mutter over her aches and to rub her pains.

A hot spot of fear formed in her stomach. She had been lucky in her first husband. He was weak and she soon found the valve of his weakness. He was hopelessly in love with her, so much so that when she needed a divorce he did not ask for a remarriage clause in his alimony settlement.

Her second husband thought she had a private fortune and so she had. He didn't leave her much when he died, but, with the alimony from her first husband, she could live decently, dress well, and cast about at leisure. Suppose her first husband should die! There was the fear spot. There was the night- or daymare—the monthly-check-mare.

In January she had seen him at that great wide cross of Madison Avenue and Fifty-seventh Street. He looked old and gaunt. She was haunted with his mortality. If the bastard died, the money would stop. She thought she might be the only person in the world who wholeheartedly prayed for his health.

His lean, silent face and dead eyes came on her memory screen now and touched off the hot spot in her stomach. If the son of a bitch should die . . . !

Margie, leaning toward the mirror, paused and hurled her will like a javelin. Her chin rose; the ropes dropped back; her eyes shone; the skin snuggled close to her skull; her shoulders squared. She stood up and waltzed in a deft circle on the deep-piled red carpet. Her feet were bare, with gleaming pinkened toenails. She must rush, she must hurry, before it was too late.

She flung open her closet and laid hands on the sweet, provocative dress she had been saving for the Fourth of July weekend, the shoes with pencil heels, the stockings more sheer than no stockings at all. There was no languor in her now. She dressed as quickly and efficiently as a butcher whets his knife and she checked against a full-length mirror the way that same butcher tests his blade against his thumb. Speed but no rush, speed for the man who will not wait, and then—the casual slowness of the in-formed, the smart, the chic, the confident, the lady with pretty legs and immaculate white gloves. No man she passed failed to look after her. Miller Brothers' truckdriver whistled as he lumbered by with lumber and two high-school boys leveled slitted Valentino eyes at her and painfully swallowed the saliva that flooded their half-open mouths.

"How about that?" said one.

And, "Yeah!" the other replied.

"How'd you like—"

"Yeah!"

A lady does not wander—not in New Baytown. She must be going someplace, have some business, however small and meaningless. As she walked in dotted steps along the High Street, she bowed and spoke to passers-by and reviewed them automatically.

Mr. Hall—he was living on credit, had been for some time.

Stoney—a tough, male man, but what woman could live on a cop's salary or pension? Besides, he was her friend.

Harold Beck with real estate and plenty of it, but Harold was queer as a duck. He himself was probably the only person in the world who didn't know it.

MacDowell— "So nice to see you, sir. How's Milly?" Impossible—Scottish, tight, tied to his wife—an invalid, the kind who lives forever. He was a secret. No one knew what he was worth.

Dew-eyed Donald Randolph—wonderful on the next bar stool, a barroom gentleman whose manners penetrated deep into his drunkenness, but useless unless you wanted to keep house on a bar stool.

Harold Luce—it was said that he was related to the publisher of *Time* magazine but who said it, himself? A flinty man who had a reputation for wisdom based on his lack of the power of speech.

Ed Wantoner—a liar, a cheat, and a thief. Supposed to be loaded and his wife was dying, but Ed trusted no one. He didn't even trust his dog not to run away. Kept it tied up and howling.

Paul Strait—a power in the Republican party. His wife was named Butterfly—not a nickname. Butterfly Strait, christened Butterfly, and that's the truth. Paul did well if New York State had a Republican governor. He owned the city dump, where it cost a quarter to dump a load of garbage. It was told that when the rats got so bad and big as to be dangerous, Paul sold tickets for the privilege of shooting them, rented flashlights and rifles—stocked .22-caliber cartridges to shoot them with. He looked so like a president that many people called him Ike. But Danny Taylor while quietly drunk had referred to him as the Noblest Paul of them Aul, and that stuck. Noble Paul became his name when he wasn't present.

Marullo—he's sicker than he was. He's gray sick. Marullo's eyes were those of a man shot in the stomach with a .45. He had walked past the doorway of his own store without going in. Margie entered the store, bouncing her neat buttocks.

Ethan was talking to a stranger, a youngish dark-haired man, Ivy League pants and hat with a narrow brim. Forty-ish, hard, tough, and devoted to whatever he was doing. He leaned over the counter and seemed about to inspect Ethan's tonsils.

Margie said, "Hi! You're busy. I'll come back later."

There are endless idle but legitimate things a strolling woman can do in a bank. Margie crossed the alley mouth and went into the marble and brushed-steel temple.

Joey Morphy lighted up the whole barred square of his teller's window when he saw her. What a smile, what a character, what a good playmate, and what a lousy prospect as a husband. Margie properly appraised him as a born bachelor who would die fighting to remain one. No double grave for Joey.

She said, "Please, sir, do you have any fresh unsalted money?"

"Excuse me, ma'am, I'll see. I'm almost positive I saw some somewhere. How much of it would you like to have?"

"About six ounces, m'sieur." She took a folding book from her white kid bag and wrote a check for twenty dollars.

Joey laughed. He liked Margie. Once in a while, not too

often, he took her out to dinner and laid her. But he also liked her company and her sense of play.

Joey said, "Mrs. Young-Hunt, that reminds me of a friend I had who was in Mexico with Pancho Villa. Remember him?"

"Never knew him."

"No jazz. It's a story the guy told me. He said when Pancho was in the north, he worked the mint printing twenty-peso notes. Made so many his men stopped counting them. They weren't so hot at counting anyway. Got to weighing them on a balance scale."

Margie said, "Joey, you can't resist autobiography."

"Hell, no, Mrs. Young-Hunt. I'd have been about five years old. It's a story. Seems a fine stacked dame, Injun but stacked, came in and said, 'My general, you have executed my husband and left me a poor widow with five children, and is that any way to run a popular revolution?'"

"Pancho went over her assets the way I'm doing now."

"You got no mortgage, Joey."

"I know. It's a story. Pancho said to an aide-de-camp, 'Weigh out five kilos of money for her.'

"Well, that's quite a bundle. They tied it together with a piece of wire and the woman went out, dangling the bale of kale. Then a lieutenant stepped out and saluted and he said, 'My general (they say it *mi gral*—like *hral*), we did not shoot her husband. He was drunk. We put him in the jail around the corner.'

"Pancho had never taken his eyes off the dame walking away with the bundle. He said, 'Go out and shoot him. We cannot disappoint that poor widow.'"

"Joey, you're impossible."

"It's a true story. I believe it." He turned her check around. "Do you want this in twenties, fifties, or hundreds?"

"Give it to me in two-bitses."

They enjoyed each other.

Mr. Baker looked out of his frosted-glass office.

Now there was a bet. Baker had made a grammatically correct but obscure pass at her once. Mr. Baker was Mr. Money. Sure he had a wife, but Margie knew the Bakers of this world. They could always raise a moral reason for doing what they wanted to do anyway. She was glad she had turned him down. It left him still in the book.

She gathered the four five-dollar bills Joey had given her and moved toward the gray banker, but at that moment the man she had seen talking to Ethan came in quietly, passed in front of her, presented a card, and was taken into Mr. Baker's office and the door closed.

"Well, kiss my foot," she said to Joey.

"Prettiest foot in Wessex County," Joey said. "Want to go out tonight? Dance, eat, all that?"

"Can't," she said. "Who is that?"

"Never saw him before. Looks like a bank-examiner type. It's times like this I'm glad I'm honest and even gladder I can add and subtract."

"You know, Joey, you're going to make some faithful woman a hell of a fine fugitive."

"That is my prayerful hope, ma'am."

"See you."

She went out, crossed the alley, and entered Marullo's grocery again.

"Hi, Eth."

"Hello, Margie."

"Who was the handsome stranger?"

"Don't you carry your crystal ball?"

"Secret agent?"

"Worse than that. Margie, is everybody afraid of cops? Even if I haven't done anything I'm scared of cops."

"Was that curly-haired piece of the true cross a dick?"

"Not exactly. Said he was a federal man."

"What you been up to, Ethan?"

"Up to? Me? Why 'up to'?"

"What did he want?"

"I only know what he asked but I don't know what he wanted."

"What did he ask?"

"How long do I know my boss? Who else knows him? When did he come to New Baytown?"

"What did you tell him?"

"When I joined up to fight the foe, I didn't know him. When I came back he was here. When I went broke, he took over the store and gave me a job."

"What do you suppose it's about?"

"God knows."

Margie had been trying to look past his eyes. She thought, He's pretending to be a simpleton. I wonder what the guy really wanted!

He said it so quietly it frightened her. "You don't believe me. You know, Margie, no one ever believes the truth."

"The whole truth? When you carve a chicken, Eth, it's all chicken, but some is dark meat and some white."

"I guess so. Frankly, I'm worried, Margie. I need this job. If anything happened to Alfio I'd be pounding the street."

"Aren't you forgetting you're going to be rich?"

"Kind of hard to remember when I'm not."

"Ethan, I wonder if you remember back. It was in the spring right near Easter. I came in and you called me Daughter of Jerusalem."

"That was Good Friday."

"You do remember. Well, I found it. It's Matthew, and it's pretty wonderful and—scary."

"Yes."

"What got into you?"

"My Great-Aunt Deborah. She got me crucified once a year. It still goes on."

"You're kidding. You weren't kidding then."

"No, I wasn't. And I'm not now."

She said playfully, "You know, the fortune I read you is coming true."

"I know it is."

"Don't you think you owe me something?"

"Sure."

"When are you going to pay?"

"Would you care to step into the back room?"

"I don't think you could do it."

"You don't?"

"No, Ethan, and you don't either. You've never had a quick jump in the hay in your life."

"I could learn, maybe."

"You couldn't fornicate if you wanted to."

"I could try."

"It would take love or hatred to arouse you, and either one would require a slow and stately procedure."

"Maybe you're right. How did you know?"

"I never know how I know."

He slid the door of the cold cabinet open, took out a Coke, which instantly grew a jacket of frost, opened it, and handed the bottle to her while he opened a second.

"What is it you want of me?"

"I've never known a man like that. Perhaps I want to see what it's like to be loved or hated that much."

"You're a witch! Why don't you whistle up a wind?"

"I can't whistle. I can raise a puny little storm in most men with my eyebrows. How do I go about lighting your fire?"

"Maybe you have."

He studied her closely and did not try to conceal his inspection. "Built like a brick outhouse," he said, "soft and smooth and strong and good."

"How do you know? You've never felt me."

"If I ever do, you'd better run like hell."

"My love."

"Come off it. There's something wrong here. I'm conceited enough to know the caliber of my attractiveness. What do you want? You're a fine broth of a dame but you're also smart. What do you want?"

"I told your fortune and it's coming true."

"And you want to suck along?"

"Yes."

"Now I can believe you." He raised his eyes. "Mary of my heart," he said, "look on your husband, your lover, your dear friend. Guard me against evil from within me and from harm without. I pray for your help, my Mary, for a man has a strange and wind-troubled need and the ache of the ages is on him to spread his seeds everywhere. *Ora pro me.*"

"You're a fake, Ethan."

"I know it. But can't I be a humble fake?"

"I'm afraid of you now. I wasn't before."

"I can't think why."

She had that tarot look and he saw it.

"Marullo."

"What about him?"

"I'm asking."

"Be with you in a moment. Half a dozen eggs, square of butter, right. How are you for coffee?"

"Yes, a can of coffee. I like to have it on the shelf. How is that Whumpdum corned-beef hash?"

"I haven't tried it. They say it's very good. Be with you in a moment, Mr. Baker. Didn't Mrs. Baker get some of that Whumpdum corned-beef hash?"

"I don't know, Ethan. I eat what's put before me. Mrs. Young-Hunt, you get prettier every day."

"Kind sir."

"It's true. And—you dress so well."

"I was thinking the same about you. Now you're not pretty but you have a wonderful tailor."

"I guess I have. He charges enough."

"Remember the old boy who said, 'Manners maketh man'? Well that's changed now. Tailors make men in any image they want."

"The trouble with a well-made suit, it lasts too long. This is ten years old."

"I can't believe it, Mr. Baker. How is Mrs. Baker?"

"Well enough to complain. Why don't you call on her, Mrs. Young-Hunt? She gets lonely. There aren't many people in this generation who can carry on a literate conversation. It was Wickham who said it. It's the motto of Winchester College."

She turned to Ethan. "You show me another American banker who knows that."

Mr. Baker grew ruddy. "My wife subscribed to Great Books. She's a great reader. Please call on her."

"I'd love to. Put my things in a bag, Mr. Hawley. I'll pick them up on my way home."

"Right, ma'am."

"That's quite a remarkable young woman," Mr. Baker said.

"She and Mary hit it off."

"Ethan, did that government man come here?"

"Yes."

"What does he want?"

"I don't know. He asked some questions about Mr. Marullo. I didn't know the answers."

Mr. Baker released the image of Margie as slowly as an anemone opens and casts out the shell of a sucked-clean crab. "Ethan, have you seen Danny Taylor?"

"No, I haven't."

"Do you know where he is?"

"No, I don't."

"I have to get in touch with him. Can't you think where he might be?"

"I haven't seen him for—well, since May. He was going to try the cure again."

"Do you know where?"

"He didn't say. But he wanted to try."

"Was it a public institution?"

"I don't think so, sir. He borrowed some money from me."

"What!"

"I loaned him a little money."

"How much?"

"*I beg your pardon?*"

"Sorry, Ethan. You are old friends. Sorry. Did he have other money?"

"I think so."

"You don't know how much?"

"No sir. I just had a feeling he had more."

"If you know where he is, please tell me."

"I would if I knew, Mr. Baker. Maybe you could make a list of the places and phone."

"Did he borrow cash?"

"Yes."

"Then that's no good. He'd change his name."

"Why?"

"They always do from good families. Ethan, did you get the money from Mary?"

"Yes."

"She didn't mind?"

"She didn't know."

"Now you're being smart."

"I learned from you, sir."

"Well, don't forget it."

"Maybe I'm learning little by little. Mostly I'm learning how much I don't know."

"Well, that's healthy. Is Mary well?"

"Oh, she's strong and tough. Wish I could take her on a little vacation. We haven't been out of town in years."

"That will come, Ethan. I think I'll go to Maine over the Fourth of July. I can't take the noise any more."

"I guess you bankers are the lucky ones. Weren't you in Albany lately?"

"What gave you that idea?"

"I don't know—heard it someplace. Maybe Mrs. Baker told Mary."

"She couldn't. She didn't know it. Try to think where you heard it."

"Maybe I only imagined it."

"This troubles me, Ethan. Think hard where you heard it."

"I can't, sir. What does it matter if it isn't true?"

"I'll tell you in confidence why I'm worried. It's because it is true. The Governor called me in. It's a serious matter. I wonder where the leak could be."

"Anyone see you there?"

"Not that I know of. I flew in and out. This is serious. I'm going to tell you something. If it gets out I'll know where it came from."

"Then I don't want to hear it."

"You haven't any choice now that you know about Albany. The state is looking into county and town affairs."

"Why?"

"I guess because the smell has got as far as Albany."

"No politics?"

"I guess anything the Governor does can be called politics."

"Mr. Baker, why can't it be in the open?"

"I'll tell you why. Upstate the word got out and by the time the examiners got to work most of the records had disappeared."

"I see. I wish you hadn't told me. I'm not a talker but I wish I didn't know."

"For that matter, I wish the same thing, Ethan."

"The election is July seventh. Will it break before that?"

"I don't know. That's up to the state."

"Do you suppose Marullo is mixed in it? I can't afford to lose my job."

"I don't think so. That was a federal man. Department of Justice. Didn't you ask for his credentials?"

"Didn't think of it. He flashed them but I didn't look."

"Well, you should. You always should."

"I wouldn't think you'd want to go away."

"Oh, that doesn't matter. Nothing happens over Fourth of July weekend. Why, the Japs attacked Pearl Harbor on a weekend. They knew everyone would be away."

"I wish I could take Mary someplace."

"Maybe you can later. I want you to whip your brains and try to find where Taylor is."

"Why? Is it so important?"

"It is. I can't tell you why right now."

"I sure wish I could find him, then."

"Well, if you could turn him up maybe you wouldn't need this job."

"If it's that way, I'll sure try, sir."

"That's the boy, Ethan. I'm sure you will. And if you do locate him, you call me—any time, day or night."

CHAPTER XIII

I WONDER about people who say they haven't time to think. For myself, I can double think. I find that weighing vegetables, passing the time of day with customers, fighting or loving Mary, coping with the children—none of these prevents a second and continuing layer of thinking, wondering, conjecturing. Surely this must be true of everyone. Maybe not having time to think is not having the wish to think.

In the strange, uncharted country I had entered, perhaps I had no choice. Questions boiled up, demanding to be noticed. And it was a world so new to me that I puzzled over matters old residents probably solved and put away when they were children.

I had thought I could put a process in motion and control it at every turn—even stop it when I wanted to. And now the frightening conviction grew in me that such a process may become a thing in itself, a person almost, having its own ends and means and quite independent of its creator. And another troublesome thought came in. Did I really start it, or did I simply not resist it? I may have been the mover, but was I not also the moved? Once on the long street, there seemed to be no crossroads, no forked paths, no choice.

The choice was in the first evaluation. What are morals? Are they simply words? Was it honorable to assess my father's weakness, which was a generous mind and the ill-founded dream that other men were equally generous? No, it was simply good business to dig the pit for him. He fell

186 / The Winter of Our Discontent

into it himself. No one pushed him. Was it immoral to strip him when he was down? Apparently not.

Now a slow, deliberate encirclement was moving on New Baytown, and it was set in motion by honorable men. If it succeeded, they would be thought not crooked but clever. And if a factor they had overlooked moved in, would that be immoral or dishonorable? I think that would depend on whether or not it was successful. To most of the world success is never bad. I remember how, when Hitler moved unchecked and triumphant, many honorable men sought and found virtues in him. And Mussolini made the trains run on time, and Vichy collaborated for the good of France, and whatever else Stalin was, he was strong. Strength and success—they are above morality, above criticism. It seems, then, that it is not what you do, but how you do it and what you call it. Is there a check in men, deep in them, that stops or punishes? There doesn't seem to be. The only punishment is for failure. In effect no crime is committed unless a criminal is caught. In the move designed for New Baytown some men had to get hurt, some even destroyed, but this in no way deterred the movement.

I could not call this a struggle with my conscience. Once I perceived the pattern and accepted it, the path was clearly marked and the dangers apparent. What amazed me most was that it seemed to plan itself; one thing grew out of another and everything fitted together. I watched it grow and only guided it with the lightest touch.

What I had done and planned to do was undertaken with full knowledge that it was foreign to me, but necessary as a stirrup is to mount a tall horse. But once I had mounted, the stirrup would not be needed. Maybe I could not stop this process, but I need never start another. I did not need or want to be a citizen of this gray and dangerous country. I had nothing to do with the coming tragedy of July 7. It was not my process, but I could anticipate and I could use it.

One of our oldest and most often disproved myths is that a man's thoughts show in his face, that the eyes are the windows of the soul. It isn't so. Only sickness shows, or defeat or despair, which are different kinds of sickness. Some rare people can feel beneath, can sense a change or hear a secret signal. I think my Mary felt a change, but she misinterpreted it, and I think Margie Young-Hunt knew— but she was a witch and that is a worrisome thing. It seemed to me that she was intelligent as well as magic—and that's even more worrisome.

I felt sure that Mr. Baker would go on a holiday, probably on Friday afternoon of the Fourth of July weekend. The storm would have to break Friday or Saturday to give it time to take effect before election and it was logical to suppose that Mr. Baker would want to be away when the shock came. Of course that didn't matter much to me. It was more an exercise in anticipation, but it did make several moves necessary on Thursday, just in case he left that night. My Saturday matter was so finely practical that I could move through it in my sleep. If I had any fear of that, it was more like a small stage fright.

On Monday, June 27, Marullo came in soon after I had opened up. He walked about, looking strangely at the shelves, the cash register, the cold counter, and he walked back to the storeroom and looked about. You would have thought from his expression that he was seeing it for the first time.

I said, "Going to take a trip over the Fourth?"

"Why do you say that?"

"Well, everybody does who can afford it."

"Oh! Where would I go?"

"Where's anybody go? Catskills, even out to Montauk and fish. School tuna running."

The very thought of fighting a thirty-pound plunging fish drove arthritic pains up his arms so that he flexed them and winced.

I very nearly asked him when he planned to go to Italy, but that seemed too much. Instead, I moved over to him and took him gently by his right elbow. "Alfio," I said, "I think you're nuts. Why don't you go into New York to the best specialist? There must be something to stop that pain."

"I don't believe it."

"What have you got to lose? Go ahead. Try it."

"What do you care?"

"I don't. But I've worked here a long time for a stupid son of a bitch dago. If a yellow dog hurt that much, I'd get to feeling it myself. You come in here and move your arms and it's half an hour before I can straighten up."

"You like me?"

"Hell, no. I'm buttering you up for a raise."

He looked at me with hound's eyes, rimmed with red, and dark brown iris and pupil all one piece. He seemed about to say something but changed his mind about it. "You're a good kid," he said.

"Don't depend on it."

"A good kid!" he said explosively and as though shocked by his show of emotion he went out of the store and walked away.

I was weighing out two pounds of string beans for Mrs. Davidson when Marullo came charging back. He stood in the doorway and shouted at me.

"You take my Pontiac."

"What?"

"Go someplace Sunday and Monday."

"I can't afford it."

"You take the kids. I told the garage for you to get my Pontiac. Tank full of gas."

"Wait a minute."

"You go to hell. Take the kids." He tossed something like a spitball at me and it fell among the string beans. Mrs. Davidson watched him plunge away again down the street. I picked the green wad from the string beans—three twenty-dollar bills folded in a tight square.

"What's the matter with him?"

"He's an excitable Italian."

"He must be, throwing money!"

He didn't show up the rest of the week, so that was all right. He'd never gone away before without telling me. It was like watching a parade go by, just standing and watching it go by and knowing what the next float would be but watching for it just the same.

I hadn't expected the Pontiac. He never loaned his car to anybody. It was a strange time. Some outside force or design seemed to have taken control of events so that they were crowded close the way cattle are in a loading chute. I know the opposite can be true. Sometimes the force or design deflects and destroys, no matter how careful and deep the planning. I guess that's why we believe in luck and unluck.

On Thursday, the thirtieth of June, I awakened as usual in the black pearl light of the dawn, and that was early now in the lap of midsummer. Chair and bureau were dark blobs and pictures only lighter suggestions. The white window curtains seemed to sigh in and out as though they breathed, because it's a rare dawn that does not wave a small wind over the land.

Coming out of sleep, I had the advantage of two worlds, the layered firmament of dream and the temporal fixtures of the mind awake. I stretched luxuriously—a good and tingling sensation. It's as though the skin has shrunk in the night and one must push it out to daytime size by bulging the muscles, and there's an itching pleasure in it.

First I referred to my remembered dreams as I would glance through a newspaper to see if there was anything of interest or import. Then I explored the coming day for events that had not happened. Next I followed a practice learned from the best officer I ever had. He was Charley Edwards, a major of middling age, perhaps a little too far along to be a combat officer but he was a good one. He had a large family, a pretty wife and four children in steps, and his heart could ache with love and longing for them if he allowed it to. He told me about it. In his deadly business he could not afford to have his attention warped and split by love, and so he had arrived at a method. In the morning, that is if he were not jerked from sleep by an alert, he opened his mind and heart to his family. He went over each one in turn, how they looked, what they were like; he caressed them and reassured them of his love. It was as though he picked precious things one by one from a cabinet, looked at each, felt it, kissed it, and put it back; and last he gave them a small good-by and shut the door of the cabinet. The whole thing took half an hour if he could get it and then he didn't have to think of them again all day. He could devote his full capacity, untwisted by conflicting thought and feeling, to the job he had to do—the killing of men. He was the best officer I ever knew. I asked his permission to use his method and he gave it to me. When he was killed, all I could think was that his had been a good and effective life. He had taken his pleasure, savored his love, and paid his debts, and how many people even approached that?

I didn't always use Major Charley's method, but on a day like this Thursday, when I knew my attention should be as uninterrupted as possible, I awakened when the day opened its door a crack and I visited my family as Major Charley had.

I visited them in chronological order, bowed to Aunt Deborah. She was named for Deborah the Judge of Israel and I have read that a judge was a military leader. Perhaps she responded to her name. My great-aunt could have led armies. She did marshal the cohorts of thought. My joy in learning for no visible profit came from her. Stern though she was, she was charged with curiosity and had little use for anyone who was not. I gave her my obeisance. I offered a spectral toast to old Cap'n and ducked my head to my father. I even made my duty to the untenanted hole in the past I knew as my mother. I never knew her. She died before I could, and left only a hole in the past where she should be.

One thing troubled me. Aunt Deborah and old Cap'n and my father would not come clear. Their outlines were vague and wavery where they should have been sharp as photographs. Well, perhaps the mind fades in its memories as old tintypes do—the background reaching out to engulf the subjects. I couldn't hold them forever.

Mary should have been next but I laid her aside for later.

I raised Allen. I could not find his early face, the face of joy and excitement that made me sure of the perfectability of man. He appeared what he had become—sullen, conceited, resentful, remote and secret in the pain and perplexity of his pubescence, a dreadful, harrowing time when he must bite everyone near, even himself, like a dog in a trap. Even in my mind's picture he could not come out of his miserable discontent, and I put him aside, only saying to him, I know. I remember how bad it is and I can't help. No one can. I can only tell you it will be over. But you can't believe that. Go in peace—go with my love even though during this time we can't stand each other.

Ellen brought a surge of pleasure. She will be pretty, prettier even than her mother, because when her little face jells into its final shape she will have the strange authority of Aunt Deborah. Her moods, her cruelties, her nervousness are the ingredients of a being quite beautiful and dear. I know, because I saw her standing in her sleep holding the pink talisman to her little breast and looking a woman fulfilled. And as the talisman was important and still is to me, so it is to Ellen. Maybe it is Ellen who will carry and pass on whatever is immortal in me. And in my greeting I put my arms around her and she, true to form, tickled my ear and giggled. My Ellen. My daughter.

I turned my head to Mary, sleeping and smiling on my right. That is her place so that, when it is good and right and ready, she can shelter her head on my right arm, leaving my left hand free for caressing.

A few days before, I snicked my forefinger with the curved banana knife at the store, and a callusy scab toughened the ball of my fingertip. And so I stroked the lovely line from ear to shoulder with my second finger but gently enough not to startle and firmly enough not to tickle. She sighed as she always does, a deep, gathered breath and a low release of luxury. Some people resent awakening, but not Mary. She comes to a day with expectancy that it will be good. And, knowing this, I try to offer some small gift to justify her conviction. And I try to hold back gifts for occasions, such as the one I now produced from my mind's purse.

Her eyes opened, hazed with sleep. "Already?" she asked, and she glanced at the window to see how near the day had come. Over the bureau the picture hangs—trees and a lake and a small cow standing in the water of the lake. I made out the cow's tail from my bed, and knew the day had come.

"I bring you tidings of great joy, my flying squirrel."

"Crazy."

"Have I ever lied to you?"

"Maybe."

"Are you awake enough to hear the tidings of great joy?"

"No."

"Then I will withhold them."

She turned on her left shoulder and made a deep crease in her soft flesh. "You joke so much. If it's like you're going to cement over the lawn—"

"I am not."

"Or you're starting a cricket farm—"

"No. But you do remember old discarded plans."

"Is it a joke?"

"Well, it's a thing so strange and magic that you are going to have to buttress your belief."

Her eyes were clear and wakeful now and I could see the little trembles around her lips preparing for laughter. "Tell me."

"Do you know a man of Eyetalian extraction named Marullo?"

"Crazy—you're being silly."

"You will find it so. Said Marullo has gone from here for a time."

"Where?"

"He didn't say."

"When will he be back?"

"Stop confusing me. He didn't say that either. What he did say and, when I protested, what he ordered was that we should take his car and go on a happy trip over the holiday."

"You're joking me."

"Would I tell a lie that would make you sad?"

"But why?"

"That I can't tell you. What I can swear to from Boy

Scout oath to papal oath is that the mink-lined Pontiac with a tank full of virgin gasoline awaits your highness's pleasure."

"But where shall we go?"

"That, my lovely insect-wife is what you are going to decide, and take all day today, tomorrow, and Saturday to plan it."

"But Monday's a holiday. That's two full days."

"That's correct."

"Can we afford it? It might mean a motel or something."

"Can or not, we will. I have a secret purse."

"Silly, I know your purse. I can't imagine him lending his car."

"Neither can I, but he did."

"Don't forget he brought candy Easter."

"Perhaps it is senility."

"I wonder what he wants."

"That's not worthy of my wife. Perhaps he wants us to love him."

"I'll have to do a thousand things."

"I know you will." I could see her mind plowing into the possibilities like a bulldozer. I knew I had lost her attention and probably couldn't get it back, and that was good.

At breakfast before my second cup of coffee she had picked up and discarded half the pleasure areas of eastern America. Poor darling hadn't had much fun these last few years.

I said, "Chloe, I know I'm going to have trouble getting your attention. A very important investment is offered. I want some more of your money. The first is doing well."

"Does Mr. Baker know about it?"

"It's his idea."

"Then take it. You sign a check."

"Don't you want to know how much?"

"I guess so."

"Don't you want to know what the investment is? The figures, the flotage, the graphs, the probable return, the fiscal dinkum, and all that?"

"I wouldn't understand it."

"Oh, yes you would."

"Well, I wouldn't want to understand it."

"No wonder they call you the Vixen of Wall Street. That ice-cold, diamond-sharp business mind—it's frightening."

"We're going a trip," she said. "We're going a trip for two days."

And how the hell could a man not love her, not adore her? "Who is Mary—what is she?" I sang and collected the empty milk bottles and went to work.

I felt the need to catch up with Joey, just to get the feel of him, but I must have been a moment late or he a moment early. He was entering the coffee shop when I turned into the High Street. I followed him in and took the stool beside him. "You got me into this habit, Joey."

"Hi, Mr. Hawley. It's pretty good coffee."

I greeted my old school girl friend. "Morning, Annie."

"You going to be a regular, Eth?"

"Looks like. One cuppa and black."

"Black it is."

"Black as the eye of despair."

"What?"

"Black."

"You see any white in that, Eth, I'll give you another."

"How are things, Morph?"

"Just the same, only worse."

"Want to trade jobs?"

"I would, just before a long weekend."

"You're not the only one with problems. People stock up on food too."

"I guess they do. I hadn't thought of that."

"Picnic stuff, pickles, sausages, and, God help us, marshmallows. This a big one for you?"

"With the Fourth on Monday and nice weather, you kidding? And what makes it worse, God Almighty feels the need of rest and recreation in the mountains."

"Mr. Baker?"

"Not James G. Blaine."

"I want to see him. I need to see him."

"Well, try to catch him if you can. He's jumping like a quarter in a tambourine."

"I can bring sandwiches to your battle station, Joey."

"I might just ask you to."

"I pay this time," I said.

"Okay."

We crossed the street together and went into the alley. "You sound lowy, Joey."

"I am. I get pretty tired of other people's money. I got a hot date for the weekend and I'll probably be too pooped to warm up to it." He nudged a gum wrapper into the lock, went in, saying, "See you," and closed the door. I pushed the back door open. "Joey! You want a sandwich today?"

"No thanks," he called out of the dim, floor-oil-smelling interior. "Maybe Friday, Saturday sure."

"Don't you close at noon?"

"I told you. The bank closes but Morphy don't."

"Just call on me."

"Thanks—thanks, Mr. Hawley."

I had nothing to say to my forces on the shelves that morning except "Good morning gentlemen—at ease!" At a few moments before nine, aproned and broomed, I was out front, sweeping the sidewalk.

Mr. Baker is so regular you can hear him tick and I'm sure there's a hairspring in his chest. Eight fifty-six, fifty-seven, there he came down Elm Street; eight fifty-eight, he crossed; eight fifty-nine—he was at the glass doors, where I, with broom at carry arms, intercepted him. "Mr. Baker, I want to talk to you."

"Morning, Ethan. Can you wait a minute? Come on in."

I followed him, and it was just as Joey said—like a religious ceremony. They practically stood at attention as the clock hand crossed nine. There came a click and buzzing from the great steel safe door. Then Joey dialed the mystic numbers and turned the wheel that drew the bolts. The holy of holies swung stately open and Mr. Baker took the salute of the assembled money. I stood outside the rail like a humble communicant waiting for the sacrament.

Mr. Baker turned. "Now, Ethan. What can I do for you?"

I said softly, "I want to talk to you privately, and I can't leave the store."

"Won't it wait?"

" 'Fraid not."

"You ought to have some help."

"I know it."

"If I get a moment I'll drop over. Any word about Taylor?"

"Not yet. But I've put out some lines."

"I'll try to get over."

"Thank you, sir." But I knew he would come.

And he did, in less than an hour, and stood about until the present customers were gone.

"Now—what is it, Ethan?"

"Mr. Baker, with a doctor or a lawyer or a priest there's a rule of secrecy. Is there such a thing with a banker?"

He smiled. "Have you ever heard a banker discuss a client's interests, Ethan?"

"No."

"Well, ask sometime and see how far you get. And besides that custom, I'm your friend, Ethan."

"I know. I guess I'm a little jumpy. It's been a long time since I've had a break."

"A break?"

"I'll lay them out face up, Mr. Baker. Marullo's in trouble."

He moved close to me. "What kind of trouble?"

"I don't know exactly, sir. I think it might be illegal entry."

"How do you know?"

"He told me—not in so many words. You know how he is."

I could almost see his mind leaping about, picking up pieces and fitting them together. "Go on," he said. "That's deportation."

"I'm afraid so. He's been good to me, Mr. Baker. I wouldn't do anything to hurt him."

"You owe yourself something, Ethan. What was his proposition?"

"It's not merely a proposition. I had to put it together out of a lot of excited gobbledegook. But I gathered that if I had a quick five thousand in cash, I could own the store."

"That sounds as if he's going to run for it—but you don't know that."

"I don't know anything really."

"So there's no chance of a collusion charge. He didn't tell you anything specific."

"No, sir."

"Then how did you arrive at that figure?"

"Easy, sir. That's all we've got."

"But you might get it for less?"

"Maybe."

His quick eye went over the store and valued it. "If you are right in your assumption you're in a good bargaining position."

"I'm not much good at that."

"You know I don't favor under-the-table deals. Maybe I could talk to him."

"He's out of town."

"When will he be back?"

"I don't know, sir. Remember, it's only my impression he might drop in, and if I had cash, he might deal. He likes me, you know."

"I know he does."

"I'd hate to think I was taking advantage."

"He can always get it from someone else. He could get ten thousand easy from—anybody."

"Then maybe I'm overhopeful."

"Now, don't think small. You have to look after number one."

"Number two. It's Mary's money."

"So it is. Well, what did you have in mind?"

"Well, I thought you could maybe draw some papers up and leave the date and the amount blank. Then I thought I'd draw the money Friday."

"Why Friday?"

"Well, again it's only a guess, but he did say something about how everybody's away over the holiday. I kind of figured he might show up then. Don't you have his account?"

"No, by God. He drew it out just recently. Buying stocks, he said. I didn't think anything of it because he's done that before and always brought back more than he took out." He looked full in the eyes of a high-colored Miss Rheingold on the cold counter, but he didn't respond to her laughing invitation. "You know you could take a terrible beating on this?"

"How do you mean?"

"For one thing, he could sell it to half a dozen different people and, for another, it might be neck-deep in mortgage. And no title search."

"I could maybe find out in the county clerk's office. I know how busy you are, Mr. Baker. I'm taking advantage of your friendship for my family. Besides, you're the only friend I have who knows about such things."

"I'll call Tom Watson about the title deed. Damn it, Ethan, it's a bad time. I want to take a little trip tomorrow night. If it's true and he's a crook, you could be taken. Taken to the cleaners."

"Maybe I better give it up, then. But good God, Mr. Baker, I'm tired of being a grocery clerk."

"I didn't say give it up. I said you're taking a chance."

"Mary would be so happy if I owned the store. But I guess you're right. I shouldn't gamble with her money. I suppose what I should do is call up the federal men."

"That would lose you any advantage you have."

"How?"

"If he is deported he can sell his holdings through an agent and this store will bring a lot more than you can pay. You don't *know* he's going to jump. How could you tell them he is if you don't know? You don't even know he's picked up."

"That's true."

"As a matter of fact, you don't know anything about him

—really know. All you've told me is vague suspicions, isn't that so?"

"Yes."

"And you'd better forget those."

"Wouldn't it look bad—paying in cash with no record?"

"You could write on the check—oh, something like 'For investment in grocery business with A. Marullo.' That would be a record of your intention."

"Suppose none of this works."

"Then redeposit the money."

"You think it's worth the risk?"

"Well—everything's a risk, Ethan. It's a risk to carry that much money around."

"I'll take care of that."

"I wish I didn't have to be out of town."

What I said about timing still held. In all that time nobody came into the store, but half a dozen came in now —three women, an old man, and two kids. Mr. Baker moved close and spoke softly. "I'll make it in hundred-dollar bills and note the numbers. Then if they catch him you can get it back." He nodded gravely to the three women, said, "Good morning, George," to the old man, and roughed his fingers through the kids' coarse hair. Mr. Baker is a very clever man.

CHAPTER XIV

J ULY first. It parts the year like the part in a head of hair. I had foreseen it as a boundary marker for me—yesterday one kind of me, tomorrow a different kind. I had made my moves that could not be recalled. Time and incidents had played along, had seemed to collaborate with me. I did not ever draw virtue down to hide what I was doing from myself. No one made me take the course I had chosen. Temporarily I traded a habit of conduct and attitude for comfort and dignity and a cushion of security. It would be too easy to agree that I did it for my family because I knew that in their comfort and security I would find my dignity. But my objective was limited and, once achieved, I could take back my habit of conduct. I knew I could. War did not make a killer of me, although for a time I killed men. Sending out patrols, knowing some of the men would die, aroused no joy in sacrifice in me as it did in some, and I could never joy in what I had done, nor excuse or condone it. The main thing was to know the limited objective for what it was, and, once it was achieved, to stop the process in its tracks. But that could only be if I knew what I was doing and did not fool myself—security and dignity, and then stop the process in its tracks. I knew from combat that casualties are the victims of a process, not of anger nor of hate or cruelty. And I believe that in the moment of acceptance, between winner and loser, between killer and killed, there is love.

But Danny's scribbled papers hurt like a sorrow, and Marullo's grateful eyes.

I had not lain awake as men are said to do on the eve of battle. Sleep came quickly, heavily, completely, and released me just as freely in the predawn, refreshed. I did not lie in the darkness as usual. My urge was to visit my life as it had been. I slipped quietly from bed, dressed in the bathroom, and went down the stairs, walking near to the wall. It did surprise me when I went to the cabinet, unlocked it, and recognized the rosy mound by touch. I put it in my pocket and closed and locked the cabinet. In my whole life I had never carried it away and I had not known I would do it this morning. Memory directed me through the dark kitchen and out the back door into the graying yard. The arching elms were fat with leaves, a true black cave. If I had then had Marullo's Pontiac I would have driven out of New Baytown to the awakening world of my first memory. My finger traced the endless sinuous design on the flesh-warm talisman in my pocket—talisman?

That Deborah who sent me as a child to Golgotha was a precise machine with words. She took no nonsense from them nor permitted me a laxity. What power she had, that old woman! If she wanted immortality, she had it in my brain. Seeing me trace the puzzle with my finger, she said, "Ethan, that outlandish thing could well become your talisman."

"What's a talisman?"

"If I tell you, your half-attention will only half learn. Look it up."

So many words are mine because Aunt Deborah first aroused my curiosity and then forced me to satisfy it by my own effort. Of course I replied, "Who cares?" But she knew I would creep to it alone and she spelled it so I could track it down. T-a-l-i-s-m-a-n. She cared deeply about words and she hated their misuse as she would hate the clumsy handling of any fine thing. Now, so many cycles later, I can see the page—can see myself misspelling "talisman." The Arabic was only a squiggly line with a bulb on the end of it. The Greek I could pronounce because of the blade of that old woman. "A stone or other object engraved with figures or characters to which are attributed the occult powers of the planetary influences and celestial configurations under which it was made, usually worn as an amulet to avert evil from **or** bring fortune to the bearer." I had then to look for "occult," "planetary," "celestial," and "amulet." It was always that way. One word set off others like a string of firecrackers.

When later I asked her, "Do you believe in talismans?" she replied, "What has my belief to do with it?"

I put it in her hands. "What does this figure or character mean?"

"It's your talisman, not mine. It means what you want it to mean. Put it back in the cabinet. It will wait for you."

Now, as I walked in the cavern of the elms, she was as alive as ever she had been and that's true immortality. Over and under itself the carving went, and around and over and under, a serpent with neither head nor tail nor beginning nor ending. And I had taken it away with me for the first time—to avert evil? To bring fortune? I don't believe in fortune-telling either, and immortality has always felt to me like a sickly promise for the disappointed.

The light-rimmed boundary of the east was July, for June had gone away in the night. July is brass where June is gold, and lead where June is silver. July leaves are heavy and fat and crowding. Birdsong of July is a flatulent refrain without passion, for the nests are empty now and dumpy fledglings teeter clumsily. No, July is not a month of promise or of fulfillment. Fruit is growing but unsweet and uncolored, corn is a limp green bundle with a young and yellow tassel. The squashes still wear umbilical crowns of dry blossom.

I walked to Porlock Street, Porlock the plump and satisfied. The gathering brass of dawn showed rosebushes heavy with middle-aged blooms, like women whose corseting no longer conceals a thickening stomach, no matter how pretty their legs may remain.

Walking slowly, I found myself not saying but feeling good-by—not farewell. Farewell has a sweet sound of reluctance. Good-by is short and final, a word with teeth sharp to bite through the string that ties past to the future.

I came to the Old Harbor. Good-by to what? I don't know. I couldn't remember. I think I wanted to go to the Place, but man commensal with the sea would know that the tide was at flood and the Place under dark water. Last night I saw the moon only four days grown like a thickened, curved surgeon's needle, but strong enough to pull the tide into the cave mouth of the Place.

No need to visit Danny's shack in hope. The light had come enough to see the grasses standing upright in the path where Danny's feet had stumbled them flat.

Old Harbor was flecked with summer craft, slim hulls with sails covered in grommeted coats of canvas, and here and there a morning man made ready, clearing boom and coiling jib- and mainsheets, unbagging his Genoa like a great white rumpled nest.

The new harbor was busier. Charter boats tied close for boarding passengers, the frantic summer fishermen who pay a price and glut the decks with fish and in the afternoon wonder vaguely what to do with them, sacks and baskets and mountains of porgies and blows and blackfish, sea robins, and even slender dogfish, all to be torn up greedily, to die, and to be thrown back for the waiting gulls. The gulls swarm and wait, knowing the summer fishermen will sicken of their plenty. Who wants to clean and scale a sack of fish? It's harder to give away fish than it is to catch them.

The bay was oil-smooth now and the brass light poured over it. The cans and nuns stood unswaying on the channel edge, each one with its mirror twin upside down below it in the water.

I turned at the flagpole and war memorial and found my name among the surviving heroes, the letters picked out in silver—Capt. E. A. Hawley—and below in gold the names of the eighteen New Baytown men who didn't make it home. I knew the names of most of them and once I knew the men—no different then from the rest, but different now in gold. For a brief moment I wished I could be with them in the lower files, Capt. E. A. Hawley in gold, the slobs and malingerers, the cowards and the heroes all lumped together in gold. Not only the brave get killed, but the brave have a better chance at it.

Fat Willie drove up and parked beside the monument and took the flag from the seat beside him.

"Hi, Eth," he said. He shackled the brass grommets and raised the flag slowly to the top of the staff, where it slumped limp as a hanged man. "She barely made it," Willie said, panting a little. "Look at her. Two more days for her, and then the new one goes up."

"The fifty-star?"

"You bet. We got a nylon, big devil, twice as big as this and don't weigh no more than half."

"How's tricks, Willie?"

"I can't complain—but I do. This glorious Fourth is always a mess. Coming on a Monday, there'll be just that much more accidents and fights and drunks—out-of-town drunks. Want a lift up to the store?"

"Thanks. I've got to stop at the post office and I thought I'd get a cup of coffee."

"Okay. I'll ride you. I'd even coffee you but Stoney's mean as a bull bitch."

"What's his problem?"

"God knows. Went away a couple of days and he come back mean and tough."

"Where'd he go?"

"He didn't say, but he come back mean. I'll wait while you get your mail."

"Don't bother, Willie. I've got to address some things."

"Suit yourself." He backed out and slid away up the High Street.

The post office was still dusky and the floor newly oiled, and a sign up: DANGER. SLICK FLOOR.

We'd had Number 7 drawer since the old post office was built. I dialed G ½ R and took out a pile of plans and promises addressed to "Box-Holder." And that's all there was—wastebasket fodder. I strolled up the High, intending to have a cup of coffee, but at the last moment I didn't want it, or didn't want to talk, or—I don't know why. I just didn't want to go to the Foremaster coffee shop. Good God, what a mess of draggle-tail impulses a man is—and a woman too, I guess.

I was sweeping the sidewalk when Mr. Baker ticked out of Elm Street and went in for the ceremony of the time lock. And I was halfheartedly arranging muskmelons in the doorway stands when the old-fashioned green armored car pulled up in front of the bank. Two guards armed like commandos got out of the back and carried gray sacks of money into the bank. In about ten minutes they came out and got into the riveted fortress and it drove away. I guess they had to stand by while Morph counted it and Mr. Baker checked and gave a receipt. It's an awful lot of trouble taking care of money. As Morph says, you could get a downright distaste for other people's money. And by the size and weight, the bank must have anticipated a large holiday withdrawal. If I was a run-of-the-mill bank robber, now would be the time to stick it up. But I wasn't a run-of-the-mill bank robber. I owed everything I knew to Pal Joey. He could have been a great one if he had wished. I did wonder why he didn't want to, just to try out his theory.

Business piled up that morning. It was worse than I had thought it might be. The sun turned hot and fierce and very little wind moved, the kind of weather that drives people on their vacations whether they want to go or not. I had a line of customers waiting to be served. One thing I knew, come hell or high water, I had to get some help. If Allen didn't work out, I'd fire him and get someone else.

When Mr. Baker came in about eleven, he was in a hurry. I had to stand off some customers and go into the storeroom with him.

He put a big envelope and a small one in my hands, and he was so rushed that he barked a kind of shorthand. "Tom Watson says the deed's okay. He doesn't know whether it's papered. He doesn't think so. Here are conveyances. Get signatures where I've checked. The money's marked and the numbers noted. Here's a check all made out. Just sign it. Sorry I have to rush, Ethan. I hate doing business like this."

"You really think I should go ahead?"

"Goddammit, Ethan, after all the trouble I've gone to—"

"Sorry, sir. Sorry. I know you're right." I put the check on a canned-milk carton and signed it with my indelible pencil.

Mr. Baker wasn't too rushed to inspect the check. "Offer

two thousand at first. And raise your offer two hundred at a time. You realize, of course, you've only got a five-hundred balance in the bank. God help you if you run short."

"If it's clear, can't I borrow on the store?"

"Sure you can if you want interest to eat you up."

"I don't know how to thank you."

"Don't go soft, Ethan. Don't let him poor-mouth you. He can be a spellbinder. All dagos can. Just remember number one."

"I am sure grateful."

"Got to go," he said. "Want to hit the highway before the noon traffic." And out he went and nearly knocked Mrs. Willow down in the doorway where she had been over every cantaloupe twice.

The day didn't get any less frantic. I guess the heat that splashed the streets made people edgy and downright quarrelsome. Instead of a holiday, you'd have thought they were stocking up for a catastrophe. I couldn't have got a sandwich over to the Morph if I'd wanted to.

I not only had to wait on people, I had to keep my eyes open. A lot of the customers were summer people, strangers in town, and they steal if you don't watch them. They can't seem to help it. And it's not always stuff they need either. The little jars of luxuries take the worst beating, foie gras and caviar and button mushrooms. That's why Marullo had me keep such stuff back of the counter, where the customers aren't supposed to go. He taught me it's not good business to catch a shoplifter. Makes everyone restless, maybe because—well, in his thoughts anyway—everyone is guilty. About the only way is to charge the loss off to somebody else. But if I saw someone drifting too close to certain shelves, I could forestall the impulse by saying, "Those cocktail onions are a bargain." I've seen the customer jump as though I'd read his mind. What I hate worst about it is the suspicion. It's unpleasant to be suspicious. Makes me angry, as though one person were injuring many.

The day wore on to a kind of sadness, and time slowed down. After five Chief Stoney came in, lean and grim and ulcerish. He bought a TV dinner—country steak, carrots, mashed potatoes, cooked and frozen in a kind of aluminum tray.

I said, "You look like you had a touch of sun, Chief."

"Well, I ain't. I feel fine." He looked miserable.

"Want two of those?"

"Just one. My wife's gone visiting. A cop don't get holidays."

"Too bad."

"Maybe it's just as well. With this mob hanging around, I don't get home much."

"I heard you were away."

"Who told you?"

"Willie."

"He better learn to keep his big mouth shut."

"He didn't mean harm."

"Hasn't got brains enough to mean harm. Maybe not brains enough to stay out of jail."

"Who has?" I said it on purpose and I got even more response than I had anticipated.

"Just what do you mean by that, Ethan?"

"I mean we've got so many laws you can't breathe without breaking something."

"That's the truth. Gets so you don't really know."

"I was going to ask you, Chief—cleaning up, I found an old revolver, all dirty and rusty. Marullo says it's not his, and it sure isn't mine. What do I do with it?"

"Turn it over to me, if you don't want to apply for a license."

"I'll bring it down from home tomorrow. I stuck it in a can of oil. What do you do with things like that, Stoney?"

"Oh, check to see if they're hot and then throw them in the ocean." He seemed to be feeling better, but it had been a long, hot day. I couldn't let him be.

"Remember a couple of years ago there was a case somewhere upstate? Police were selling confiscated guns."

Stoney smiled the sweet smile of an alligator and with the same gay innocence. "I had one hell of a week, Eth. One hell of a week. If you're going about needling me, why, don't do it, because I've had one hell of a week."

"Sorry, Chief. Anything a sober citizen can do to help, like getting drunk with you?"

"I wish to Christ I could. I'd rather get drunk than anything I can think of."

"Why don't you?"

"Do you know? No, how could you? If I only knew what it's for and where it's from."

"What you talking about?"

"Forget it, Eth. No—don't forget it. You're a friend of Mr. Baker. Has he got any deals on?"

"I'm not that good a friend, Chief."

"How about Marullo? Where is Marullo?"

"Went in to New York. He wants to get his arthritis checked over."

"God almighty. I don't know. I just don't know. If there was just a line, why, I'd know where to jump."

"You're not talking sense, Stoney."

"No, I'm not. I talked too much already."

"I'm not too bright but if you want to unload—"

"I don't. No, I don't. They're not going to pin a leak on me even if I knew who they were. Forget it, Eth. I'm just a worried man."

"You couldn't leak to me, Stoney. What was it—grand jury?"

"Then you do know?"

"A little."

"What's behind it?"

"Progress."

Stoney came close to me and his iron hand grasped my upper arm so tightly that it hurt. "Ethan," he said fiercely, "do you think I'm a good cop?"

"The best."

"I aim to be. I want to be. Eth—do you think it's right to make a man tell on his friends to save himself?"

"No, I don't."

"Neither do I. I can't admire such a government. What scares me, Eth, is—I won't be such a good cop any more because I won't admire what I'm doing."

"Did they catch you out, Chief?"

"It's like you said. So many laws you can't take a deep breath without you break one. But Jesus Christ! The guys were my friends. You won't leak, Ethan?"

"No I won't. You forgot your TV dinner, Chief."

"Yeah!" he said. "I'll go home and take off my shoes and watch how those television cops do it. You know, sometimes an empty house is a nice rest. See you, Eth."

I liked Stoney. I guess he is a good officer. I wonder where the line falls.

I was closing up shop, drawing in the fruit bins from the doorway, when Joey Morphy sauntered in.

"Quick!" I said, and I closed the double front doors and drew the dark green shades. "Speak in a whisper."

"What's got into you?"

"Someone might want to buy something."

"Yeah! I know what you mean. God! I hate long holidays. Brings out the worst in everybody. They start out mad and come home pooped and broke."

"Want a cold drink while I draw the coverlets over my darling?"

"I don't mind. Got some cold beer?"

"To take out only."

"I'll take it out. Just open the can."

I punched two triangular holes in the tin and he upended it, opened his throat, and drained it into him. "Ah!" he said and set the can on the counter.

"We're going on a trip."

"You poor devil. Where?"

"I don't know. We haven't fought over that yet."

"Something's going on. Do you know what it is?"

"Give me a clue."

"I can't. I just feel it. Hair on the back of my neck kind of itches. That's a sure sign. Everybody's a little out of synch."

"Maybe you just imagine it."

"Maybe. But Mr. Baker doesn't take holidays. He was in one hell of a hurry to get out of town."

I laughed. "Have you checked the books?"

"Know something? I did."

"You're kidding."

"Once I knew a postmaster, little town. Had a punk kid working there, name of Ralph—pale hair, glasses, little tiny chin, adenoids big as goiters. Ralph got tagged for stealing stamps—lots of stamps, like maybe eighteen hundred dollars' worth. Couldn't do a thing. He was a punk."

"You mean he didn't take them?"

"If he didn't it was just the same as if he did. I'm jumpy. I'm never going to get tagged if I can help it."

"Is that why you never married?"

"Come to think of it, by God, that's one of the reasons."

I folded my apron and put it in the drawer under the cash register. "Takes too much time and effort to be suspicious, Joey. I couldn't take the time."

"Have to in a bank. You only lose once. All it needs is a whisper."

"Don't tell me you're suspicious."

"It's an instinct. If anything's just a little bit out of norm, my alarm goes off."

"What a way to live! You don't really mean that."

"I guess I don't. I just thought if you'd heard something, you'd tell me—that is, if it was any of my business."

"I think I'd tell anybody anything I know. Maybe that's why nobody ever tells me anything. Going home?"

"No, I think I'll go eat across the street."

I switched the front lights off. "Mind coming out through the alley? Look, I'll make sandwiches in the morning before the rush. One ham, one cheese on rye bread, lettuce *and* mayonnaise, right? And a quart of milk."

"You ought to work in a bank," he said.

I guess he wasn't any lonelier than anybody else just because he lived alone. He left me at the door of the Foremaster and for a moment I wished I could go with him. I thought home might be a mess.

And it was. Mary had planned the trip. Out near Montauk Point there's a dude ranch with all the fancy fixings you see in what they call adult Westerns. The joke is that it's the oldest working cattle ranch in America. It was a cattle ranch before Texas was discovered. First charter came from Charles II. Originally the herds that supplied New

York grazed there and the herdsmen were drawn by lot, like jurors, for limited service. Of course now it's all silver spurs and cowboy stuff, but the red cattle still graze on the moors. Mary thought it would be nice to spend Sunday night in one of the guest houses.

Ellen wanted to go into New York, stay at a hotel, and spend two days in Times Square. Allen didn't want to go at all, any place. That's one of his ways of getting attention and proving that he exists.

The house boiled with emotion—Ellen in slow, dripping, juicy tears, Mary tired and flushed with frustration, Allen sitting sullen and withdrawn with his little radio blasting in his ear, a thumping whining song of love and loss in a voice of sub-hysteria. "You promised to be true, and then you took and threw, my lovin' lonely heart right on the floor."

"I'm about ready to give up," Mary said.

"They're just trying to help."

"They seem to go out of their way to be difficult."

"I never get to do anything." Ellen sniffled.

In the living room Allen turned up the volume. ". . . my lovin' lonely heart right on the floor."

"Couldn't we lock them in the cellar and go off by ourselves, carotene, dear."

"You know, at this point I wish we could." She had to raise her voice to be heard over the pounding roar of the lovin' lonely heart.

Without warning a rage came up in me. I turned and strode toward the living room to tear my son to shreds and throw his lonely lovin' corpse on the floor and trample it. As I went loping through the door the music stopped. "We interrupt this program to bring you a special bulletin. Officials of New Baytown and Wessex County were this afternoon subpoenaed to appear before a grand jury to answer charges ranging from fixing traffic tickets to taking bribes and kickbacks on town and county contracts. . . ."

There it came—the Town Manager, the council, the magistrates, the works. I listened without hearing—sad and heavy. Maybe they had been doing what they were charged with, but they'd been doing it so long they didn't think it was wrong. And even if they were innocent they couldn't be cleared before the local election, and even if a man is cleared the charge is remembered. They were surrounded. They must have known it. I listened for a mention of Stoney and it didn't come so I guess he had traded them for immunity. No wonder he felt so raw and alone.

Mary was listening at the door. "Well!" she said. "We haven't had so much excitement in a long time. Do you think it's true, Ethan?"

"Doesn't matter," I said. "That's not what it's for."

"I wonder what Mr. Baker thinks."

"He went on a holiday. Yes, I wonder what he feels."

Allen grew restive because his music was interrupted.

The news and dinner and dishes put off our trip problems until it was too late for a decision or for further tears and quarreling.

In bed I got to shivering all over. The cold, passionless savagery of the attack chilled right through the warm summer night.

Mary said, "You're all goose lumps, dear. Do you think you have a virus?"

"No, my fancy, I guess I was just feeling what those men must feel. They must feel awful."

"Stop it, Ethan. You can't take other people's troubles on your shoulders."

"I can because I do."

"I wonder if you'll ever be a businessman. You're too sensitive, Ethan. It's not your crime."

"I was thinking maybe it is—everybody's crime."

"I don't understand."

"I don't much either, sweetheart."

"If there was only someone who could stay with them."

"Repeat, please, Columbine!"

"How I would love to take a holiday just with you. It's been forever."

"We're short on unattached elderly female relatives. Put your mind to it. If only we could can them or salt or pickle them for a little while. Mary, madonna, put your mind to it. I ache to be alone with you in a strange place. We could walk the dunes and swim naked at night and I would tousle you in a fern bed."

"Darling, I know, darling. I know its been hard on you. Don't think I don't know."

"Well, hold me close. Let's think of some way."

"You're still shivering. Do you feel cold?"

"Cold and hot, full and empty—and tired."

"I'll try to think of something. I really will. Of course I love them but—"

"I know, and I could wear my bow tie—"

"Will they put them in jail?"

"I wish we could—"

"Those men?"

"No. It won't be necessary. They can't even appear before next Tuesday, and Thursday is election. That's what it's for."

"Ethan, that's cynical. You aren't like that. We'll have to go away if you're getting cynical because—that wasn't a joke, the way you said it. I know your jokes. You meant that."

A fear struck me. I was showing through. I couldn't let myself show through. "Oh say, Miss Mousie will you marry me?"

And Mary said, "Oho! Oho!"

My sudden fear that I might be showing through was very great. I had made myself believe that the eyes are not the mirror of the soul. Some of the deadliest little female contraptions I ever saw had the faces and the eyes of angels. There is a breed that can read through skin and through bone right into the center, but they are rare. For the most part people are not curious except about themselves. Once a Canadian girl of Scottish blood told me a story that had bitten her and the telling bit me. She said that in the age of growing up when she felt that all eyes were on her and not favorably, so that she went from blushes to tears and back again, her Highland grandfather, observing her pain, said sharply. "Ye wouldna be sae worrit wi' what folk think about ye if ye kenned how seldom they do." It cured her and the telling reassured me of privacy, because it's true. But Mary, who ordinarily lives in a house of flowers of her own growing, had heard a tone, or felt a cutting wind. This was a danger, until tomorrow should be over.

If my plan had leaped up full-grown and deadly I would have rejected it as nonsense. People don't do such things, but people play secret games. Mine began with Joey's rules for robbing a bank. Against the boredom of my job I played with it and everything along the way fell into it—Allen and his mouse mask, leaking toilet, rusty pistol, holiday coming up, Joey wadding paper in the lock of the alley door. As a game I timed the process, enacted it, tested it. But gunmen shooting it out with cops—aren't they the little boys who practiced quick draws with cap pistols until they got so good they had to use the skill?

I don't know when my game stopped being a game. Perhaps when I knew I might buy the store and would need money to run it. For one thing, it is hard to throw away a perfect structure without testing it. And as for the dishonesty, the crime—it was not a crime against men, only against money. No one would get hurt. Money is insured. The real crimes were against men, against Danny and against Marullo. If I could do what I had done, theft was nothing. And all of it was temporary. None of it would ever have to be repeated. Actually, before I knew it was not a game, my procedure and equipment and timing were as near perfection as possible. The cap-pistol boy found a .45 in his hand.

Of course an accident was possible but that is so in crossing the street or walking under a tree. I don't think I had any fear. I had rehearsed that out of me, but I did have a breathlessness, like the stage fright of an actor standing in the wings on his opening night. And it was like a play in that every conceivable mischance had been inspected and eliminated.

In my worry that I would not sleep, I slept, deeply and as far as I know without dreams, and overslept. I had planned to use the dark pre-day for the calming medicine of contemplation. Instead, when my eyes jerked open, the tail of the cow in the lake had been visible at least half an hour. I awakened with a jar like the blow of driven air from high explosive. Sometimes such an awakening sprains muscles. Mine shook the bed so that Mary awakened, saying, "What's the matter?"

"I've overslept."

"Nonsense. It's early."

"No, my ablative absolute. This is a monster day for me. The world will be grocery-happy today. Don't you get up."

"You'll need a good breakfast."

"Know what I'll do? I'll get a carton of coffee at the Foremaster and I'll raven Marullo's shelves like a wolf."

"You will?"

"Rest, little mouse of a mouseness, and try to find a way for us to escape from our darling children. We need that. I mean it."

"I know we do. I'll try to think."

I was dressed and gone before she could suggest any of the seasonal things for my protection and comfort.

Joey was in the coffee shop and he patted the stool beside him.

"Can't, Morph. I'm late. Annie, could you give me a quart of coffee in a carton?"

"It'll have to be two pints, Eth."

"Good. Even gooder."

She filled and covered the little paper buckets and put them in a bag.

Joey finished and walked across with me.

"You'll have to say mass without the bishop this morning."

"Guess so. Say, how about that news?"

"I can't take it in."

"You remember I said I smelled something."

"I thought about that when I heard it. You've got quite a nose."

"It's part of the trade. Baker can come back now. Wonder if he will."

"Come back?"

"You get no smell there?"

I looked at him helplessly. "I'm missing something and I don't even know what it is."

"Jesus God."

"You mean I should see something?"

"That's what I mean. The law of the fang is not repealed."

"Oh, Lord! There must be a whole world I miss. I was trying to remember whether it's both lettuce and mayonnaise you like."

"Both." He stripped the cellophane cover from his pack of Camels and wadded it to push in the lock.

"Got to go," I said. "We've got a special sale on tea. Send in a box top, you get a baby! Know any ladies?"

"I sure do, and that's about the last prize they want. Don't bother to bring them, I'll come for the sandwiches." He went in his door and there was no click of the spring lock. I did hope that Joey never discovered that he was the best teacher I had ever had. He not only informed, he demonstrated and, without knowing it, prepared a way for me.

Everyone who knew about such things, the experts, agreed that only money gets money. The best way is always the simplest. The shocking simplicity of the thing was its greatest strength. But I really believe it was only a detailed daydream until Marullo through none of his fault walked in his own darkness over a cliff. Once it seemed almost certain that I could get the store for my own, only then did the high-flown dreaming come down to earth. A good but ill-informed question might be: If I could get the store, why did I need money? Mr. Baker would understand, so would Joey—so, for that matter, would Marullo. The store without running capital was worse than no store at all. The Appian Way of bankruptcy is lined with the graves of unprotected ventures. I have one grave there already. The silliest soldier would not throw his whole strength at a break-through without mortars or reserves or replacements, but many a borning business does just that. Mary's money in marked bills bulged against my bottom in my hip pocket, but Marullo would take as much of that as he could get. Then the first of the month. The wholesale houses are not openhanded with credit for unproved organizations. Therefore I would still need money, and that money was waiting for me behind ticking steel doors. The process of getting it, designed as daydreams, stood up remarkably when inspected. That robbery was unlawful troubled me very little. Marullo was no problem. If he were not the victim he might have planned it himself. Danny was troubling, even though I could with perfect truth assume that he was finished anyway. Mr. Baker's ineffectual attempt to do the same thing to Danny gave me more justification than most men need. But Danny remained a burning in my guts and I had to accept that as one accepts a wound in successful combat. I had to live with that, but maybe it would heal in time or be walled off with forgetfulness the way a shell fragment gets walled off with cartilage.

The immediate was the money, and that move was as carefully prepared and timed as an electric circuit.

The Morphy laws stood up well and I remembered them and had even added one. First law: Have no past record. Well, I had none. Number two: No accomplices or confidants. I certainly had none. Number three: No dames. Well, Margie Young-Hunt was the only person I knew who could be called a dame, and I was not about to drink champagne out of her slipper. Number four: Don't splurge. Well, I wouldn't. Gradually I would use it to pay bills to wholesalers. I had a place for it. In my Knight Templar's hatbox there was a support of velvet-covered cardboard, the size and shape of my head. This was already lifted free and the edges coated with contact cement so it could be restored in an instant.

Recognition—a Mickey Mouse mask. No one would see anything else. An old cotton raincoat of Marullo's—all tan cotton raincoats look alike—and a pair of those tear-off cellophane gloves that come on a roll. The mask had been cut several days ago and the box and cereal flushed down the toilet, as the mask and gloves would be. The old silvered Iver Johnson pistol was smoked with lampblack and in the toilet was a can of crankcase oil to throw it in for delivery to Chief Stoney at the first opportunity.

I had added my own final law: Don't be a pig. Don't take too much and avoid large bills. If somewhere about six to ten thousand in tens and twenties were available, that would be enough and easy to handle and to hide. A cardboard cakebox on the cold counter would be the swap bag and when next seen it would have a cake in it. I had tried that terrible reedy ventriloquism thing to change my voice and had given it up for silence and gestures. Everything in place and ready.

I was almost sorry Mr. Baker wasn't here. There would be only Morph and Harry Robbit and Edith Alden. It was planned to the split second. At five minutes to nine I would place the broom in the entrance. I'd practiced over and over. Apron tucked up, scale weight on the toilet chain to keep it flushing. Anyone who came in would hear the water and draw his own conclusion. Coat, mask, cakebox, gun, gloves. Cross the alley on the stroke of nine, shove open the back door, put on mask, enter just after timeclock buzzes and Joey swings open the door. Motion the three to lie down, with the gun. They'd give no trouble. As Joey said, the money was insured, he wasn't. Pick up the money, put it in cakebox, cross alley, flush gloves and mask down toilet, put gun in can of oil, coat off. Apron down, money in hatbox, cake in cakebox, pick up broom, and go on sweeping sidewalk, available and visible when the alarm came. The whole thing one minute and forty seconds, timed, checked, and rechecked. But carefully as I had planned and timed, I still felt a little breathless and I swept out the store prior to opening the two front doors. I wore yesterday's apron so that new wrinkles would not be noticeable.

And would you believe it, time stood still as though a Joshua in a wing collar had shot the sun in its course. The minute hand of my father's big watch had set its heels and resisted morning.

It was long since I had addressed my flock aloud, but this morning I did, perhaps out of nervousness.

"My friends," I said, "what you are about to witness is a mystery. I know I can depend on you to keep silent. If any of you have any feeling about the moral issue involved, I challenge you and will ask you to leave." I paused. "No objections? Very well. If I ever hear of an oyster or a cabbage discussing this with strangers, the sentence is death by dinner fork.

"And I want to thank you all. We have been together, humble workers in the vineyard, and I a servant as you are. But now a change is coming. I will be master here henceforth, but I promise I will be a good and kind and understanding master. The time approaches, my friends, the curtain rises—farewell." And as I moved to the front doors with the broom, I heard my own voice cry, "Danny—Danny! Get out of my guts." A great shudder shook me so that I had to lean on the broom a moment before I opened up the doors.

My father's watch said nine with its black, stumpy hour hand and minus six with its long, thin minute hand. I could feel its heart beat against my palm as I looked at it.

CHAPTER XV

IT WAS a day as different from other days as dogs are from cats and both of them from chrysanthemums or tidal waves or scarlet fever. It is the law in many states, certainly in ours, that it must rain on long holiday weekends, else how could the multitudes get drenched and miserable? The July sun fought off a multitude of little feathered clouds and drove them scuttling, but thunderheads looked over the western rim, the strong-arm rain-bearers from the Hudson River Valley, armed with lightning and already mumbling to themselves. If the law was properly obeyed, they would hold back until a maximum number of ant-happy humans were on the highways and the beaches, summer-dressed and summer-green.

Most of the other stores did not open until nine-thirty. It had been Marullo's thought to catch a pinch of trade by having me jump the gun half an hour. I thought I would change that. It caused more ill feeling among the other stores than the profit justified. Marullo didn't care about that, if he ever knew about it. He was a foreigner, a wop, a criminal, a tyrant, a squeezer of the poor, a bastard, and eight kinds of son of a bitch. I having destroyed him, it was only natural that his faults and crimes should become blindingly apparent to me.

I felt old long hand edging around on my father's watch and I found I was sweeping viciously with tensed muscles, waiting for the moment of swift, smooth movement of my mission. I breathed through my mouth, and my stomach pushed against my lungs as I remember it did waiting for an attack.

For Saturday-morning-Fourth-of-July-weekend, there were few people about. A stranger—old man—went by, carrying a fishing rod and a green plastic tackle box. He was on his way to the town pier to sit all day dangling a limp strip of squid in the water. He didn't even look up, but I forced his attention.

"Hope you catch some big ones."

"Never catch anything," he said.

"Stripers come in sometimes."

"I don't believe it."

A red-hot optimist, but at least I had set the hook in his attention.

And Jennie Single rolled along the sidewalk. She moved as though she had casters instead of feet, probably New Baytown's least reliable witness. Once she turned on her gas oven and forgot to light it. She'd have blown herself through the roof if she could have remembered where she had put the matches.

"Morning, Miss Jenny."

"Good morning, Danny."

"I'm Ethan."

"Course you are. I'm going to bake a cake."

I tried to gouge a scar in her memory. "What kind?"

"Well, it's Fannie Farmer but the label fell off the package so I really don't know."

What a witness she would make, if I needed a witness. And why did she say "Danny"?

A piece of tinfoil on the pavement resisted the broom. I had to stoop down and lift it with a fingernail. Those assistant bank mice were really mousing the hour with Cat Baker away. They were the ones I wanted. It was less than one minute to nine when they burst from the coffee shop and sprinted across the street.

"Run—run—run!" I called and they grinned self-consciously as they charged the bank doors.

Now it was time. I must not think of the whole thing— just one step at a time and each in its place, as I had practiced. I folded my anxious stomach down where it belonged. First lean the broom against the doorjamb where it could be seen. I moved with slow, deliberate speed.

From the corner of my eye I saw a car come along the street and I paused to let it go by.

"Mr. Hawley!"

I whirled the way cornered gangsters do in the movies. A dusty dark green Chevrolet had slid to the curb and, great God! that Ivy League government man was getting out. My stone-built earth shuddered like a reflection in water. Paralyzed, I saw him cross the pavement. It seemed to take ages, but it was simple as that. My long-planned perfect structure turned to dust before my eyes the way a long-buried artifact does when the air strikes it. I thought of rushing for the toilet and going through with it. It wouldn't work. I couldn't repeal the Morphy law. Thought and light must travel at about the same speed. It's a shock to throw out a plan so long considered, so many times enacted that its consummation is just one more repetition, but I tossed it out, threw it away, closed it off. I had no choice. And light-speed thought said, Thank God he didn't come one minute later. That would have been the fatal accident they write about in crime stories.

And all this while the young man moved stiffly four steps across the pavement.

Something must have showed through to him.

"What's the matter, Mr. Hawley? You look sick."

"Skitters," I said.

"That'll wait for no man. Run for it. I'll wait."

I dashed for the toilet, closed the door, and pulled the chain to make a rush of water. I hadn't switched on the light. I sat there in the dark. My quaking stomach played along. In a moment I really had to go, and I did, and slowly the beating pressure in me subsided. I added a by-law to the Morphy code. In case of accident, change your plan—instantly.

It has happened to me before that in crisis or great danger I have stepped out and apart and as an interested stranger watched myself, my movements and my mind, but immune to the emotions of the thing observed. Sitting in the blackness, I saw the other person fold his perfect plan and put it in a box and close the lid and shove the thing not only out of sight but out of thought. I mean that by the time I stood up in the darkness and zipped and smoothed and laid my hand on the flimsy plywood door, I was a grocery clerk prepared for a busy day. It was no secretiveness. It was really so. I wondered what the young man wanted, but only with the pale apprehension that comes from a low-grade fear of cops.

"Sorry to keep you waiting," I said. "Can't remember what I ate to cause that."

"There's a virus going around," he said. "My wife had it last week."

"Well, this virus carried a gun. I nearly got caught short. What can I do for you?"

He seemed embarrassed, apologetic, almost shy. "A guy does funny things," he said.

I overcame an impulse to say, It takes all kinds—and I'm glad I did because his next words were, "In my business you meet all kinds."

I walked behind the counter and kicked the leather Knight Templar hatbox closed. And I leaned my elbows on the counter.

Very odd. Five minutes earlier I saw myself through the eyes of other people. I had to. What they saw was important. And as he came across the pavement, this man had been a huge, dark, hopeless fate, an enemy, an ogre. But with my project tucked away and gone as a part of me, I saw him now as an object apart—no longer linked with me for good or bad. He was, I think, about my age, but shaped in a school, a manner, perhaps a cult—a lean face and hair carefully trimmed short and standing straight up, white shirt of a coarse woven linen with the collar buttoned down and a tie chosen by his wife, and without doubt patted and straightened by her as he left the house. His suit a gray darkness and his nails home cared for but well cared for, a wide gold wedding ring on his left hand, a tiny bar in his buttonhole, a suggestion of the decoration he would not wear. His mouth and dark blue eyes were schooled to firmness, which made it all the more strange that they were not firm now. In some way a hole had been opened in him. He was not the same man whose questions had been short, squared bars of steel spaced perfectly, one below its fellow.

"You were here before," I said. "What is your business?"

"Department of Justice."

"Your business is justice?"

He smiled. "Yes, at least that's what I hope. But I'm not on official business—not even sure the department would approve. But it's my day off."

"What can I do for you?"

"It's kind of complicated. Don't know quite where to begin. It's not in the book. Hawley, I've been in the service twelve years and I've never had anything like this before."

"Maybe if you tell me what it is I can help you do it."

He smiled at me. "Hard to set it up. I've been driving three hours from New York and I've got to drive three hours back in holiday traffic."

"Sounds serious."

"It is."

"I think you said your name was Walder."

"Richard Walder."

"I'm going to be swamped with customers, Mr. Walder. Don't know why they haven't started. Hot-dog-and-relish trade. You'd better start. Am I in trouble?"

"In my job you meet all kinds. Tough ones, liars, cheats, hustlers, stupid, bright. Mostly you can get mad at them, get an attitude to carry you through. Do you see?"

"No, I guess not. Look, Walder, what in hell's bothering you? I'm not completely stupid. I've talked to Mr. Baker at the bank. You're after Mr. Marullo, my boss."

"And I got him," he said softly.

"What for?"

"Illegal entry. It's not my doing. They throw me a dossier and I follow it up. I don't judge him or try him."

"He'll be deported?"

"Yes."

"Can he make a fight? Can I help him?"

"No. He doesn't want to. He's pleading guilty. He wants to go."

"Well, I'll be damned!"

Six or eight customers came in. "I warned you," I called to him, and I helped them select what they needed or thought they did. Thank heaven I had ordered a mountain of hot-dog and hamburger rolls.

Walder called, "What do you get for piccalilli?"

"It's marked on the label."

"Thirty-nine cents, ma'am," he said. And he went to work, measuring, bagging, adding. He reached in front of me to ring up cash on the register. When he moved away I took a bag from the pile, opened the drawer, and, using the bag like a potholder, I picked up the old revolver, took it back to the toilet, and dropped it in the can of crankcase oil that waited for it.

"You're good at this," I said when I came back.

"I used to have a job at Grand Union after school."

"It shows."

"Don't you have anybody to help?"

"I'm going to bring my boy in."

Customers always come in coveys, never in evenly spaced singles. A clerk gets set in the interval to meet the next flight. Another thing, when two men do something together they become alike, differences of mind become less ragged. The Army discovered that black and white no longer fight each other when they have something else to fight in company. My subcutaneous fear of a cop dissipated when Walder weighed out a pound of tomatoes and totted up a list of figures on a bag.

Our first flight took off.

"Better tell me quick what you want," I said.

"I promised Marullo I'd come out here. He wants to give you the store."

"You're nuts. I beg your pardon, ma'am. I was speaking to my friend."

"Oh, yes. Of course. Well, there are five of us—three children. How many frankfurters will I need?"

"Five apiece for the children, three for your husband, two for you. That's twenty."

"You think they'll eat five?"

"They think they will. Is it a picnic?"

"Uh-huh."

"Then get five extra for dropping in the fire."

"Where do you keep the Plug-O for sinks?"

"Back there with the cleansers and ammonia."

It was broken up like that and was bound to be. Edited of customers, it was like this:

"I guess I'm in a state of shock. I just do my job and it's with mugs for the most part. If you get conditioned by crooks and liars and cheats, why, an honest man can shock the hell out of you."

"What do you mean, honest? My boss never gave away anything. He's a tough monkey."

"I know he is. We made him that way. He told me and I believe him. Before he came over he knew the words on the bottom of the Statue of Liberty. He'd memorized the Declaration of Independence in dialect. The Bill of Rights was words of fire. And then he couldn't get in. So he came anyway. A nice man helped him—took everything he had and dropped him in the surf to wade ashore. It was quite a while before he understood the American way, but he learned—he learned. 'A guy got to make a buck! Look out for number one!' But he learned. He's not dumb. He took care of number one."

This was interspersed with customers so it didn't build to a dramatic climax—just a series of short statements.

"That's why he wasn't hurt when somebody turned him in."

"Turned him in?"

"Sure. All it takes is a telephone call."

"Who did that?"

"Who knows? The department's a machine. You set the dials and it follows through all the steps like an automatic washer."

"Why didn't he run for it?"

"He's tired, right to his bones he's tired. And he's disgusted. He's got some money. He wants to go back to Sicily."

"I still don't get it about the store."

"He's like me. I can take care of chiselers. That's my job. An honest man gums up my works, throws me sky high. That's what happened to him. One guy didn't try to cheat him, didn't steal, didn't whine, didn't chisel. He tried to teach the sucker to take care of himself in the land of the free but the boob couldn't learn. For a long time you scared him. He tried to figure out your racket, and he discovered your racket was honesty."

"Suppose he was wrong?"

"He doesn't think he was. He wants to make you a kind of monument to something he believed in once. I've got the conveyance out in the car. All you have to do is file it."

"I don't understand it."

"I don't know whether I do or not. You know how he talks—like corn popping. I'm trying to translate what he tried to explain. It's like a man is made a certain way with a certain direction. If he changes that, something blows, he strips a gear, he gets sick. It's like a—well, like a do-it-yourself police court. You have to pay for a violation. You're his down payment, kind of, so the light won't go out."

"Why did you drive out here?"

"Don't know exactly. Had to—maybe—so the light won't go out."

"Oh, God!"

The store clouded up with clamoring kids and damp women. There wouldn't be any more uncluttered moments until noon at least.

Walder went out to his car, and came back and parted a wave of frantic summer wives to get to the counter. He laid down one of those hard board bellows envelopes tied with a tape.

"Got to go. Four hours' drive with this traffic. My wife's mad. She said it could wait. But it couldn't wait."

"Mister, I been waiting ten minutes to get waited on."

"Be right with you, ma'am."

"I asked him if he had any message and he said, 'Tell him good-by.' You got any message?"

"Tell him good-by."

The wave of ill-disguised stomachs closed in again and it was just as well for me. I dropped the envelope in the drawer below the cash register and with it—desolation.

CHAPTER XVI

THE day went quickly and yet was endless. Closing time had no relation to opening time, so long ago it was that I could hardly remember it. Joey came in as I was about to close the front doors and without asking him I punched a beer can and handed it to him, and then I opened one for myself and I have never done that before. I tried to tell him about Marullo and the store, and found I could not, not even the story I had accepted in exchange for the truth.

"You look tired," he said.

"I guess I am. Look at those shelves—stripped. They bought things they didn't want and didn't need." I unloaded the cash register into the gray canvas bag, added the money Mr. Baker had brought, and on top I put the bellows envelope and tied up the bag with a piece of string.

"You oughtn't to leave that around."

"Maybe not. I hide it. Want another beer?"

"Sure."

"Me too."

"You're too good an audience," he said. "I get to believing my own stories."

"Like what?"

"Like my triple-deck instincts. I had one this morning. Woke up with it. Guess I dreamed it, but it was real strong, hair on the back of my neck and everything. I didn't think the bank was going to get stuck up today. I knew it. I knew it, lying in bed. We keep little wedges under the foot alarms so we won't tramp them by mistake. First thing this morning I took them out. I was that sure of it, braced for it. Now how do you explain that?"

"Maybe somebody planned it and you read his mind and he gave it up."

"You make it easy for a guy to guess wrong with honor."

"How do you figure it?"

"God knows. I think I've been Mr. Know-It-All to you so much I got to believe it. But it sure shook me up."

"You know, Morph, I'm too tired even to sweep out."

"Don't leave that dough here tonight. Take it home."

"Okay, if you say so."

"I still got the feeling something's screwy."

I opened the leather box and put the money sack in with my plumed hat and strapped it closed. Joey, watching me, said, "I'm going in to New York and get a room at a hotel and I'm going to watch the waterfall across Times Square for two solid days with my shoes off."

"With your date?"

"I called that off. I'll order up a bottle of whisky and a dame. Don't have to talk to either of them."

"I told you—maybe we're going on a little trip."

"Hope so. You need it. Ready to go?"

"Couple of things to do. You go on, Joey. Get your shoes off."

First thing to do was to call Mary and tell her I had to be a little late.

"Yes, but hurry, hurry, hurry. News, news, news."

"Can't you tell me now, sweetheart?"

"No. I want to see your face."

I hung the Mickey Mouse mask on the cash register by its rubber band so that it covered the little window where the numbers show. Then I put on my coat and hat and turned out the lights and sat on the counter with my legs dangling. A naked black banana stalk nudged me on one side and the cash register fitted against my left shoulder like a bookend. The shades were up so that the summer late light strained through the crossed-wire grating, and it was very quiet, a quiet like a rushing sound, and that's what I needed. I felt in my left side pocket for the lump the cash register pushed against me. The talisman—I held it in my two hands and stared down at it. I had thought I needed it yesterday. Had I forgot to put it back or was my keeping it with me no accident? I don't know.

As always it put its power on me as I traced its design with my finger. At midday it was the pink of a rose, but in the evening it picked up a darker tone, a purplish blush as though a little blood had got in it.

It wasn't thought I needed but rearrangement, change of design, as though I were in a garden from which the house had been moved in the night. Some kind of make-shift had to be set up to shelter me until I could rebuild. I had retired into busyness until I could let new things enter slowly and count and identify them as they came. The shelves, all day assaulted, showed many gaps where their defenses had been breeched by the hungry horde, a snaggle-toothed effect, a walled town after artillery fire.

"Let us pray for our departed friends," I said. "The thin red line of catsup, the gallant pickles and condiments down to the small bald capers of vinegar. We cannot dedicate, we cannot consecrate—no not that. It is rather to us the living—no not that. Alfio—I wish you luck and surcease from pain. You are wrong, of course, but wrongness can be a poultice to you. You made a sacrifice for having been a sacrifice."

People passing in the street flickered the light inside the store. I dug back in the debris of the day for Walder's words and for his face when he said them: "A do-it-yourself police court. You have to pay for a violation. You're his down payment, kind of, so the light won't go out." That's what the man said. Walder in his safe world of crooks shaken by one gleaming shaft of honesty.

So the light won't go out. Did Alfio say it that way? Walder didn't know, but he did know that's what Marullo meant.

I traced the serpent on the talisman and came back to the beginning, which was the end. That was an old light— Marulli three thousand years ago found their way through the lupariae to the Lupercal on the Palatine to offer a votive to Lycean Pan, protector of the flocks from wolves. And that light had not gone out. Marullo, the dago, the wop, the guinea, sacrificed to the same god for the same reason. I saw him again raise his head out of the welter of fat neck and aching shoulders, I saw the noble head, the hot eyes—and the light. I wondered what my payment would be and when demanded. If I took my talisman down to the Old Harbor and threw it in the sea—would that be acceptable?

I did not draw the shades. On long holidays we left them up so the cops could look in. The storeroom was dark. I locked the alley door and was halfway across the street when I remembered the hatbox behind the counter. I did not go back for it. It would be a kind of question asked. The wind was rising that Saturday evening, blowing shrill and eagerly from the southeast as it must to bring the rain to soak the vacationers. I thought to put out the milk for that gray cat on Tuesday and invite it in to be a guest in my store.

CHAPTER XVII

I DON'T know for sure how other people are inside—all different and all alike at the same time. I can only guess. But I do know how I will squirm and wriggle to avoid a hurtful truth and, when finally there is no choice, will put it off, hoping it will go away. Do other people say primly, "I'll think about that tomorrow when I am rested," and then draw on a hoped-for future or an edited past like a child playing with violence against the inevitability of bedtime?

My dawdled steps toward home led through a minefield of the truth. The future was sowed with fertile dragon's teeth. It was not unnatural to run for a safe anchorage in the past. But on that course, set square across it was Aunt Deborah, a great wing shot on a covey of lies, her eyes gleaming question marks.

I had looked in the window of the jewelry store at expanding watch bands and glasses frames as long as was decent. The humid, windy evening was breeding a thunderstorm.

There were many like Great-Aunt Deborah early in the last century, islands of curiosity and knowledge. Maybe it was being cut off from a world of peers that drove the few into books or perhaps it was the endless waiting, sometimes three years, sometimes forever, for the ships to come home, that pushed them into the kind of books that filled our attic. She was the greatest of great-aunts, a sibyl and a pythoness in one, said magic nonsense words to me, which kept their magic but not their nonsense when I tracked them down.

"Me beswac fah wyrm thurh faegir word," she said and

the tone was doom. And, "Seo leo gif heo blades onbirigth abit aerest hire ladteow." Wonder-words they must be, since I still remember them.

The Town Manager of New Baytown went crab-scuttling by me, head down, and only gave me good evening in return for mine first offered.

I could feel my house, the old Hawley house, from half a block away. Last night it huddled in a web of gloom but this thunder-bordered eve it radiated excitement. A house, like an opal, takes on the colors of the day. Antic Mary heard my footsteps on the walk and she flickered out the screen door like a flame.

"You'll never guess!" she said, and her hands were out, palms in, as though she carried a package.

It was in my mind so I replied "Seo leo gif heo blades onbirigth abit aerest hire ladteow."

"Well, that's a pretty good guess but it's not right."

"Some secret admirer has given us a dinosaur."

"Wrong, but it's just as wonderful. And I won't tell till you wash up, because you'll have to be clean to hear it."

"What I hear is the love music of a blue-bottom baboon." And I did—it blatted from the living room, where Allen importuned his soul in a phlegm of revolt. "Just when I was ready, to ask you to go steady, they said I didn't know my mind. Your glance gives me ants whenever we romance, and they say I couldn't know my mind."

"I think I'll burn him up, heaven wife."

"No, you won't. Not when you hear."

"Can't you tell me dirty?"

"No."

I went through the living room. My son responded to my greeting with the sharp expression of a piece of chewed gum.

"I hope you got your lonely lovin' heart swept up."

"Huh?"

"Huh, *sir!* Last I heard, somebody had took and threw it on the floor."

"Number one," he said, "number one in the whole country. Sold a million copies in two weeks."

"Great! I'm glad the future is in your hands." I joined the next chorus as I went up the stairs. " 'Your glance gives me ants whenever we romance, and they say I couldn't know my mind.' "

Ellen was stalking me with a book in her hand, one finger between the pages. I know her method. She would ask me what she thought I might think an interesting question and then let slip whatever it was Mary wanted to tell me. It's a kind of triumph for Ellen to tell first. I wouldn't say she is a tattletale, but she is. I waved crossed fingers at her.

"King's X."

"But, Daddy—"

"I said King's X, Miss Hothouse Rhubarb, and I meant King's X." I slammed the door and shouted, "A man's bathroom is his castle." And I heard her laugh. I don't trust children when they laugh at my jokes. I scrubbed my face raw and brushed my teeth until my gums bled. I shaved, put on a clean shirt and the bow tie my daughter hated, as a declaration of revolt.

My Mary was flittered with impatience when I faced her.

"You won't believe it."

"Seo leo gif heo blades onbirigth. Speak."

"Margie is the nicest friend I ever had."

"I quote—'The man who invented the cuckoo clock is dead. This is old news but good!' "

"You'll never guess—she's going to keep the children so we can have our trip."

"Is this a trick?"

"I didn't ask. She offered."

"They'll eat her alive."

"They're crazy about her. She's going to take them to New York on the train Sunday, stay all night in a friend's apartment, and Monday see the new fifty-star flag-raising in Rockefeller Center and the parade and—everything."

"I can't believe it."

"Isn't that the nicest thing?"

"The very nicest. And we will flee to the Montauk moors, Miss Mousie?"

"I've already called and reserved a room."

"It's delirium. I shall burst. I feel myself swelling up."

I had thought to tell her about the store, but too much news is constipating. Better to wait and tell her on the moor.

Ellen came slithering into the kitchen. "Daddy, that pink thing's gone from the cabinet."

"I have it. I have it here in my pocket. Here, you may put it back."

"You told us never to take it away."

"I still tell you that, on pain of death."

She snatched it almost greedily and carried it in both hands to the living room.

Mary's eyes were on me strangely, somberly. "Why did you take it, Ethan?"

"For luck, my love. And it worked."

CHAPTER XVIII

Iᴛ ʀᴀɪɴᴇᴅ on Sunday, July third, as it must, fat drops more wet than usual. We nudged our way in the damp segmented worms of traffic, feeling a little grand and helpless and lost, like cage-bred birds set free, and frightened as freedom shows its teeth. Mary sat straight, smelling of fresh-ironed cotton.

"Are you happy—are you gay?"

"I keep listening for the children."

"I know. Aunt Deborah called it happy-lonesome. Take flight, my bird! Those long flaps on your shoulders are wings, you juggins."

She smiled and nuzzled close. "It's good, but I still listen for the children. I wonder what they are doing now?"

"Almost anything you can guess except wondering what we are doing."

"I guess that's right. They aren't really interested."

"Let us emulate them, then. When I saw your barge slide near, O Nile serpent, I knew it was our day. Octavian will beg his bread tonight from some Greek goatherd."

"You're crazy. Allen never looks where he's going. He might step right out in traffic against a light."

"I know. And poor little Ellen with her club foot. Well, she has a good heart and a pretty face. Perhaps someone will love her and amputate her feet."

"Oh! let me worry a little. I'll feel better if I do."

"I never heard it better put. Shall we together go over all the horrid possibilities?"

"You know what I mean."

"I do. But you, highness, brought it to the family. It only travels in the female line. The little bleeders."

"No one loves his children more than you."

"My guilt is as the guilt of ten because I am a skunk."

"I like you."

"Now that's the kind of worrying I approve of. See that stretch? Look how the gorse and heather hold and the sand cuts out from under like solid little waves. The rain hits the earth and jumps right up in a thin mist. I've always thought it is like Dartmoor or Exmoor, and I've never seen them except through the eyes of print. You know the first Devon men must have felt at home here. Do you think it's haunted?"

"If it isn't, you'll haunt it."

"You must not make compliments unless you mean them."

"It's not for now. Watch for the side road. It will say 'Moorcroft.'"

It did, too, and the nice thing about that lean spindle end of Long Island is that the rain sinks in and there is no mud.

We had a doll's house to ourselves, fresh and ginghamy, and nationally advertised twin beds, fat as muffins.

"I don't approve of those."

"Silly—you can reach across."

"I can do one whole hell of a lot better than that, you harlot."

We dined in greasy dignity on broiled Maine lobsters sloshed down with white wine—lots of white wine to make my Mary's eyes to shine, and I plied her with cognac seductively until my own head was buzzing. *She* remembered the number of our doll house and *she* could find the keyhole. I wasn't too buzzed to have my way with her, but I think she could have escaped if she had wanted to.

Then, aching with comfort, she drowsed her head on my right arm and smiled and made small yawny sounds.

"Are you worried about something?"

"What a thought. You're dreaming before you're asleep."

"You're working so hard to make me happy. I can't get past into you. Are you worried?"

A strange and seeing time, the front steps of sleep.

"Yes, I'm worried. Does that reassure you? I wouldn't want you to repeat it, but the sky is falling and a piece of it fell on my tail."

She had drifted sweetly off with her Panic smile. I slipped my arm free and stood between the beds. The rain was over except for roof drip, and the quarter-moon glistened its image in a billion droplets. "*Beaux rêves*, my dearling dear. Don't let the sky fall on us!"

My bed was cool and oversoft but I could see the sharp moon driving through the sea-fleeing clouds. And I heard the ghost-cry of a bittern. I crossed the fingers of both hands —King's X for a little while. Double King's X. It was only a pea that fell on my tail.

If the dawn came up with any thunder, I didn't hear it. All golden green it was when I came to it, dark of heather and pale with fern and yellowy red with wet dune sand, and not far away the Atlantic glittering like hammered silver. A twisted gaffer oak beside our house had put out near its root a lichen big as a pillow, a ridge-waved thing of gray pearly white. A curving graveled path led among the small township of doll houses to the shingled bungalow that had spawned them all. Here were office, postcards, gifts, stamps, and also dining room with blue-checkered tablecloths where we dolls could dine.

The manager was in his counting house, checking some kind of list. I had noticed him when we registered, a man of wisped hair and little need to shave. He was a furtive and a furthy man at once, and he had so hoped from our gaiety our outing was clandestine that I nearly signed his book "John Smith and wife" to give him pleasure. He sniffed for sin. Indeed he seemed to see with his long tender nose as a mole does.

"Good morning," I said.

He leveled his nose at me. "Slept well?"

"Perfectly. I wonder if I can carry a tray of breakfast to my wife."

"We only serve in the dining room, seven-thirty to nine-thirty."

"But if I carry it myself—"

"It's against the rules."

"Couldn't we break them this once? You know how it is."
I threw that in because that's how he hoped it was.

His pleasure was reward enough. His eyes grew moist and
his nose trembled. "Feeling a little shy, is she?"

"Well, you know how it is."

"I don't know what the cook will say."

"Ask him and tell him a dollar stands tiptoe on the misty
mountaintop."

The cook was a Greek who found a dollar attractive. In
time I toted a giant napkin-covered tray along the graveled
path and set it on a rustic bench while I picked a bouquet
of microscopic field flowers to grace the royal breakfast of
my dear.

Perhaps she was awake, but she opened her eyes anyway
and said, "I smell coffee. Oh! Oh! What a nice husband—
and—and flowers"—all the little sounds that never lose their
fragrance.

We breakfasted and coffeed and coffeed again, my Mary
propped up in bed, looking younger and more innocent
than her daughter. And each of us spoke respectfully of how
well we had slept.

My time had come. "Get comfortable. I have news both
sad and glad."

"Good! Did you buy the ocean?"

"Marullo is in trouble."

"What?"

"A long time ago he came to America without asking
leave."

"Well—what?"

"Now they are asking him to leave."

"Deported?"

"Yes."

"But that's awful."

"It's not nice."

"What will we do? What will you do?"

"Playtime is over. He sold me the store—or rather he sold
you the store. It's your money. He has to convert his prop-

erty and he likes me; he practically gave it to me—three thousand dollars."

"But that's awful. You mean—you mean you own the store?"

"Yes."

"You're not a clerk! Not a clerk!"

She rolled face down in the pillows and wept, big, full-bosomed sobs, the way a slave might when the collar is struck off.

I went out on the doll's front stoop and sat in the sun until she was ready, and when she had finished and washed her face and combed her hair and put on her dressing gown, she opened the door and called to me. And she was different, would always be different. She didn't have to say it. The set of her neck said it. She could hold up her head. We were gentlefolks again.

"Can't we do anything to help Mr. Marullo?"

"I'm afraid not."

"How did it happen? Who found out?"

"I don't know."

"He's a good man. They shouldn't do it to him. How is he taking it?"

"With dignity. With honor."

We walked on the beach as we had thought we might, sat in the sand, picked up small bright shells and showed them to each other, as we must do, spoke with conventional wonder about natural things, the sea, the air, the light, the wind-cooled sun, as though the Creator were listening in for compliments.

Mary's attention was split. I think she wanted to be back home in her new status, to see the different look in the eyes of women, the changed tone of greetings in the High Street. I think she was no more "poor Mary Hawley, she works so hard." She had become Mrs. Ethan Allen Hawley and would ever be. And I had to keep her that. She went through the day because it was planned and paid for, but the real shells she turned over and inspected were the shining days to come.

We had our lunch in the blue-checked dining room,

where Mary's manner, her certainty of position and place, disappointed Mr. Mole. His tender nose was out of joint that had so joyously quivered at the scent of sin. His disillusion was complete when he had to come to our table and report a telephone call for Mrs. Hawley.

"Who knows we're here?"

"Why, Margie, of course. I had to tell her because of the children. Oh! I do hope— He doesn't look where he's going, you know."

She came back trembling like a star. "You'll never guess. You couldn't."

"I can guess it's good."

"She said, 'Have you heard the news? Have you heard the radio?' I could tell by her voice it wasn't bad news."

"Could you tell it and then flash back to how she said it?"

"I can't believe it."

"Could you let me try to believe it?"

"Allen has won honorable mention."

"What? Allen? Tell me!"

"In the essay contest—in the whole country—honorable mention."

"No!"

"He has. Only five honorable mentions—and a watch, and he's going on television. Can you believe it? A celebrity in the family."

"I can't believe it. You mean all that slob stuff was a sham? What an actor! His lonely lovin' heart wasn't throwed on the floor at all."

"Don't make fun. Just think, our son is one of five boys in the whole United States to get honorable mention—and television."

"And a watch! Wonder if he can tell time."

"Ethan, if you make fun, people will think you're jealous of your own son."

"I'm just astonished. I thought his prose style was about the level of General Eisenhower's. Allen doesn't have a ghost-writer."

"I know you, Eth. You make a game of running them

down. But it's you who spoil them. It's just your secret way. I want to know—did you help him with his essay?"

"Help him! He didn't even let me see it."

"Well—that's all right then. I didn't want you looking smug because you wrote it for him."

"I can't get over it. It goes to show we don't know much about our own children. How's Ellen taking it?"

"Why, proud as a peacock. Margie was so excited she could hardly talk. The newspapers want to interview him—and television, he's going to be on television. Do you realize we don't even have a set to see him on? Margie says we can watch on hers. A celebrity in the family! Ethan, we ought to have a television."

"We'll get one. I'll get one first thing tomorrow morning, or why don't you order one?"

"Can we—Ethan, I forgot you own the store, I clean forgot. Can you take it in? A celebrity."

"I hope we can live with him."

"You let him have his day. We should start home. They're coming in on the seven-eighteen. We should be there, you know, to kind of receive him."

"And bake a cake."

"I will."

"And string crepe paper."

"You aren't being jealous mean, are you?"

"No. I'm overcome. I think crepe paper is a fine thing, all over the house."

"But not outside. That would look—ostentatious. Margie said why don't we pretend we don't know and let him tell us?"

"I disagree. He might turn shy. It would be as though we didn't care. No, he should come home to cheers and cries of triumph and a cake. If there was anything open, I'd get sparklers."

"The roadside stands—"

"Of course. On the way home—if they have any left."

Mary put down her head a moment as though she were saying grace. "You own the store and Allen's a celebrity.

Who would have thought all that could happen all at once? Ethan, we should get started home. We ought to be there when they come. Why are you looking that way?"

"It just swept over me like a wave—how little we know about anyone. It gives me a shiver of mullygrubs. I remember at Christmas when I should be gay I used to get the Welsh rats."

"What's that?"

"It's the way I heard it when Great-Aunt Deborah pronounced *Weltschmerz.*"

"What's that?"

"A goose walking over your grave."

"Oh! That! Well, don't get it. I guess this is the best day of our whole lives. It would be—ungrateful if we didn't know it. Now you smile and chase off those Welsh rats. That's funny, Ethan, 'Welsh rats.' You pay the bill. I'll put our things together."

I paid our bill with money that had been folded in a tight little square. And I asked Mr. Mole, "Do you have any sparklers left at the gift counter?"

"I think so. I'll see. . . . Here they are. How many do you want?"

"All you have," I said. "Our son has become a celebrity."

"Really? What kind?"

"There's only one kind."

"You mean like Dick Clark or like that?"

"Or Chessman or Dillinger."

"You're joking."

"He'll be on television."

"What station? What time?"

"I don't know—yet."

"I'll watch for it. What's his name?"

"The same as mine. Ethan Allen Hawley—called Allen."

"Well it's been an honor to have you and Mrs. Allen with us."

"Mrs. Hawley."

"Of course. I hope you'll come again. Lots of celebrities have stayed here. They come for—the quiet."

Mary sat straight and proud on the golden road toward home in the slow and glittering snake of the traffic.

"I got a whole box of sparklers. Over a hundred."

"Now that's more like you, dear. I wonder if the Bakers are back yet."

CHAPTER XIX

My son conducted himself well. He was relaxed and kind to us. He took no revenge, ordered no executions. His honors and our compliments he accepted as his due, without vanity and also without overdone humility. He advanced to his chair in the living room and switched on his radio before the hundred sparklers had fizzed out to black sticks. It was obvious that he forgave us our trespasses. I never saw a boy accept greatness with more grace.

It was truly a night of wonders. If Allen's easy ascent into heaven was surprising, how much more so was Ellen's reaction. Some years of close and enforced observation told me Miss Ellen would be tattered and storm-blown with envy, would in fact look out for some means of minimizing his greatness. She fooled me. She became her brother's celebrator. It was Ellen who told how they were sitting in an elegant apartment on Sixty-seventh Street, after an evening of magic, casually watching the C.B.S. late news on television, when the word of Allen's triumph was announced. It was Ellen who recounted what they said and how they looked and how you could have knocked them over with a feather. Allen sat remote and calm during Ellen's telling of how he would appear with the four other honorables, how he would read his essay while millions looked and listened, and Mary clucked happily in the pauses. I glanced at Margie Young-Hunt. She was indrawn as she was during card-reading. And a dark quiet crept into the room.

"No escaping it," I said. "This calls for ice-cold root beer all around."

"Ellen will get it. Where is Ellen? She drifts in and out like smoke."

Margie Young-Hunt stood up nervously. "This is a family party. I've got to go."

"But Margie, you're part of it. Where did Ellen go?"

"Mary, don't make me admit I'm a trifle on the pooped side."

"You have had it, dear. I keep forgetting. We had such a rest, you'll never know—and thanks to you."

"I loved it. I wouldn't have missed it."

She wanted to be away, and quickly. She took our thanks and Allen's thanks and fled.

Mary said quietly, "We didn't tell about the store."

"Let it ride. It would be robbing His Pink Eminence. It's his right. Where did Ellen go?"

"She went to bed," said Mary. "That's thoughtful, darling, and you're right. Allen, it's been a big day. Time you went to bed."

"I think I'll sit here a while," Allen said kindly.

"But you need rest."

"I'm resting."

Mary looked to me for help.

"These are the times that try men's souls. I can dust him, or we can let him have his victory even over us."

"He's just a little boy, really. He needs his rest."

"He needs several things, but rest isn't one of them."

"Everyone knows children need their rest."

"The things everyone knows are most likely to be wrong. Did you ever know a child to die of overwork? No—only adults. Children are too smart for that. They rest when they need rest."

"But it's after midnight."

"So it is, darling, and he will sleep until noon tomorrow. You and I will be up at six."

"You mean you'll go to bed and leave him sitting there?"

"He needs his revenge on us for having borne him."

"I don't know what you're talking about. What revenge?"

"I want to make a treaty with you because you're growing angry."

"So I am. You're being stupid."

"If within half an hour after we go to bed he does not creep to his nest, I will pay you forty-seven million, eight hundred and twenty-six dollars and eighty cents."

Well, I lost, and I must pay her. It was thirty-five minutes after we said good night that the stair creaked under our celebrity.

"I hate you when you're right," my Mary said. She had prepared herself to spend the night listening.

"I wasn't right, dear. I lost by five minutes. It's just that I remember."

She went to sleep then. She didn't hear Ellen creep down the stairs, but I did. I was watching my red dots moving in the dark. And I did not follow, for I heard the faint click of the brass key in the lock of the cabinet and I knew my daughter was charging her battery.

My red spots were active. They dashed about and ran away when I centered on them. Old Cap'n was avoiding me. He hadn't come clear since—well, since Easter. It's not like Aunt Harriet—"up in heben she be"—but I do know that when I am not friends with myself old Cap'n doesn't come clear. That's a kind of test of my personal relations with myself.

This night I forced him. I lay straight and rigid, far over on my side of the bed. I tightened every muscle of my body, particularly my neck and jaw, and doubled my fists on my belly and I forced him, bleak little eyes, white spiky mustache, and the forward-curving shoulders that proved he had once been a powerful man of his body and had used it. I even made him put on the blue cap with the short shiny visor and the gold H contrived of two anchors, the cap he hardly ever wore. The old boy was reluctant, but I made him come and I set him on the crumbling sea wall of Old Harbor near the Place. I sat him firmly on a heap of ballast stone and fixed his cupped hands on the head of the narwhal cane. That cane could have knocked over an elephant.

"I need something to hate. Being sorry and understanding—that's pap. I'm looking for a real hate to take the heat off."

Memory's a spawner. Start with one clear detailed print, and it springs into action and it can go forward or back like a film, once it starts.

Old Cap'n moved. He pointed with his cane. "Line the third rock beyond the breakwater with the tip of Porty Point at high water, then out that line half a cable-length she lies, what's left of her."

"How far is half a cable-length, sir?"

"How far? Why, half a hundred fathom, of course. She was anchored to swing and the tide flowing. Two bad-luck years. Half the oil casks empty. I was ashore when she caught fire, about midnight. When the oil fired she lit the town like midday and flames running on the oil slick as far as Osprey Point. Couldn't beach her for fear of burning the docks. She burned to the water in an hour. Her keel and false keel are down there now—and sound. Shelter Island virgin oak they were, and her knees too."

"How'd it start?"

"I never thought it started. I was ashore."

"Who'd want to burn her?"

"Why, her owners."

"You owned her."

"I was half-owner. I couldn't burn a ship. I'd like to see those timbers—like to see what shape they're in."

"You can go now, Cap'n, sir."

"That's slim fare to hate on."

"It's better than nothing. I'll get that keel up—soon as I'm rich. I'll do that for you—line the third rock with Porty Point at high water, fifty fathoms out." I was not sleeping. My fists and forearms were rigid and pressed against my stomach to prevent old Cap'n from fading, but when I let him go, sleep lapped over me.

When Pharaoh had a dream he called in the experts and they told him how it was and would be in the kingdom, and that was right because he was the kingdom. When some of us have a dream, we take it to an expert and he tells us how it is in the country of ourselves. I had a dream that didn't need an expert. Like most modern people, I don't believe in prophecy or magic and then spend half my time practicing it.

In the springtime Allen, feeling low and lonely, announced that he was an atheist to punish God and his parents. I told him not to go out on a limb or he wouldn't have leeway to not walk under ladders and cancel black cats with spit and thumb and wish on the new moon.

People who are most afraid of their dreams convince themselves they don't dream at all. I can explain my dream easily enough, but that doesn't make it any less frightening.

An order came through from Danny, I don't know how. He was going away by aircraft and he wanted certain things of me, things I had to make myself. He wanted a cap for Mary. It had to be of dark brown sueded lambskin with the wool on the inside. It had to be of skin like an old pair of sheep-lined slippers I have, had to be like a baseball cap with a long beak. Also he wanted a wind gauge—not the little whirling metal cups but handmade from the thin, stiff cardboard of government postcards, mounted on strips of bamboo. And he called me to meet him before he took off. I carried old Cap'n's narwhal stick with me. It stands in the elephant's-foot umbrella stand in our hall.

When we got the elephant's foot as a present I looked at the big ivory-colored toenails, I told my children, "The first kid who puts nail polish on those toenails gets clobbered—understand?" They obeyed me, so I had to paint them myself—bright red fingernail enamel from Mary's harem table.

I went to meet Danny in Marullo's Pontiac and the airport was the New Baytown post office. When I parked I laid the twisted stick on the back seat and two mean-looking cops in a squad car drove up and said, "Not on the seat."

"Is it against the law?"

"So you want to be a wise guy!"

"No. I was just asking."

"Well, don't put it on the seat."

Danny was in the back of the post office, sorting packages. He was wearing the lambskin cap and whirling the cardboard wind gauge. His face was thin and his lips very chapped but his hands were swollen like hot-water bottles, as though they had been wasp-stung.

He stood up to shake hands and my right hand was folded in the warm, rubbery mass. He put something in my hand, something small and heavy and cool, about the size of a key but not a key—a shape, a metal thing that felt sharp-edged and polished. I don't know what it was because I didn't look at it, I only felt it. I leaned near and kissed him on the mouth and with my lips felt his dry lips all chapped and rough. I awakened then, shaken and cold. The dawn had come. I could see the lake but not the cow standing in it, and I could still feel the chapped dry lips. I got up instantly because I didn't want to lie there thinking about it. I didn't make coffee but I went to the elephant's foot and saw that the wicked club called a cane was still there.

It was the throbbing time of dawn, and hot and humid, for the morning wind had not started to blow. The street was gray and silver and the sidewalk greasy with the deposit of humanity. The Foremaster coffee shop wasn't open, but I didn't want coffee anyway. I went through the alley and opened my back door—looked in the front and saw the leather hatbox behind the counter. I opened a coffee can, poured the coffee in the garbage pail. Then I punched two holes in a can of condensed milk and squirted it into the coffee can, propped the back door open, and put the can in the entrance. The cat was in the alley all right, but he wouldn't come to the milk until I went into the front of the store. From there I could see him, gray cat in gray alley, lapping the milk. When he raised his head he was mustached with milk. He sat down and wiped his mouth and licked his pads.

I opened the hatbox and took out the Saturday receipts, all listed and held together with paper clips. From the brown bank envelope I removed thirty one-hundred-dollar bills and replaced the other twenty of them. This three thousand dollars would be my margin of safety until the store's economy could balance. Mary's other two thousand would go back to her account and, as soon as I could do it safely, I would replace the three thousand. The thirty bills I put in my new wallet, which made it very fat in my hip pocket. Then I brought cases and cartons from the storeroom, ripped and tore them open, and began to replenish my exhausted shelves, while on a strip of wrapping paper I listed the goods that had to be reordered. Cartons and boxes I piled in the alley for the collection truck, and I refilled the coffee can with milk but the cat did not return. Either he had had enough or he took pleasure only in what he could steal.

It must be that there are years unlike other years, as different in climate and direction and mood as one day can be from another day. This year of 1960 was a year of change, a year when secret fears come into the open, when discontent stops being dormant and changes gradually to anger. It wasn't only in me or in New Baytown. Presidential nominations would be coming up soon and in the air the discontent was changing to anger and with the excitement anger brings. And it wasn't only the nation; the whole world stirred with restlessness and uneasiness as discontent moved to anger and anger tried to find an outlet in action, any action so long as it was violent—Africa, Cuba, South America, Europe, Asia, the Near East, all restless as horses at the barrier.

I knew that Tuesday, July fifth, was going to be a day larger than other days. I even think I knew what things would happen before they happened, but since they did I will never be sure whether I really knew.

I think I knew that the seventeen-jewel, shockproof Mr. Baker, who ticked the hours, would come rattling at my front door an hour before the bank opening time. He did before I had opened for business. I let him in and closed the doors after him.

"What an awful thing," he said. "I was out of touch. I came back as soon as I heard."

"Which awful thing, sir?"

"Why, the scandal! Those men are my friends, my old friends. I've got to do something."

"They won't even be questioned before election—just charged."

"I know. Couldn't we issue a statement of our belief in their innocence? Even a paid advertisement if necessary."

"In what, sir? The *Bay Harbor Messenger* doesn't come out until Thursday."

"Well, something should be done."

"I know."

It was so formal. He must have known I knew. And yet he met my eyes and he seemed genuinely worried.

"The crazy fringe will ruin town elections unless we do something. We've got to offer new candidates. We don't have any choice. It's a terrible thing to do to old friends, but they'd be the first to know we can't let the egghead fringe get in."

"Why don't you talk to them?"

"They're bruised and mad. They haven't had time to think it out. Did Marullo come?"

"He sent a friend. I bought the store for three thousand."

"That's good. You got a bargain. Get the papers?"

"Yes."

"Well, if he jumps, the bills are listed."

"He won't jump. He wants to go. He's tired."

"I never trusted him. Never knew what he had his fingers in."

"Was he a crook, sir?"

"He was tricky, played both sides of the street. He's worth a lot if he can dispose of his property, but three thousand—that's a giveaway."

"He liked me."

"He must have. Who did he send, the Mafia?"

"A government man. You see, Marullo trusted me."

Mr. Baker clasped his brow, and that was out of character. "Why didn't I think of it? You're the man. Good family, reliable, property-owner, businessman, respected. You don't have an enemy in town. Of course you're the man."

"The man?"

"For town manager."

"I've only been a businessman since Saturday."

"You know what I mean. Around you we could get respectable new faces. Why, it's the perfect way."

"From grocery clerk to town manager?"

"Nobody ever thought of a Hawley as a grocery clerk."

"I did. Mary did."

"But you aren't. We can announce it today before that crazy fringe gets set."

"I'll have to consider it from keelson to skys'l."

"There's no time."

"Who had you thought of before?"

"Before what?"

"Before the council burned. I'll talk to you later. Saturday was a big day. I could have sold the scales."

"You can make a nice thing of this store, Ethan. I advise you to build it up and sell it. You're going to be too big to wait on customers. Is there any word at all about Danny?"

"Not yet. Not so far."

"You shouldn't have given him money."

"Perhaps not. I thought I was doing a good deed."

"Of course you did. Of course you did."

"Mr. Baker, sir—what happened to the *Belle-Adair?*"

"What happened? Why, she burned."

"In the harbor—how did it start, sir?"

"Funny time to ask. I only know what I heard. I was too little even to remember. Those old ships got oil-soaked. I suppose some sailor dropped a match. Your grandfather was master. I think he was ashore. Just came in."

"Bad voyage."

"That's what I heard."

"Any trouble collecting the insurance?"

"Well, they always send investigators. No, as I remember, it took some time but we collected, Hawleys and Bakers."

"My grandfather thought she was set afire."

"Why, for heaven's sake?"

"To get the money. The whaling industry was gone."

"I never heard that he said that."

"You never heard it?"

"Ethan—what are you getting at? Why are you bringing up something that happened so long ago?"

"It's a horrible thing to burn a ship. It's a murder. I'm going to bring up her keel someday."

"Her keel?"

"I know just where she lies. Half a cable offshore."

"Why would you do that?"

"I'd like to see if the oak is sound. It was Shelter Island virgin oak. She's not all dead if her keel's alive. You'd better go, if you're going to bless the opening of the safe. And I've got to open up."

Then his balance wheel started and he ticked off to the bank.

I think now I had expected Biggers too. Poor fellow must spend most of his time watching doorways. And he must have been waiting somewhere in peeking range for Mr. Baker to leave.

"I hope you're not going to jump down my throat."

"Why should I?"

"I can understand why you were huffy. I guess I wasn't very—diplomatic."

"Maybe that was it."

"Have you chewed on my proposition?"

"Yes."

"What do you think?"

"I think six per cent would be better."

"I don't know whether B. B. will go for it."

"It's up to them."

"They might go five and a half."

"And you might go the other half."

"Jesus, man. I thought you were being a country boy. You cut deep."

"Take it or leave it."

"Well, what kind of volume would it be?"

"There's a partial list over by the cash register."

He studied the strip of wrapping paper. "Looks like I'm hooked. And, brother, I'm bleeding. Can I get the full order today?"

"Tomorrow would be better and bigger."

"You mean you'll switch the whole account?"

"If you play nice."

"Brother, you must have your boss by the throat. Can you get away with it?"

"Just have to see."

"Well, maybe I could get a crack at the drummer's friend. Brother, you must be cold as a herring. I tell you that dame's a dish."

"Friend of my wife."

"Oh! Yeah! I see how it could be. Too close to home is bad news. You're smart. If I didn't know it before, I know it now. Six per cent. Jesus! Tomorrow in the morning."

"Maybe late this afternoon if I get time."

"Make it tomorrow morning."

On Saturday business came in bursts. This Tuesday the whole tempo had changed. People took time. They wanted to talk about the scandal, saying it was bad, awful, sad, disgraceful, but enjoying it too. We haven't had a scandal for a long time. Nobody mentioned the Democratic National Convention coming up in Los Angeles—not even once. Of course New Baytown is a Republican town, but I think mostly they were interested in what was close to home. We knew the men whose graves we danced on.

Chief Stonewall Jackson came in during the noon hour and he looked tired and sad.

I put the can of oil on the counter and fished out the old pistol with a piece of wire.

"Here's the evidence, Chief. Take it away, will you? It makes me nervous."

"Well, wipe it off, will you? Look at that! That's what they used to call a two-dollar pistol—top-latch Iver Johnson. You got anybody that can mind the store?"

"No, I haven't."

"Where's Marullo?"

"He's out of town."

"Guess maybe you might have to close up for a while."

"What is this, Chief?"

"Well, Charley Pryor's boy ran away from home this morning. Got a cold drink there somewhere?"

"Sure. Orange, cream, lemon, Coke?"

"Give me a Seven-Up. Charley's a funny kind of guy. His boy Tom is eight. He figures the world's against him and he's going to run away to be a pirate. Anybody else would of give him a crack acrost the behind, but not Charley. Aren't you going to open this?"

"Sorry. There you are. What's Charley got to do with me? I like him, of course."

"Well, Charley don't do things like other people. He figures the best way to cure Tom is to help him. So after breakfast they get a bedroll together and a big lunch. Tom wants to take a Jap sword for self-protection, but it drags so he settles for a bayonet. Charley loads him in the car and drives him out of town to give him a good start. He let him out over near Taylor Meadow—you know, the old Taylor place. That's about nine o'clock this morning. Charley watched the kid a while. First thing he did was sit down and eat six sandwiches and two hard-boiled eggs. And then he went on acrost the meadow with his brave little bindle and his bayonet and Charley drove home."

Here it came. I knew it, I knew it. It was almost a relief to get it over.

" 'Bout eleven he come slobbering out on the road and hooked a ride home."

"I think I can guess, Stoney—is it Danny?"

" 'Fraid so. Down in the cellar hole of the old house. Case of whisky, only two empties, and a bottle of sleeping pills. Sorry I got to ask you this, Eth. Been there a long time and something got at him, at his face. Cats, maybe. You remember any scars or marks on him?"

"I don't want to look at him, Chief."

"Well, who does? How about scars?"

"I remember a barb-wire cut above the knee on his left leg, and—and"—I rolled up my sleeve—"a heart just like this tattooed. We did it together when we were kids. Cut in with a razor blade and rubbed ink in. It's still pretty clear, see?"

"Well—that may do it. Anything else?"

"Yes—big scar under his left arm, piece of the rib cut

out. He had pleural pneumonia before the new drugs and they put in a drain."

"Well, of course if there was a rib cut, that'll do it. I won't even have to go back myself. Let the coroner get off his ass. You'll have to swear to those marks if it's him."

"Okay. But don't make me look at him, Stoney. He was —you know—he was my friend."

"Sure, Eth. Say is there anything in what I hear about you running for town manager?"

"It's news to me. Chief—could you stay here two minutes—"

"I got to go."

"Just two minutes while I run across the street and get a drink?"

"Oh! Sure! I get it. Sure—go ahead. I got to get along with the new town manager."

I got the drink and a pint too to bring back with me. When Stoney had gone, I printed BACK AT TWO on a card, closed the doors, and drew the shades.

I sat on the leather hatbox behind the counter in my store, sat in the dim green darkness of my store.

CHAPTER XX

At ten minutes to three I went out the back door and around the corner to the front of the bank. Morph in his bronze cage drew in the sheaf of money and checks, the brown envelope, and the deposit slips. He spread the little bank books with a Y of fingers and wrote small angled numbers with a steel pen that whispered on the paper. As he pushed the books out to me he looked up with veiled and cautious eyes.

"I'm not going to talk about it, Ethan. I know he was your friend."

"Thanks."

"If you slip out quick you might avoid the Brain."

But I didn't. For all I know Morph may have buzzed him. The frosted-glass door of the office swung open and Mr. Baker, neat and spare and gray, said quietly, "Can you spare a moment, Ethan?"

No use to put it off. I walked into his frosty den and he closed the door so softly that I did not hear the latch click. His desk was topped with plate glass, under which were lists of typed numbers. Two customers' chairs in echelon stood by his tall chair like twin suckling calves. They were comfortable but lower than the desk chair. When I sat down I had to look up at Mr. Baker and that put me in the position of supplication.

"Sad thing."

"Yes."

"I don't think you ought to take all the blame. Probably would have happened anyway."

"Probably."

"I'm sure you thought you were doing the right thing."

"I thought he had a chance."

"Of course you did."

My hatred was rising in my throat like a yellow taste, more sickening than furious.

"Apart from the human tragedy and waste, it raises a difficulty. Do you know whether he had relatives?"

"I don't think so."

"Anybody with money has relatives."

"He had no money."

"He had Taylor Meadow, free and clear."

"Did he? Well, a meadow and a cellar hole—"

"Ethan, I told you we planned an airfield to service the whole district. The meadow is level. If we can't use it, it will cost millions to bulldoze runways in the hills. And now, even if he has no heirs, it will have to go through the courts. Take months."

"I see."

His ire fissured. "I wonder if you do see! With your good intentions you've thrown the thing sky high. Sometimes I think a do-gooder is the most dangerous thing in the world."

"Perhaps you're right. I ought to get back to the store."

"It's your store."

"It is, isn't it? I can't get used to it. I forget."

"Yes, you forget. The money you gave him was Mary's money. She'll never see it now. You threw it away."

"Danny was fond of my Mary. He knew it was her money."

"Fat lot of good that will do her."

"I thought he was making a joke. He gave me these." I pulled the two pieces of ruled paper from my inside pocket, where I had put them, knowing I would have to draw them out like this.

Mr. Baker straightened them on his glass-topped desk. As he read them a muscle beside his right ear twitched so that his ear bobbed. His eyes went back over them, this time looking for a hole.

When the son of a bitch looked at me there was fear in

him. He saw someone he hadn't known existed. It took him a moment to adjust to the stranger, but he was good. He adjusted.

"What is your asking price?"

"Fifty-one per cent."

"Of what?"

"Of the corporation or partnership or whatever."

"That's ridiculous."

"You want an airfield. I have the only one available."

He wiped his glasses carefully on a piece of pocket Kleenex, then put them on. But he didn't look at me. He looked a circle all around me and left me out. Finally he asked, "Did you know what you were doing, Ethan?"

"Yes."

"Do you feel good about it?"

"I guess I feel as the man felt who took him a bottle of whisky and tried to get him to sign a paper."

"Did he tell you that?"

"Yes."

"He was a liar."

"He told me he was. He warned me he was. Maybe there's some trick in these papers." I swept them gently from in front of him and folded the two soiled pencil-written sheets.

"There's a trick all right, Ethan. Those documents are without a flaw, dated, witnessed, clear. Maybe he hated you. Maybe his trick was the disintegration of a man."

"Mr. Baker, no one in my family ever burned a ship."

"We'll talk, Ethan, we'll do business. We'll make money. A little town will spring up on the hills around the meadow. I guess you'll have to be town manager now."

"I can't, sir. That would constitute a conflict of interest. Some pretty sad men are finding that out right now."

He sighed—a cautious sigh as though he feared to awaken something in his throat.

I stood up and rested my hand on the curved and padded leather back of the supplicant's chair. "You'll feel better, sir, when you have got used to the fact that I am not a pleasant fool."

"Why couldn't you have taken me into your confidence?"

"An accomplice is dangerous."

"Then you do feel you have committed a crime."

"No. A crime is something someone else commits. I've got to open the store, even if it is my own store."

My hand was on the doorknob when he asked quietly, "Who turned Marullo in?"

"I think you did, sir." He leaped to his feet, but I closed the door after me and went back to my store.

CHAPTER XXI

No ONE in the world can rise to a party or a plateau of celebration like my Mary. It isn't what she contributes but what she receives that makes her glow like a jewel. Her eyes shine, her smiling mouth underlines, her quick laughter builds strength into a sickly joke. With Mary in the doorway of a party everyone feels more attractive and clever than he was, and so he actually becomes. Beyond this Mary does not and need not contribute.

The whole Hawley house glowed with celebration when I came home. Bright-colored plastic flags were strung in canopies from center light to picture molding, and lines of colored plastic bannerets hung from the banisters.

"You wouldn't believe it," Mary cried. "Ellen got them from the Esso Service Station. George Sandow loaned them."

"What's it about?"

"About everything. It's a glory thing."

I don't know whether she had heard of Danny Taylor or had heard and retired him. Certainly I didn't invite him to the feast, but he paced about outside. I knew I would have to go out to meet him later but I did not ask him in.

"You'd think it was Ellen had won honorable mention," Mary said. "She's even prouder than if *she* was the celebrity. Look at the cake she baked." It was a tall white cake with HERO written on its top in red, green, yellow, and blue letters. "We're having roast chicken *and* dressing *and* giblet gravy *and* mashed potatoes, even if it is summer."

"Good, darling, good. And where's the young celebrity?"

"Well, it's changed him too. He's taking a bath and changing for dinner."

"It's a day of portent, sibyl. Somewhere you will find a mule has foaled and a new comet come into the sky. A bath before dinner. Imagine!"

"I thought you might like to change too. I have a bottle of wine and I thought maybe a speech or a toast or something like that, even if it's just the family." She fairly flooded the house with party. I found myself rushing up the stairs to bathe and be a part of it.

Passing Allen's door, I knocked, heard a grunt, and went in.

He was standing in front of his mirror, holding a hand-glass so he could see his profile. With some dark stuff, maybe Mary's mascara, he had painted on a narrow black mustache, had darkened his brows and raised the outer ends to satanic tips. He was smiling a world-wise, cynical charm into the mirror when I entered. And he was wearing my blue polka-dot bow tie. He did not seem embarrassed at being caught.

"Rehearsing for a turn," he said and put the hand-mirror down.

"Son, in all the excitement I don't think I've told you how proud I am."

"It's—well, it's only a start."

"Frankly, I didn't think you were even as good a writer as the President. I'm as much surprised as I am pleased. When are you going to read your essay to the world?"

"Sunday, four-thirty *and* a national hookup. I have to go into New York. Special plane flying me."

"Are you well rehearsed?"

"Oh, I'll do all right. It's just a start."

"Well, it's more like a jump to be one of five in the whole country."

"National hookup," he said. He began to remove the mustache with a cotton pad and I saw with amazement that he had a make-up kit, eye-shadow, grease paint, cold cream.

"Everything's happened at once to all of us. Do you know I've bought the store?"

"Yeah! I heard."

"Well, when the bunting and the tinsel come down, I'm going to need your help."

"How do you mean?"

"I told you before, to help me in the store."

"I couldn't do that," he said, and he inspected his teeth in the hand-mirror.

"You couldn't do what?"

"I've got a couple of guest shots and then 'What's My Line?' and 'Mystery Guest.' Then there's a new quiz coming up called Teen Twisters. I might even get to M.C. that. So you see I won't have time." He sprayed something sticky on his hair from a pressure can.

"So your career is all set, is it?"

"Like I told you, it's just a start."

"I'll not let loose the dogs of war tonight. We'll discuss it later."

"There's a guy from N.B.C. been trying to get you on the phone. Maybe it's a contract because like I'm not of age."

"Have you thought of school, my son?"

"Who needs it if you got a contract?"

I got out fast and closed the door and in my bathroom I ran the water cold and iced my skin and let the cold penetrate deep to control my shaking rage. And when I emerged clean and shining and smelling of Mary's perfume, my control was back. In the few moments before dinner, Ellen sat on the arm of my chair and then rolled over in my lap and put her arms around me.

"I do love you," she said. "Isn't it exciting? And isn't Allen wonderful? It's like he's born to it." And this was the girl I had thought very selfish and a little mean.

Just before the cake I toasted the young hero and wished him luck and I finished, " 'Now is the winter of our discontent made glorious summer by this son of York.' "

"That's Shakespeare," Ellen said.

"Yes, muggins, but what play, who says it, and where?"

"I wouldn't know," said Allen. "That's for squares."

I helped carry the dishes to the kitchen. Mary still carried her glow. "Don't fret," she said. "He'll find his line. He'll be all right. Please be patient with him."

"I will, my holy quail."

"There was a man calling from New York. I guess about Allen. Isn't it exciting, their sending a plane for him? I can't get used to you owning the store. I know—it's all over town you're going to be town manager."

"I'm not."

"Well, I heard it a dozen times."

"I have a business deal that makes it impossible. I have to go out for a while, my darling. I have a meeting."

"Maybe I'll get to wish you were back a clerk. You were home nights then. What if the man calls back?"

"He can wait."

"He didn't want to. Will you be late?"

"Can't tell. Depends on how it goes."

"Wasn't it sad about Danny Taylor? Take a raincoat."

"Sure was."

In the hall I put on my hat and on an impulse picked old Cap'n's narwhal cane from the elephant foot. Ellen materialized beside me.

"Can I go with you?"

"Not tonight."

"I do love you."

I stared deep into my daughter for a moment. "I love you too," I said. "I'll bring you jewels—any favorites?"

She giggled. "You going to carry a cane?"

"For self-protection." I held the spiraled ivory at parry, like a broadsword.

"You going to be gone long?"

"Not long."

"Why do you take the cane?"

"Pure decoration, a boast, a threat, a fear, a vestigial need to bear arms."

"I'll wait up for you. Can I hold the pink thing?"

"Oh, no you won't, my little dung-flower. Pink thing? You mean the talisman? Sure you may."

"What's a talisman?"

"Look it up in the dictionary. Know how to spell it?"

"T-a-l-e-s-m-a-n."

"No, t-a-l-*i*-s-m-a-n."

"Why don't you tell me?"

"You'll know it better if you look it up."

She locked her arms around me and squeezed and as quickly let me go.

The night closed thick and damp about me, humid air about the consistency of chicken broth. The street lights hiding among the fat leaves of Elm Street sprouted damp, hairy halos of moisture.

A man with a job sees so little of the normal daylight world. No wonder he must get his news and his attitudes from his wife. She knows what happened and who said what about it, but it is strained through her womanness, wherefore most working men see the daylight world through women's eyes. But in the night, when his store or his job is closed, then is a man's world risen—for a time.

The twisted staff of narwhal ivory felt good in my hand, its heavy silver knob polished by old Cap'n's palm.

Once long ago when I lived in a daylight world, the world being too much with me, I would have gone to grass. Face downward and very close to the green stems, I became one with ants and aphids and sow bugs, no longer a colossus. And in a ferocious jungle of the grass I found the distraction that meant peace.

Now in the night I wanted Old Harbor and the Place, where an inevitable world of cycles of life and time and of tide could smooth my raggedness.

I walked quickly to the High Street, and only glanced across at my green-curtained store as I passed the Foremaster. In front of the fire station fat Willie sat in the police car, red of face and sweating like a pig.

"You on the prowl again, Eth?"

"Yep."

"Terrible sad about Danny Taylor. Nice fella."

"Terrible," I said and hurried on.

A few cars cruised about, building a breeze, but there were no strollers. No one risked the sweat of walking.

I turned at the monument and walked toward Old Harbor and saw the anchor lights of a few yachts and offshore fishing craft. Then I saw a figure turn out of Porlock Street and come toward me and I knew by walk and posture it was Margie Young-Hunt.

She stopped in front of me, gave me no chance of passing. Some women can look cool on a hot night. Perhaps it was the breezy movement of her cotton skirt.

She said, "I guess you're looking for me." She replaced a strand of hair that wasn't out of place.

"Why do you say that?"

She turned and took my arm and with her fingers urged me to walk on. "That's the kind I get. I was in the Foremaster. I saw you go by and I thought you might be looking for me, so I whipped around the block and intercepted you."

"How'd you know which way I would turn?"

"I don't know. I knew. Listen to the cicadas—that's more hot weather and no wind. Don't worry, Ethan, we'll be out of the light in a moment. You can come to my place if you want. I'll give you a drink—a tall cold drink, from a tall hot woman."

I let her fingers guide me into the shadows of a grove of outgrown privet. Some kind of yellow blossoms near the ground burned the darkness.

"This is my house—a garage with a pleasure dome over it."

"What makes you think I was looking for you?"

"Me or someone like me. Ever see a bullfight, Ethan?"

"Once at Arles just after the war."

"My second husband used to take me. He loved them. I think bullfights are for men who aren't very brave and wish they were. If you saw one you'll know what I mean. Remember after all the cape work when the bull tries to kill something that isn't there?"

"Yes."

"Remember how he gets confused and uneasy, sometimes just stands and looks for an answer? Well, then they have to give him a horse or his heart will break. He has to get his horns into something solid or his spirit dies. Well, I'm that horse. And that's the kind of men I get, confused and puzzled. If they can get a horn into me, that's a little triumph. Then they can go back to *muleta* and *espada*."

"Margie!"

"Just a moment. I'm trying to find my key. Smell the honeysuckle!"

"But I've just had a triumph."

"You have? Hooked a cape—trampled it?"

"How do you know?"

"I just know when a man is looking for me, or some other Margie. Watch the stairs, they're narrow. Don't hit your head at the top. Now, here's the switch—you see? A pleasure dome, soft lights, smell of musk—down to a sunless sea!"

"I guess you're a witch all right."

"You know goddam well I am. A poor, pitiful small-town witch. Sit there, near the window. I'll turn on the fake breeze. I'm going to what they call 'slip into something comfortable,' then I'll get you a tall cool skull-buster."

"Where'd you hear that word?"

"You know where I heard it."

"Did you know him well?"

"Part of him. The part of a man a woman can know. Sometimes that's the best part, but not often. It was with Danny. He trusted me."

The room was a memory album of other rooms, bits and pieces of other lives like footnotes. The fan at the window made a small whispering roar.

She came back soon in long, loose, billowing blue and brought a cloud of scent. When I breathed it in she said, "Don't worry. It's a cologne Mary has never smelled on me. Here's a drink—gin and tonic. I rubbed the glass with tonic. It's gin, just gin. If you rattle the ice, you'll think it's cool."

I drank it down like beer and felt its dry heat reach out over my shoulders and down my arms so that my skin shimmered.

"I guess you needed that," she said.

"I guess so."

"I'll make a brave bull of you—enough resistance so you'll think you have a triumph. That's what a bull needs."

I stared at my hands, crisscrossed with scratches and tiny cuts from opening boxes, and my nails, not too clean.

She took the ivory stick from the couch where I had dropped it. "I hope you don't need this for your drooping passion."

"Are you my enemy, now?"

"Me, New Baytown's playmate, your enemy?"

I was silent so long that I could feel her growing restless. "Take your time," she said. "You've got all your life to answer. I'll get you a drink."

I took the full glass from her and my lips and mouth were so dry I had to sip from it before I could speak, and when I did my throat wore a husk.

"What do you want?"

"I might have settled for love."

"From a man who loves his wife?"

"Mary? You don't even know her."

"I know she's tender and sweet and kind of helpless."

"Helpless? She's tough as a boot. She'll go right on long after you've rattled your engine to pieces. She's like a gull that uses the wind to stay aloft and never beats a wing."

"That's not true."

"Comes a big trouble, she'll breeze through while you burn up."

"What do you want?"

"Aren't you going to make a pass? Aren't you going to beat out your hatred with your hips on good old Margie?"

I set my half-emptied glass down on a side table, and quick as a snake she lifted it and put an ash tray under it, and dried the ring of moisture with her hand.

"Margie—I want to know about you."

"No kidding. You want to know what I thought of your performance."

"I can't figure what you want until I know who you are."

"I believe the man means it—the dollar tour. Through Margie Young-Hunt with gun and camera. I was a good little kid, a smart little kid and a medium lousy dancer. Met what they call an older man and married him. He didn't love me—he was in love with me. That's on a silver platter for a good smart little kid. I didn't like to dance much and I sure as hell didn't like to work. When I dumped him he was so mixed up he didn't even put a remarriage clause in the settlement. Married another guy and led a big world whirl that killed him. For twenty years that check has zeroed in on the first of every month. For twenty years I haven't done a lick of work, except pick up a few presents from admirers. Doesn't seem like twenty years, but it is. I'm not a good little kid any more."

She went to her little kitchen and brought three ice cubes in her hand, dumped them into her glass, and sloshed gin over them. The muttering fan brought in the smell of sea flats exposed by the dropping tide. She said softly, "You're going to make a lot of money, Ethan."

"You know about the deal?"

"Some of the noblest Romans of them all are creepers."

"Go on."

She made a sweeping gesture with her hand and her glass went flying; the ice cubes bounced back from the wall like dice.

"Lover boy had a stroke last week. When he cools, the checks stop. I'm old and lazy and I'm scared. I set you up as a backlog, but I don't trust you. You might break the rules. You might turn honest. I tell you I'm scared."

I stood up and found my legs were heavy, not wavery— just heavy and remote.

"What have you got to work with?"

"Marullo was my friend too."

"I see."

"Don't you want to go to bed with me? I'm good. That's what they tell me."

"I don't hate you."

"That's why I don't trust you."

"We'll try to work something out. I hate Baker. Maybe you can clip him."

"What language. You're not working on your drink."

"Drink's for happy times with me."

"Does Baker know what you did to Danny?"

"Yes."

"How'd he take it?"

"All right. But I wouldn't like to turn my back."

"Alfio should have turned his back to you."

"What do you mean by that?"

"Only what I guess. But I'd make book on my guess. Don't worry, I won't tell him. Marullo is my friend."

"I think I understand; you're building up a hate so you can use the sword. Margie, you've got a rubber sword."

"Think I don't know it, Eth? But I've got my money on a hunch."

"Do you want to tell me?"

"Might as well. I'm betting ten generations of Hawleys are going to kick your ass around the block, and when they leave off you'll have your own wet rope and salt to rub in the wounds."

"If that were so—where does it leave you?"

"You're going to need a friend to talk to and I'm the only person in the world who fills the bill. A secret's a terribly lonesome thing, Ethan. And it won't cost you much, maybe only a small percentage."

"I think I'll go now."

"Drink your drink."

"I don't want it."

"Don't bump your head going downstairs, Ethan."

I was halfway down when she followed me. "Did you mean to leave your stick?"

"Lord, no."

"Here it is. I thought it might be a kind of—sacrifice."

It was raining and that makes honeysuckle smell sweet in the night. My legs were so wobbly that I really needed the narwhal stick.

Fat Willie had a roll of paper towels on the seat beside him to mop the sweat from his head.

"I'll give you odds I know who she is."

"You'd win."

"Say, Eth, there's been a guy looking for you—guy in a big Chrysler, with a chauffeur."

"What'd he want?"

"I don't know. Wanted to know if I seen you. I didn't give a peep."

"You'll get a Christmas present, Willie."

"Say, Eth, what's the matter with your feet?"

"Been playing poker. They went to sleep."

"Yeah! they'll do that. If I see the guy, shall I tell him you've went home?"

"Tell him to come to the store tomorrow."

"Chrysler Imperial. Big son of a bitch, long as a freight car."

Joey-boy was standing on the sidewalk in front of the Foremaster, looking limp and humid.

"Thought you were going into New York for a cold bottle."

"Too hot. Couldn't put my heart in it. Come in and have a drink, Ethan. I'm feeling low."

"Too hot for a drink, Morph."

"Even a beer?"

"Beer heats me up."

"Story of my life. When the cards are down—no place to go. Nobody to talk to."

"You should get married."

"That's nobody to talk to in spades."

"Maybe you're right."

"Damn right I am. There's nobody as lonely as an all-married man."

"How do you know?"

"I see 'em. I'm looking at one. Guess I'll get a bag of cold beer and see if Margie Young-Hunt will play. She don't keep hours."

"I don't think she's in town, Morph. She told my wife—at least I think she did—that she was going up to Maine till the heat is over."

"Goddam her. Well—her loss is the barkeep's gain. I'll tell him the sad episodes of a misspent life. He don't listen either. So long, Eth. Walk with God! That's what they say in Mexico."

The narwhal stick tapped on the pavement and punctuated my wondering about why I told Joey that. She wouldn't talk. That would spoil her game. She had to keep the pin in her hand grenade. I don't know why.

I could see the Chrysler standing at the curb by the old Hawley house when I turned into Elm Street from the High, but it was more like a hearse than a freight car, black but not gleaming by reason of the droplets of rain and the greasy splash that rises from the highways. It carried frosted parking lights.

It must have been very late. No lights shone from the sleeping houses on Elm Street. I was wet and I must somewhere have stepped in a puddle. My shoes made a juicy squidging sound as I walked.

I saw a man in a chauffeur's cap through the musty windshield. I stopped beside the monster car and rapped with my knuckles on the glass and the window slid down with an electric whine. I felt the unnatural climate of air-conditioning on my face.

"I'm Ethan Hawley. Are you looking for me?" I saw teeth in the dimness—gleaming teeth picked out by our street light.

The door sprang open of itself and a lean, well-tailored man stepped out. "I'm Dunscombe, Brock and Schwin, television branch. I have to talk to you." He looked toward the driver. "Not here. Can we go inside?"

"I guess so. I think everyone's asleep. If you talk quietly . . ."

He followed me up our walk of flagstones set in the spongy lawn. The night light was burning in the hall. As we went in I put the narwhal stick in the elephant's foot.

I turned on the reading light over my big sprung-bottomed chair.

The house was quiet, but it seemed to me the wrong kind of quiet—a nervous quiet. I glanced up the stairwell at the bedroom doors above.

"Must be important to come this late."

"It is."

I could see him now. His teeth were his ambassadors, unhelped by his weary but wary eyes.

"We want to keep this private. It's been a bad year, as

you well know. The bottom fell out with the quiz scandals and then the payola fuss and the Congressional committees. We have to watch everything. It's a dangerous time."

"I wish you'd tell me what you want."

"You've read your boy's I Love America essay?"

"No, I haven't. He wanted to surprise me."

"He has. I don't know why we didn't catch it, but we didn't." He held out a folded blue cover to me. "Read the underlining."

I sank into my chair and opened it. It was either printed or typed by one of those new machines that looks like type, but it was marred with harsh black pencil lines down both margins.

I LOVE AMERICA

by
ETHAN ALLEN HAWLEY II

"What is an individual man? An atom, almost invisible without a magnifying glass—a mere speck upon the surface of the universe; not a second in time compared to immeasurable, never-beginning and never-ending eternity, a drop of water in the great deep which evaporates and is borne off by the winds, a grain of sand, which is soon gathered to the dust from which it sprung. Shall a being so small, so petty, so fleeting, so evanescent oppose itself to the onward march of a great nation which is to subsist for ages and ages to come, oppose itself to that long line of posterity which springing from our loins will endure during the existence of the world? Let us look to our country, elevate ourselves to the dignity of pure and disinterested patriots, and save our country from all impending dangers. What are we—what is any man—worth who is not ready and willing to sacrifice himself for his country?"

I riffled through the pages and saw the black marks everywhere.

"Do you recognize it?"

"No. It sounds familiar—sounds like maybe somewhere in the last century."

"It is. It's Henry Clay, delivered in 1850."

"And the rest? All Clay?"

"No—bits and pieces, some Daniel Webster, some Jefferson, and, God help me, a swatch from Lincoln's Second Inaugural. I don't know how that got past. I guess because there were thousands of them. Thank Christ we caught it in time—after all the quiz troubles and Van Doren and all."

"It doesn't sound like the prose style of a boy."

"I don't know how it happened. And it might have gone through if we hadn't got the postcard."

"Postcard?"

"Picture postcard, picture of the Empire State Building."

"Who sent it?"

"Anonymous."

"Where was it mailed from?"

"New York."

"Let me see it."

"It's under lock and key in case there's any trouble. You don't want to make trouble, do you?"

"What is it you want?"

"I want you to forget the whole thing. We'll just drop the whole thing and forget it—if you will."

"It's not a thing easy to forget."

"Hell, I mean just keep your lip buttoned—don't give us any trouble. It's been a bad year. Election year anybody will dig up anything."

I closed the rich blue covers and handed it back to him. "I won't give you any trouble."

His teeth showed like matched pearls. "I knew it. I told them. I looked you up. You have a good record—good family."

"Will you go away now?"

"You've got to know I understand how you feel."

"Thank you. And I know how you feel. What you can cover up doesn't exist."

"I don't want to go away leaving you angry. Public relations is my line. We could work something out. Scholarship or like that—something dignified."

"Has sin gone on strike for a wage raise? No, just go away now—please!"

"We'll work something out."

"I'm sure you will."

I let him out and sat down again and turned out the light and sat listening to my house. It thudded like a heart, and maybe it was my heart and a rustling old house. I thought to go to the cabinet and take the talisman in my hand—had stood up to get it.

I heard a crunching sound and a whinny like a frightened colt, and quick steps in the hall and silence. My shoes squidged on the stairs. I went in to Ellen's room and switched on the light. She was balled up under a sheet, her head under her pillow. When I tried to lift the pillow she clung to it and I had to yank it away. A line of blood ran from the corner of her mouth.

"I slipped in the bathroom."

"I see. Are you badly hurt?"

"I don't think so."

"In other words, it's none of my business."

"I didn't want him to go to jail."

Allen was sitting on the edge of his bed, naked except for jockey shorts. His eyes—they made me think of a mouse in a corner, ready at last to fight a broom.

"The stinking sneak!"

"Did you hear it all?"

"I heard what that stinking sneak did."

"Did you hear what you did?"

The driven mouse attacked. "Who cares? Everybody does it. It's the way the cooky crumbles."

"You believe that?"

"Don't you read the papers? Everybody right up to the top—just read the papers. You get to feeling holy, just read the papers. I bet you took some in your time, because they all do. I'm not going to take the rap for everybody. I don't care about anything. Except that stinking sneak."

Mary awakens slowly, but she was awake. Perhaps she

hadn't been asleep. She was in Ellen's room, sitting on the edge of the bed. The street light made her plain enough with shadows of leaves moving on her face. She was a rock, a great granite rock set in a tide race. It was true. She was tough as a boot, unmoving, unyielding, and safe.

"Will you be coming to bed, Ethan?"

So she had been listening too.

"Not now, my darling dear."

"Are you going out again?"

"Yes—to walk."

"You need your sleep. It's still raining. Do you have to go?"

"Yes. There's a place. I have to go there."

"Take your raincoat. You forgot it before."

"Yes, my darling."

I didn't kiss her then. I couldn't with the balled and covered figure beside her. But I touched her shoulder and I touched her face and she was tough as a boot.

I went to the bathroom for a moment for a package of razor blades.

I was in the hall, reaching in the closet for a raincoat as Mary wished, when I heard a scuffle and a scramble and a rush and Ellen flung herself at me, grunting and snuffling. She buried her bleeding nose against my breast and pinned my elbows down with encircling arms. And her whole little body shook.

I took her by the forelock and pulled her head up under the hall night light.

"Take me with you."

"Silly, I can't. But if you'll come in the kitchen, I'll wash your face."

"Take me with you. You're not coming back."

"What do you mean, skookum? Of course I'm coming back. I'm always coming back. You go up to bed and rest. Then you'll feel better."

"You won't take me?"

"Where I'm going they wouldn't let you in. Do you want to stand outside in your nightgown?"

"You can't."

She grappled me again and her hands caressed and stroked my arms, my sides, dug her balled fists into my side pockets so that I was afraid she might find the razor blades. She was always a caressing girl, a stroking girl, and a surprising girl. Suddenly she released me and stood back with her head raised and her eyes level and without tears. I kissed her dirty little cheek and felt the dried blood against my mouth. And then I turned to the door.

"Don't you want your stick?"

"No, Ellen. Not tonight. Go to bed, darling. Go to bed."

I ran away fast. I guess I ran away from her and from Mary. I could hear Mary coming down the stairs with measured steps.

CHAPTER XXII

THE tide was on the rise. I waded into the warm bay water and clambered into the Place. A slow ground swell moved in and out of the entrance, flowed through my trousers. The fat billfold in my hip pocket swelled against my hip and then grew thinner under my weight as it water-soaked. The summer sea was crowded with little jellyfish the size of gooseberries, dangling their tendrils and their nettle cells. As they washed in against my legs and belly I felt them sting like small bitter fires, and the slow wave breathed in and out of the Place. The rain was only a thin mist now and it accumulated all the stars and town lamps and spread them evenly—a dark, pewter-colored sheen. I could see the third rock, but from the Place it did not line up with the point over the sunken keel of the *Belle-Adair*. A stronger wave lifted my legs and made them feel free and separate from me, and an eager wind sprang from nowhere and drove the mist like sheep. Then I could see a star—late rising, too late rising over the edge. Some kind of craft came chugging in, a craft with sail, by the slow, solemn sound of her engine. I saw her mast light over the toothy tumble of the breakwater but her red and green were below my range of sight.

My skin blazed under the lances of the jellyfish. I heard an anchor plunge, and the mast light went out.

Marullo's light still burned, and old Cap'n's light and Aunt Deborah's light.

It isn't true that there's a community of light, a bonfire of the world. Everyone carries his own, his lonely own.

A rustling school of tiny feeding fish flicked along the shore.

My light is out. There's nothing blacker than a wick.

Inward I said, I want to go home—no not home, to the other side of home where the lights are given.

It's so much darker when a light goes out than it would have been if it had never shone. The world is full of dark derelicts. The better way—the Marulli of that old Rome would have known it—there comes a time for decent, honorable retirement, not dramatic, not punishment of self or family—just good-by, a warm bath and an opened vein, a warm sea and a razor blade.

The ground swell on the rising tide whished into the Place and raised my legs and hips and swung them to the side and carried my wet folded raincoat out with it.

I rolled on one hip and reached in my side pocket for my razor blades and I felt the lump. Then in wonder I remembered the caressing, stroking hands of the light-bearer. For a moment it resisted coming out of my wet pocket. Then in my hand it gathered every bit of light there was and seemed red—dark red.

A surge of wave pushed me against the very back of the Place. And the tempo of the sea speeded up. I had to fight the water to get out, and I had to get out. I rolled and scrambled and splashed chest deep in the surf and the brisking waves pushed me against the old sea wall.

I had to get back—had to return the talisman to its new owner.

Else another light might go out.